JOURNEY TO DUNCANS MILLS

John Michael McCarty
Inspired by True Events

JOURNEY TO DUNCANS MILLS
Copyright © 2023 by John Michael McCarty

All rights reserved. No portion of this book may be reproduced in any form—mechanically, electronically, or by any other means, including photocopying, recording, or by any information storage and retrieval system—without permission in writing from the author except for use of brief quotations in a book review or by a reviewer, who may quote brief passages in a periodical.

ISBN: 9798851338007

Printed in the United States of America
First Printing, 2023

This book is a work of fiction. Names, characters, businesses, organizations, places, events, and incidents either are the product of the author's imagination or are used fictitiously. Any resemblance to actual persons, living or dead, events or locales is entirely coincidental.

Cover design by Ron Friedland. All rights reserved.

Praises For John McCarty

National winner for best historical fiction, 2022
    San Francisco Book Festival

Notable winner for best Indie book in the United States, 2018
    Shelf Unbound National Competition

"John's works are something out of the world of John Steinbeck's *Cannery Row*, with all the colorful characters and lively situations!"
    Dave Pelzer, #1 International Bestselling Author, National Jefferson Award Recipient, Former Monte Rio Firefighter

"Nostalgic trips back to the day. Grand accomplishments."
    Benny Barth, recording artist ("Stranger in Paradise") and drummer for Peggy Lee, Mel Torme and Barbra Streisand

"John McCarty's novels are the best mix of eclectic characters since *On the Road*. His wild rides through the anti-establishment denizens of the Russian River in Sonoma County are throwback treats."
    Mike Reilly, former county supervisor and president of the California Coastal Commission

"The author captures the heart of local politics in its most basic and repugnant form. Must reads."
    Gil Loescher, former professor of International Politics at Oxford University, England

"Crafty and intriguing stories."
    San Francisco Historical Society

"Charming tales of the past."
    Sonoma County Historical Society

"Nice intertwining of City and River. Well researched."
　Russian River Historical Society

"John McCarty's novels capture the flavor of our past through his vivid characters. As John Dryden said of Chaucer's *The Canterbury Tales*, 'Here is God's plenty.'"
　Fulbright Association

"Familiar folks, home-grown scenery, and candid attitudes will put you happily in the middle of all the action. Tasty well-paced reads."
　The Press Democrat

"Fun, historical novels of the Russian River."
　Bohemian

"This is history."
　Sonoma County Gazette

"Armed with a sharp wit, John McCarty weaves iconic characters through historic mazes with ease and color."
　Russian River Times

"McCarty's novels shine with the tough and unsentimental way of talking you can find in these parts (Russian River Valley)."
　Sonoma West Times & News

"Grand peeks into another era."
　Windsor Times

"The author gives us characters and plots that seem beyond the pale but are actually rooted in history. Delightful reads."
　The Upbeat Times

Acknowledgements

The author wishes to express his gratitude to the following individuals for their contributions: Patricia Morrison, Sean McCarty and Jim Berry. Also, thank you to the following organizations: San Francisco, Sonoma County and Russian River Historical Societies as well as the Sonoma County Library and Google Earth. Finally, appreciation is extended to Ron Friedland for the cover design and Cris Wanzer for her technical assistance.

Though *Journey to Duncans Mills* is fiction, the novel is the result of extensive research. The author combed twenty-one nonfiction books as well as four historical fiction works. In addition, over two hundred articles provided invaluable fodder from personal diaries, periodicals of the day, census reports, county records, academic theses, etc.

"Judas is among the Brethren...Every home has its cesspool and California has its Sonoma County."
Samuel Cassiday, editor of the *Petaluma Argus-Courier*, 1864

Other Novels by John McCarty:

Memories That Linger

In the Rough

Stumptown Daze

A Thousand Slippers

Don't Stop the Music

Hunting Ground: The Forgotten Story of Cazadero

For more information regarding the author or to purchase his novels, visit http://www.johnmccarty.org

JOURNEY TO DUNCANS MILLS

Chapter One

The old man circled the jaunty with a fine eye. The open sidecar appeared in superb condition. Both wheels boasted new metal bands while the wooden spokes were attached to refreshed felloes. The rear seats, set back-to-back, would allow his son to render a proper *adieu* as he paraded through the streets of Strabane on the following day. The event would bring out a handful of well-wishers who were mainly dirt farmers with a penchant for a pint of Guinness and a taste for the irreverent.

Samuel Duncan resembled your typical senior in this rural town of Northern Ireland—hard working with a rich brogue and harsh features. His hands thick and hardened. His posture bent from decades of farming. While two hectares of land would not promote advancement in life, it did furnish the family with enough sustenance on most days.

His wife, Lucinda, doted over their two sons and dreaded the inevitability that had finally arrived. Manhood had taken a firm grasp on the eldest, Alex, who would soon celebrate his twentieth birthday by leaving the fold.

He exited school at age fourteen—as did many teenagers in 1840—and sought a trade other than farming to avoid being reduced to another forgotten statistic at the local almshouse. Harbingers of the ill-fated were everywhere. Crops were succumbing to disease. British landlords were raising rents. The government refused to provide assistance. It was time to leave.

The father shook the hand of a hearty individual with a rust-colored beard, thanking him for the loan of the wagon. Nathaniel Bosworth was the manager of an ironworks factory. Having inherited a limp from a British bullet at the Battle of

Bonnymuir, he was always happy to help a fellow Scot. Bosworth went further, saying that Samuel Duncan's son was as good an apprentice to come along in quite some time.

Square-shoulders and a barrel chest provided the boy with a no-nonsense demeanor. Deep-set eyes rested below a thinning scalp, accentuating a business-like aura. Hidden under this fleshy armor, however, was the soul of a light-hearted and witty fellow. Alex Duncan would need to utilize all of these tools if he was to survive the rigors of the outside world.

A draft horse led all from the factory toward the Duncan farm, five kilometers from town. Along the way, Alex noticed a soldier who was engaged in a heated argument with a neighbor. The animated Redcoat shook his finger and pointed in a threatening manner to this and that. Pyres dotted the field. Dark soot climbed from bricks of burning peat, meandering into the ether. The scene could be mistaken as a backdrop for some macabre event as if heralding the beginning of the apocalypse.

The son tapped his father on the shoulder. The old man anticipated the question and answered, "Shite in a bucket. Nothin' more, nothin' less."

The statement didn't furnish much of an explanation, but Alex knew when to leave well enough alone. While his father was a man of few words, he was a man of even less patience.

Samuel Duncan and Lucinda Montgomery emigrated from Scotland to the Emerald Isle with the hope of cheaper land. It was all part of England's scheme to populate the northern sector of Ireland with more Protestants. It didn't take long for people like the Duncans to feel the squeeze from both ends. On the one hand, there was the ire of the Irish Catholics. On the other, there was the pressure from the Brits to produce more from the land.

Stone walls bordering the Duncan property came to them as they passed through an unhinged gate. Alex hopped from the jaunty, hitched the mare to a post and stepped into the cottage. Dirty plates and saucers lay stacked in the sink while dust flittered in and out of a slant of light, which pushed through the bubbled window. No reason for Alex to call out as the space provided little in the way of concealment, not even for the resident mouse seen skittering across the earthen floor.

Must be in the fields, Alex thought and exited to investigate his hunch.

Wrinkles were wedged into the folds of his mother's face, deep enough to hold the disappointments of recent months. The hem of her skirt skimmed across the field while her sleeves offered a modicum of protection against the unholy fog. It was a soft day by Irish standards, the drizzle lingering in suspended animation as the sun slipped beneath the horizon.

The youngest, Sam Montgomery Duncan, worked alongside, plucking tubers and green stalks, tossing all into burlap bags as if throwing out the garbage. While the brothers retained the same Christian name, there rested a vast difference in both physique and attitude. Sam was more wasted in appearance, thin as a matchstick and tight-mouthed, preferring the quiet confines of the family farm. Alex, however, possessed a stout physique with a personality to fit, able to charm the muck off a sow.

The patriarch eyed the activity, working his mind to attach meaning to the destruction before him. "What in the name of Jesus is goin' on here, if I might ask?"

No words, however, rose to elucidate the matter as wife and youngest continued to spade the furrows with their splintered hands.

"Can't be makin' the rent if there be no product to sell," the father persisted. "Ya understand this, don't ya woman?"

Alex held a different slant on the invading silence. He was annoyed by the lack of a proper greeting since this was his last day with the family. He threw a glare to the back of his brother, thinking the lad deserved a double dose of the devil's lip.

Nothing more *disrespectful* than a younger sibling's noncompliance, Alex thought as the blunt of his finger found the spine of Sam.

The adolescent spun around on his knees. "Quit acting the maggot."

"*Tabhair amach,*" Alex retorted in Gaelic. "You're giving out the stink. About that hour for a good wash, don't you think?" and he motioned to a stream beyond the bog.

"The good book says all men are brothers," Sam argued,

"but it doesn't seem to cut much ice with the like of us."

The mother put away the exchange between her sons and bolted to her feet with more pressing issues on her mind. Displeasure showed in her tired countenance, saying that both husband and eldest could lend a hand.

Alex, feeling his opinion should not be so easily dismissed, insisted that the day called for celebration and well wishes, not labor. "If you put everything on the long finger, then the long finger will soon be too short."

"Let the work cut me short. So be it," the mother said. "Better than standin' idly by, watchin' certain death come to the place," and she shoved a green stalk into the chest of her son to make her point.

Alex brought the leafy bunch to his vision. Little life presented itself. A black malignancy coursed its way through the vascular tissue of the plant. The son raised his head and looked toward the barren Sperrin Mountains as if an answer alighted there. He returned his disbelief to the crop, feathering the leaves with his fingers as might a veterinarian in search of fleas amidst a Wolfhound's coat.

"Blight?" he said in a startled voice.

No one answered to confirm. No need to. Alex realized the emergency. It gave meaning to the scene earlier when he saw a British soldier arguing with a neighbor. Rumors traveled. The English saw fit to shutter farms by the bushel, sending families to the poor house. If one could hide the evidence before a Redcoat came calling, perhaps another day might show itself.

Alex, however, harbored doubts on the subject. His family's enterprise was a microcosm of half the farms in Ireland. It was meager by any standard with potatoes being the sole crop of choice. Putting all your tubers in one basket simplified things, but it also invited economic calamity. One not-so-healthy swipe of blight and a family's finances could be swept away on the next refuse wagon out of town.

The family worked into the evening to purge the crop of the infestation. A moonless sky arrived to act as a co-conspirator, masking their actions. Tired bodies slid from one row to the next, examining the leaves as best as the darkness allowed.

Limbs sagged while the hours passed in steady determination.

Dawn arrived to showcase the future. Splotches of greenery flecked the field in broken harmony. Plumes of breath escaped from husband and wife as they gazed at each other without a word. There was nothing more that could be said. Eyes fell as if unable to bear the truth that rested in the other's countenance.

There was little time to lament as the new day showed itself with the next hardship. The eldest had booked passage aboard the packet ship *Roscoe* out of Liverpool.

Needed to get cracking. Alex washed up, threw his meager belongings together and hurried into the only suit he had ever owned.

The mother nodded and surrendered a final hug, whispering in his ear: "A man is only a son until he takes to the road. God be with you," and she withdrew, folding her arms across her chest as if restraining emotions long held captive.

Sam refused his brother's handshake. Though the youngest was nothing more than a *tattie-hoker* with no useful skills or savings, he saw no reason as to why he should remain behind.

In a final effort to change his brother's mind, Sam said, "Two people shorten the road," and he raised his hand to signal his willingness to play the part.

"Best you stay with mum and da," Alex answered. They had discussed this previously. Because of the old man's poor health, it would be necessary for one of the boys to stay behind and assist wherever needed.

Sam knew he didn't possess the fortitude to reverse the decision and stuffed his hands in his pockets. The mother blinked away a tear, her face crumpled with sadness.

The father climbed onto his perch in the jaunty and said he would return in a day. The old man whipped the draft horse into a trot while Alex held onto his valise in the backseat. Mother and youngest stood stiff and wooden, fixing their eyes on the retreating cart as it dwarfed from sight.

Alex's mind stirred within a soup of mixed emotions. The idea of embarking on a venture caused his skin to tingle with a buzz but leaving his family in such a state promoted a sense of guilt. If there was one institution with which the Scottish could claim mastery of, it was guilt. The very notion of the word would stay attached for life, festering like some unborn demon ready to hatch.

Cobbled streets made their way through a cluster of two-story stone enterprises while the stench of burning coal drifted from chimneys. They passed the Farmer's Home Public House where a couple of patrons raised their mugs in a final salute. Steel workers ceased their jawing in front of the foundry and tapped the rims of their caps while a beefy individual with a rusty beard clapped a single clap to signal his approval.

The scene, however, was much different at a place known to all as the Strabane Union Workhouse. Defeated figures stood in line to greet a fate from which they would not return. Authorities separated family members, directing males to one wing of the almshouse and females to another.

The image had no effect on the patriarch. The impoverished had become an everyday occurrence throughout Tyrone County. His son, however, imprinted the spectacle into his mindscape, never to be forgotten. It was at that very moment when he made a solemn oath to make a better path for himself, one that did not include pauperism or permanent residence at a public tenement for the poor.

The city dimmed behind them as their travels took them to the River Foyle where a mighty oak stood proud along its bank. It was once king of the forest, its seed flown here by cranes and other fowl from the continent.

Good riddance, Alex thought as his body jounced in rhythm with the cart. If you're going to decimate the entire woodlands, it might as well be the oak of the English *bosthoons*.

The two-wheel cart kept its course through the Foyle River Valley with nary a soul in sight. Mushrooms of smoke rose a kilometer to the east. Probably the potato fields of Dunamanagh Parish, Alex thought.

He brought his head back around and lost himself in the wheel's shadow twirling along the road. Its repetitive nature took him captive and he surrendered his thoughts to the distraction.

A passing road sign barely caught his attention.

LONDONDERRY had been defaced with LONDON crossed out. Thoughts of its meaning disappeared under the veil of self-hypnosis until the jaunty creaked to a halt.

"Where are we?" the son asked, snapping out of his wanderings.

"Bishop's Gate, home to those Union Jack-waving eejits," the father answered.

Some forty thousand citizens lived within the walled city of Londonderry. For people like the Duncans, however, the preferred title for their beloved city was *Derry* in keeping with tradition before British guilds forced the name change.

"Best hitch your sourness to a post," the son said.

"Sassing your father, are ya, boy?"

"Well, no. I...I just thought this place might not—"

"Shut your gob. My belt still fits the length of your backside. Best not forget that."

Silence.

It was difficult for Alex to read his father's moods. Harsh words often disguised his true design. Was this act another life lesson or a show of anger or an attempt to appear strong in the face of losing a son? While Alex rarely had trouble interpreting people's intentions with a snappy reply, such was not the case with his father.

Samuel Duncan clicked his tongue, urging on the draft horse. Jumbles of Hansom cabs, pedestrians, commercial wagons and men on horseback crisscrossed each other. The barks of tinkers selling their wares mixed with the neighing of beasts and the general discord of the city. The Duncans' jaunty weaved in and out of the crowd, passing row houses down untidy avenues.

The father's nerves began to unravel, unaccustomed to such frenzy. He pulled hard on the reins to avoid a gaggle of Redcoats.

"Shite!" Samuel Duncan roared.

The British presence was visible on every corner. *Jakeens and Tories, from the first to the last,* Alex thought. He recalled from one of his father's discourses that the word Tory came from the Irish *toraidhe*, referring to "bandit". In the mind of

Samuel Duncan, the Brits were indeed nothing more than a gang of bandits, stealing land that wasn't theirs.

An industrial district rushed upon them. The flickering of flames shone from forging shops. A wool-carding store butted up against a string of decaying enterprises. A tannery, machine outlet and harness shop appeared listless. The glumness proceeded to Gilmour's, a factory on Artillery Street. Many of the windows were boarded up giving some credence to rumors circulating the countryside. The decline in the production of linen cloth served as a warning. The women who staffed such factories would most likely emigrate and join their husbands on the continent in search of employment.

Hard times.

The jaunty made its way downhill along Shipquay Street and thru Shipquay Gate to the port. Wharves extended from stone platforms, which protruded into Loch Foyle. Warehouses lined the estuary, occupying shipbuilders while steamers and clippers sat at berths ready to transport multitudes across the channel.

A swarm of bar-tailed godwits swirled over the brick structure of William McCorkell & Company where a queue of defeated-looking people stretched from the ticket office and disappeared around the corner. Mismatched patches scarred outfits while twine secured valises.

The corners of Alex's mouth sagged with the reality that he was soon to become one of them. And these were the lucky few, those who were able to fetch a passage out of hell. He had tried to procure the same ticket but space aboard the vessels *Caroline* and *Erin* of the McCorkell Line had been booked for months. Like many other Johnnies-come-lately, Alex would have to make his way to Liverpool. It seemed like a minor setback, but it was not how he wanted to start his new life.

Samuel Duncan brought the cart to a halt, alighted and tied the reins to a hitching post. He turned to his son who stationed himself beside the jaunty with suitcase in hand.

"No doubt there'll be plenty of shites waitin' for your Irish arse," the father said as he took a step closer. "And don't be a lick. Stand up for yourself. Ya hear me, son?"

"I do, father," Alex said. "And while we're on the subject of life-lessons, make sure my little brother earns his keep."

"I appreciate the concern ya be dishing out, but your mum and I been here before." The old man picked a wad of bills from his coat pocket along with a watch and extended the batch to his son.

Alex Duncan opened the casing and studied a photo of his mum and da before gazing at the gift of cash, shaking his head. "You need this more than I do," and he pushed the offer away.

"It be your inheritance," Samuel Duncan said and returned the currency to his son's hand. "And remember, lad, if ya look after the pennies, the pounds will look after themselves."

During their final embrace, Alex secreted the money back into his father's waistcoat. The gold watch would be kept as a remembrance of all that once was.

Alex made his way to the vessel's deck and turned for one last farewell, but his father wasn't there.

Chapter Two

Naked breasts decorated the bowsprit, which pointed the way to Liverpool. For the next sixteen hours, Alex would keep company aboard the *Mona's Isle* with other emigrants as well as thirty-five tons of coal. Black dust flitted in a beam of light from an open hatch. Coughs and hacking mingled with an infant's cry while the gaiety from the first-class cabins above did little to assuage the gloom.

A throaty blast from a horn signaled departure as twin engines churned. A tugboat edged the *Mona's Isle* from its berth and escorted her past the last quay and through the green-brown algae of Loch Foyle. Flocks of pale-bellied geese and whooper swans honked as if to signal a farewell.

The warehouses and pilot station at Inishown came and went as the loch opened to the North Channel and the Irish Sea. Nary a word was exchanged within the tight circles of the passengers except for a whisper or a subtle gesture. Arms cradled belongings while eyes scoured the hold for any conspiratorial plots. Such was the new order of things.

In these initial hours of independence, Alex began to question his ability to deal with the uncertainty that lay ahead. British jack-waving eejits and Irish Paddies were one thing. He had been equipped by his sermonizing father to deal with them back in Strabane, but the future would present foes of an unspeakable nature, both human and of the earth.

The display on the paddle boxes of the vessel returned to his memory as if offering a clue—the Three Legs of Man (a trio of interlocking spirals). It was one of the oldest Celtic symbols in existence, representing the three worlds of the celestial, physical and spiritual. His mindscape tried to paint a picture of these creations even though his attention started to wane. A gradual drowsiness soon took over and he fell into a hazy slumber.

A crusty fellow with wiry hair and a gray beard stretched his ancient finger and poked the lad on his forehead. Alex blinked away the fuzziness as the stranger came into focus bit by bit.

"'Bout time to rise and git," and the stranger motioned to the inners of the ship.

Alex traced the gesture and surveyed the emptiness. "What's the *craic*?"

"Devil a bit, not much," the stranger answered. "Except you 'bout to be left behind with the vermin and such."

Alex bolted up and started to sprint out of the hold before returning to claim his valise. But it wasn't there. He brushed aside coal and trash and peeked between crates. Nothing. He gazed into the spent eyes of the stranger as if to say "What the hell," and dashed up the steps and through the hatch. Another sprint took him along the Liverpool waterfront past a string of ships and up a gangplank.

"Not so fast there, lad," an officer said in a blue uniform with gold-gilded epaulets and buttons.

Joseph Clement Delano was captain of the packet vessel. It was one of several owned by his grandfather, Warren Delano, who evidently came by his money in nefarious ways.

"Is this the *Roscoe*?" the young man asked with a distinctive brogue.

"Ya be an Ulster Scot, I be guessing," Captain Delano said.

The young man caught the disdain in the captain's look and said, "This Scot has a ticket to board your ship."

"Own a bit of an attitude, do ya? It was your kind that came uninvited onto the land of my ancestors and took it with no one's permission."

"The colonization was fostered by the Brits," the young man argued.

"Don't hold much favor with them either," the captain retorted.

"Nor do I," the young man said while searching for his ticket. His countenance grew serious as pocket after pocket showed no more than a ball of lint and a handkerchief. His wallet and watch missing as well.

Christ on a bike!

"What be your name?"

"Alex Duncan. From Strabane, Tyrone County. Of the United Kingdom of Great—"

"I be well aware of where Strabane be situated," the captain interrupted before requesting the passenger list from the first mate.

The second page of the catalogue showed the name DUNCAN, ALEXANDER. "Appears ya already boarded. At 7:34 a.m. to be precise," and the captain lifted his vision from the clipboard to the face of the young man.

Alex's countenance drooped. Visions of the past few days paraded across his mind: the infected crop of his family's farm; the theft of his possessions. Penniless without an identity, standing alone before a man who most likely could give a rat's arse.

"Off with ya now," the captain said before gesturing to his first mate. The officer didn't hesitate and passed the request to a couple of deckhands who started to escort the intruder from the ship.

"Wait," the lad said to the captain. "You said that you knew where Strabane was? Then you should be familiar with the owner of the town foundry."

With a sense that there might be some truth to what the lad claimed, Captain Delano asked, "Can ya be describin' this man you speak of?"

"Yes...Yes, I can."

"And?" the captain said with a note of frustration as he studied the line growing behind the lad along the gangplank.

"He's a kind gentleman, a bit beefy around the edges with a rusty beard and a limp he received from his injuries in the Battle of Bonnymuir. Has acquired a penchant for an ale or two down at the—"

"The name, damn it. The name."

"Ah, yes, of course. His name is Nathaniel Bosworth."

The captain ordered the second mate to find the other "Alexander Duncan" and bring him forth. The previous line of questioning was repeated and it was determined in short order who was the imposter. All belongings, including wallet and pocket watch, were returned to their rightful owner.

* * *

A blue and white flag rippled in the breeze from the main mast, the signature of the Blue Swallowtail Line. The *Roscoe* was a three-masted, merchant-class ship with a capacity for eighteen cabin passengers and three hundred in steerage. In addition, bales of cotton, sugar, rice, flour, tobacco and woolens rested in the hold.

Alexander Duncan looked past the crates to a bank of bunks. Four young girls, one with an infant, squeezed into a single berth. It wasn't clear if the females knew each other, as all kept to themselves. A sixty-something haggard-looking man, with the breath of a stink bug, grinned a lustful grin when assigned to join the female quartet.

The parade didn't stop until each bunk held more than its allotted sum, which was both illegal and sufferable yet tolerated with the greasing of the harbor master's palm.

On March 19, 1840 at approximately 8:00 a.m., Alex felt the sway of the 400-ton vessel. The blast of a steamer's horn could be heard. Must belong to a tugboat, Alex guessed. A steady stream of cheers from the wharf came next, a sendoff worthy of a queen's departure. The gloom in the cargo hold, however, bared little resemblance to the gaiety heard from atop deck.

With the passing of another hour, two blows from the tugboat sounded. The flap of sails mixed with the barking of orders and the patter of busy feet as the *Roscoe* began to heel, running free but uneven. Alex knew the reputation of these waters where the Mersey River collided with the Atlantic. It was as rocky as the potato fields of Strabane.

Sickness and wrenching ensued as a gale rushed upon the *Roscoe*. Most took to masking themselves with shirt sleeves and handkerchiefs while the queasiness of others found the bottom of various containers. The moaning lasted through the night as the stench swelled from the pens of livestock. Cattle and sheep, ducks and geese, and chickens and hens all did their part to assure the growing discomfort. The air grew thick within the pressing masses, threatening to suffocate all.

The weather calmed itself as the next morning arrived. Captain Delano ordered the passengers from steerage on deck. Crew tossed buckets of water onto all. The sting of sea salt accompanied the embarrassment associated with being treated like a pack of critters. Mothers from first-class corralled little ones and shepherded them around the mess.

Alex returned to the cargo hold and dried off his clothes as best he could when he noticed the old man with the stink-bug breath attempting to mount one of the young females in the next berth. "Perhaps you should take your hand off the girl," Alex Duncan said as he jabbed his finger into the spine of the old man.

Lost in lust, Stink Bug threw a second leg over the girl. She cried out. Alex latched onto Stink Bug by his scalp and pitched him against a bundle of tobacco. The old man sprung to his feet with the agility of a much younger fellow and flashed a dagger along with a toothy grin.

"What's going on here?" a Negro said from the hatch. He showed a straight back and wore a noble face, which complimented his scarlet-colored uniform with matching shoes.

"Mind your business, Sambo," Stink Bug said.

"Such words will bring you no favors with me," and the black man raised his silver-tip cane and clubbed the arm of Stink Bug, sending the dagger to the floor. Stink Bug lunged for the weapon but another wallop across the head put him out.

"Much obliged," Alex Duncan said before introducing himself.

"And I'm Mr. Ogden," the Negro said. "Steward of the *Roscoe*," and he ordered a second mate to haul away Stink Bug. While this was happening, Mr. Ogden explained that although he was not in charge of the vessel's security, he nevertheless abhorred any lack of manners.

"I was returning from first-class when I overheard the disturbance. Such behavior will not be tolerated," Mr. Ogden said.

The quiet of the young female went unnoticed until Duncan spied the quiver aboard her expression. An infant lay cradled in her arms, looking worn and listless. Duncan wrapped a blanket around both while Mr. Ogden mentioned that the woman was Elizabeth Holmes of Leicestershire, England.

"Not aware of her relation to the child as the young one is not on the manifesto," the steward said to Duncan before returning his attention to Elizabeth Holmes, saying that there was no further need to concern herself, that her former bunkmate would be in chains until surrendered to port authorities.

Elizabeth Holmes did not respond, her eyes frozen to the planks below her feet. Mr. Ogden surveyed her expression, which hung gaunt and absence of life. Her lips pasty and parched. With a suspicion, the steward went to a barrel, took a sip of its contents and then spit the liquid to the side.

"Water is foul," the steward said. "Someone's tainted the batch. Seen this before." He leaned into the ear of Duncan, saying, "Mind your back, lad," and then he glanced toward Elizabeth Holmes and the child as if to include them with his warning.

* * *

On the third day out, a gale sent the *Roscoe* off course. Alex spent most of the time in bed, sharing a bucket with others who had fallen ill. While the girl and infant joined the list of infirmed, at least they were no longer harassed as a strong message had been delivered to any who might harbor similar intentions as Stink Bug.

Due to the storm, the vessel retreated further south where they were caught up in a series of whirlpools. Fears ran rampant when bits of rigging blew away.

The tempest abated and passengers began to brighten up with the exception of a few, including Elizabeth Holmes and the infant. Alex, through his connections with Mr. Ogden, was able to procure goat's milk and a fresh supply of water.

"It's a right bloody shame," the steward said as he handed a gourd to Duncan who crunched up his face in question.

"What I mean to say," the steward explained, "is that the division of goods seems to be greater than ever before."

"Just last evening," the steward continued, "my charges in first-class dined on terrapin, salmon, peas, asparagus and strawberries all the while pretending to be heartbroken about the famine."

"No need to look further than beneath them if it's suffering they seek," Duncan said.

Conditions became worse with the robbing of passengers' valuables. Money, spirits, tea, coffee and sugar were but a few of the items disappearing from lockers and luggage.

Alex Duncan led a small contingent to voice their complaints to Captain Delano, but he rebutted, saying to take up the matter with the ticket agents as they were the ones responsible.

"That doesn't leave us with much recourse for the moment," Duncan argued.

"It not be my concern," the captain retorted.

"These passengers are in need of the few provisions they brought with them, seeing as how the vessel has reneged on its promise of fresh vittles and water."

"You best be leavin' now."

"And what about the crew's attitude toward the females?" Duncan persisted in a defiant tone. "The Blue Swallowtail Line promised safe passage. Is this not still the case?"

The captain studied the man. "Mind your attitude, sir."

But Duncan wouldn't relent, saying that certain members of the crew prowled about the ship in the hopes of finding girls who would hearken to them.

"And where might you be obtaining such ridiculous notions, Mr. Duncan?" the captain asked.

"With my own eyes, sir."

The captain allowed a pause to build during which he regarded the man before him. "I have seen you and my steward, Mr. Ogden, engaged in several exchanges. Might he be—"

"No reason to bring him into this," Duncan interrupted.

"These findings belong to no one other than myself and my fellow passengers," and he motioned to the men alongside.

"Perhaps."

Chapter Three

Unseaworthy, overcrowded and with inadequate provisions, the *Roscoe* was more than worthy of the title "coffin ship". Duncan recalled reading an editorial in the *Irish Times* describing passengers such as himself as "…flying from one form of death to another." While his fellow travelers had escaped the potato blight, many were in bad health and ill-equipped to fend off diseases. A single case of typhus could spread like a greased pig ablaze.

Three children appeared to have contracted the malady. Some doubted their recovery. Those who had brought faith with them, prayed over the ill. But as far as Duncan could see, God had taken a holiday.

Without warning, color began to find its way back into the cheeks of Elizabeth Holmes. Most gave thanks to the Almighty for the young girl's renewed vibrancy while Duncan was of the opinion that the recovery was in no small measure due to the stolen bits of salt pork provided by Mr. Ogden.

Lizzy, as she was called, began to converse with the person in the next bunk. She told Duncan of her story, how she had agreed to care for the bastard child of her sister. Since Lizzy had no immediate promise of marriage and had been recently laid off at the local textile factory, the prospect of a new beginning in America sounded appealing. For both her and the infant.

In the days that followed, Lizzy's health continued to rebound. Regrettably, the same could not be said for the infant who no longer possessed the capacity to feed.

"It's time," Alex said to Lizzy, gesturing to the infant. "She has a right to a name, if though but for a short time."

"Alexandra," she said in a spurt, showing a weak grin

before taking the child into her arms for the last time.

Honor filled Alex Duncan and he nodded a quiet assent as emotions blocked his efforts to speak.

* * *

Captain Delano was ordering the child to be sealed in a flour sack when a square-shouldered man with a receding hairline moved forward. "The child deserves a proper burial."

The captain gazed past the words of Duncan to others who had ascended from the hold with similar beliefs. Dissentions amongst the passengers had increased in recent days. No reason to stir the pot any further than necessary, the captain thought and told Duncan to make it quick.

Lizzy came forward and kissed the mummified body of Alexandra before Duncan recited a passage from Luke, chapter 18, verse 16: "'But Jesus called them to Him, saying, *Let the children come to me, and do not hinder them, for to such belongs the kingdom of God.*'"

Alexandra was committed to the sea on May 10, 1840, owning a name and some dignity.

Duncan approached Lizzy and started to put an arm around her but she stiffened. Her discomfort with a man's touch was understandable and he backed away. A moistness joined the dark, which swelled below her eyes. To measure her sorrow was futile.

Lizzy's head drooped from the bent shoulders of Duncan who tried again, saying that he would be there for her. She lifted her eyes, but little hope resided there.

Captain Delano ordered everyone to return to their berths, a command aided by the nudging from a gang of sailors. Upon arriving in the hold, a surprise inspection was made. It was the captain's way of saying that he would have the last word, that he was in charge, not some Ulster Scot who was weak in the knees for some no-count woman and a bastard child.

The first mate sermonized the importance of cleanliness. Between his phrasing, he would finger-scoop a speck of dirt from a berth. On one occasion a stench penetrated his nostrils and he covered his nose with the back of his gloved hand.

"Many of you see fit to remain clothed in the same filth day after bleeding day," the first mate said, his boots clicking the planks in a steady beat.

"A sorry lot, indeed," he continued.

Alex Duncan and others felt demeaned by the approach of the sailor, a man who was paid to serve them. The Ulster Scot thought about voicing his displeasure but resisted.

Commands to undress were passed down the line. Those that resisted had the clothes stripped off their backs. Buckets of salt water found the open sores of the ill. The yelps of old folks and the cries of children filled the darkness.

A crewman lit kerosene lamps to sweeten the air and prevent disease. Typhus, typhoid, scurry, pneumonia, small pox and any other number of ailments could easily accompany such a voyage.

Duncan wondered what tomorrow would bring. Would he join the infant Alexandra and call the Atlantic his final resting place? Perhaps such a sentence was all that he deserved.

* * *

The Delano Blue Swallowtail Line provided weekly service between Liverpool and New York, employing five packet ships to assure the scheduled sailings. Normally the crossing took six weeks but if the Atlantic misbehaved it might take as long as fourteen.

A storm began to brew and crewmen were reefing the sails when a rogue gust took away three sheets. The following night the *Roscoe* lost another sail and several of its blocks.

On the fourth day out a dead calm engulfed all. The sails went limp and orders from the bridge were given to hove to. Sailors began the task of bringing about the spars and yardarms to catch what little wind existed. With the job done, a few crewmen went below to lighten the load.

The footfalls of the first mate were unmistakable. Trouble would soon be at hand. Mr. Ogden hurried ahead to alert Duncan.

"The girl," the steward said, motioning to Lizzy, "hide away her extra valise."

Duncan used Mr. Ogden as a shield and slinked to the next berth and slipped the luggage in question behind a sack of flour. Half way back to his bunkbed, a boot crossed his path. Duncan looked up at the first mate, flashed an unconvincing grin and asked the officer if he had seen a pocket watch lying about.

"It has sentimental value," Duncan said. "A gift from my da."

"Most likely his entire endowment," the first mate said in a clipped tone.

"Very clever, sir. No doubt you are the product of a witty and prodigious *breagan*."

The first mate was unfamiliar with the Gaelic term but assumed it was not of a flattering nature and let his study linger to instill a remembrance of the man.

Duncan rose and stepped away to avoid any further interaction. He weaved his way through a swarm of sailors, catching pieces of conversations, overhearing the placing of a wager or two. Shillings passed hands. Duncan wondered if the silver represented the sea burial of Alexandra, using the infant's date of death for nothing more than cheap entertainment.

The first mate and his charges exited the hold and scampered in different directions. Mr. Ogden lingered behind to ask Duncan if he and Lizzy would like to join him on the quarterdeck to escape the musty confines for a bit. Lizzy did not respond except to scratch at the hem of her dress. Whether her melancholy was due to the recent burial of Alexandra or the introduction of some other distress was not known.

Duncan took Mr. Ogden up on his offer and went topside. The sudden brightness caused him to blink, black pinholes dotting his vision. Laughter drew his attention and he gazed overboard where members of first-class swam in the flattened sea.

Others nearby were entertaining themselves in a dingy. Men wore starched white shirts with bow ties and colorful vests while ladies donned puffy dresses with parasols in hand. One crewman rowed while another dangled a fishing rod over the side. A whitetip shark took the bait and flailed about as it was hauled onboard. Women screeched and slapped at husbands to do something.

"It never ceases to amaze me how a pampered life ill prepares one for the goings-on of the real world," Mr. Ogden observed.

"A sheltered existence will do that," Duncan confirmed.

"Perhaps they are blessed," Mr. Ogden added. "After all, ignorance is not easily acquired. One has to work at it."

Much of that night was spent arranging for payment of potatoes. The cost was £8 for three. Duncan paid for Lizzy's share though she showed no signs of wanting to eat.

Gaiety could be heard from the cabins above. Feet moved to a lively tune. The strumming of fiddles and the organ-like sound of a squeezebox, however, did not lift the mood in the cargo hold. An affliction of sorts had spread to many who muffled coughs so as not to inflame the angst of the first mate.

Mr. Ogden came below with leftovers from first-class. He and Duncan brought the victuals to Lizzy, shaking her awake. She rolled over to comply with the request, groaning a dissent. Mr. Ogden felt her forehead for a fever but Lizzy jerked away in pain. He continued with the examination, applying pressure to her arms, legs and feet. Her limbs were swollen, some covered with putrid sores.

Mr. Ogden pulled the blanket over her shoulders, but its weight seemed unbearable and Lizzy pushed it down her frame. Mr. Ogden looked at Duncan and motioned toward the hatch. Atop deck the steward said that the girl had typhus.

"I should have checked on her earlier," Duncan said. "I assumed she was simply distraught over the loss of Alexandra."

"The cause of her illness is not for you to carry," Mr. Ogden said.

"Is there anything that can be done?"

"Wait here," and the steward marched toward his quarters in the forecastle.

Upon his return the duo returned to Lizzy. Mr. Ogden applied a compound to the open wounds. The girl squealed with each application. Next, he sat her up and tilted a tin cup to her lips.

The two men retreated to a quiet corner where the steward explained his actions. "The compound is a combination of mercury and iodine. Unfortunately, the employment can be quite painful."

"And the drink?" Duncan asked.

"A dose of quinine. On my travels to South America, I was able to procure some from the bark of the cinchona tree. Lately, it has been used for more than managing malaria."

* * *

The next day Mr. Ogden and the first mate were charged with the task of casting overboard the Mormon son and daughter of Paul and Jane Harris. The burials ran the casualty number to three, all children under the age of eight. Evening prayer continued over the remaining sick. Lizzy's condition improved with the prolongation of her treatments, which aroused the suspicions of others who did not have the privilege of knowing the steward.

Later that evening, a sailor from the crowsnest spotted land. The ship's bell rang as a string of sandy peninsulas and barrier islands ran before them. The Outer Banks of North Carolina owned a reputation as "The Graveyard of the Atlantic" and this day would show its worth as a formidable foe to all who dare to sail its waters.

A squall rose up and the call was given for all hands on deck. The main top sail was ripped from top to bottom and the *Roscoe* began to roll. Captain Delano gave some thought to further lightening the load with the transference of passengers onto several of the fishing boats anchored nearby. With the rebuke that his grandfather's shipping line could lose a substantial amount of money with such action, the captain decided to sail onward. Though additional possessions of wayfarers were tossed overboard, the action did little to assuage the wrath of the sea.

The weather increased and pushed the *Roscoe* onto Sandy Hook. Orders were given to reef the sails. Anchors were lowered to protect the vessel from being torn asunder.

With the rocking and rolling, a mishap of undetermined proportions began. Screams from the hold sounded an alarm. Flecks of fire began to drop upon the passengers. Duncan went to protect Lizzy who responded with little emotion. A sailor investigated the trouble and sang out to another who was stationed near the opened hatch. A cry brought crewmen from the forecastle. A brigade was formed and water buckets were passed down a human chain to the galley where hot coals had spilled from a stove shorn from its foundation.

Passengers panicked and scrambled toward the topdeck, knocking over crates, bumping into each other. Duncan shoved a man to the side and brought Lizzy into his arms.

The fire was put out and the chaos simmered down. For some, however, the shock of yet another calamity was the final stroke. Four adults were added to the ship's fatalities, which had become so commonplace as to receive little attention.

With the return of calmer weather, the *Roscoe* weighed anchor and raised its sails. The vessel came about and headed 90° through the wind. After another hour of sailing, a pilot came aboard and guided the *Roscoe* into New York City harbor at 8:00 p.m. on May 28, 1840.

As there were no docks, ships pressed up against each other offshore. In the process the *Roscoe* nudged a small schooner and struck at her bulwarks, breaking some rigging. All was accounted for between the captains and the *Roscoe* made fast. A flat-bottomed lighter approached on the starboard side to receive first-class passengers and luggage.

Steerage patrons unloaded last. They were not afforded the luxury of a lighter and used the decks of various vessels as stepping stones to land. Several wore the rags with which they began the voyage some ten weeks earlier. Others, including Alex Duncan, had changed into less dingy attire, feeling fortunate to have held onto a few of their possessions.

Halfway across the gangplank to a neighboring schooner, the sound of prayer came to Duncan and he swung back around. The steward was rendering the sign of the cross over the wrapped bodies of the recent casualties. Upon one he layed his hands across the frame and mouthed something. Duncan guessed it was a special invocation for a special lady.

Chapter Four

Upon setting his feet on terra firma, Alex Duncan wobbled forward feeling a bit nauseous. The sensation of movement ebbed as the area entered his awareness. The rain did little to cheer up the cobblestone streets while murky shades of yellow from windows failed to add any spirit to nearby enterprises.

Nor did his soul emit much light either. His mind filled with his last sight of the *Roscoe*, of Mr. Ogden blessing the bodies of the dead. Was Lizzy among them? Had she joined Alexandra? Living was a rigorous ordeal. It possessed little poetry and less reason. It was beyond Duncan's understanding as to why God did not grant all humankind an equal chance at life.

As he regained his land-legs, the place overtook him. Not even in Derry or Liverpool had he witnessed such bustle. The scene began to press the thoughts of Lizzy and the infant into the background as he tried to negotiate the busyness that swallowed him. Buggies and other contrivances of varying shapes and sizes crammed the thoroughfares while pedestrians buried the sidewalks from view. Shoremen unloaded wares from wagons. Women hung laundry on catwalks. Tinkers clanged anvils. Vendors barked, advertising their products.

He continued along the waterfront where a series of five-story brick structures came into view. Above the doorway of one flew the banner of the Blue Swallowtail Line, the Delano family's signature endeavor. Duncan recalled the stories of how the grandfather of Captain Delano had started the business with the importation of illegal drugs from China.

Why do the scoundrels of the world seem to be the ones to prosper the most? Duncan thought. Perhaps he possessed the potential to be such a scoundrel. Perhaps even a first rate one. It did take gumption to abandon an ailing father and a failing potato crop, not to mention leaving a younger brother to clean up the damage.

He strolled through the Fourth Ward of Manhattan, which took up quarters along the East River. The waterfront was awash with rat pits, dives and whorehouses. Scrapers, sailors and longshoremen from all parts of the globe slipped in and out of shops and saloons.

He stepped from the madness and entered a lodging tenement. Lord only knew what awaited on the other side of the door. It did, however, provide an escape from the claustrophobic walkways.

A porky fellow with a waxed mustache greeted Duncan. Before a salutation could be returned, the fellow latched onto the valise from the newcomer's grip and guided him up the stairs, boasting along the way of how Brother Delong's provided the richest environment to be had, of how it was one of the few establishments with hot water.

"Showers are at the end of the hall. Appreciate it if you'd share the same with your roommate who would, by my reckoning, be ameniable to the arrangement."

Duncan remained silent, wondering if such a custom was common practice. Very progressive city, he thought as he marched upstairs to room 19 (the 9 hanging upside down looking like a 6).

Porky surrendered a room key after receiving a week's rent in advance. "And this is for the outhouse," and handed Duncan a second key, noticing the lost look aboard the tenant's face. "Can't be too careful," he explained. "Tricksters would just as soon set up housing back there if ya gave 'em half a chance."

* * *

Duncan met up with Mr. Ogden for dinner at 54 Pearl Street in the Financial District. Fraunces Tavern was built in 1720 and was the target of British soldiers during the Revolutionary War. But owner Samuel Fraunces took a page from his English adversaries and showed a stiff upper lip, never closing the inn even with the sending of a cannonball through its walls.

Duncan entered where a framed tooth hung nearby. A brass plate announced that the fang once belonged to George Washington who attended a banquet there in his honor.

The Ulster Scot spotted a black man in a stylish three-piece suit and approached. "Interesting place," Duncan said as he gestured back over his shoulder to the framed tooth.

"I guess it depends on your point of reference," Mr. Ogden said without further explanation, dismissing the curious look on Duncan. "Anyways, it is one of the few places where a black man can dine in this city."

"I suppose we are fortunate to be dining at all," Duncan said.

Mr. Ogden acknowledged the truth of the statement, agreeing to their arduous crossing of the Atlantic. "But that was not the end of it," he said with a tease.

Duncan gestured with his hand as if to request more.

Mr. Ogden continued, saying that Captain Delano had secretly unloaded the deceased and infirmed while communicating false information with the port authorities. "Otherwise, the ship would have been quarantined at the New York Marine Hospital on Staten Island. The *Patrick Henry* arrived two months ago with seventeen passengers recorded dead and is still in detention."

They ordered ales and a couple of meat pies. While waiting for their meals, the subject of Lizzy came up. "I made sure that she was delivered to the county coroner's office, but with no one to claim the remains she will most likely be cremated, as are all indigents."

Duncan's hand raked through what little hair he possessed. His expression tight.

"She didn't deserve such an ending," and Duncan shared Lizzy's story of trying to make a new life for herself and her sister's illegitmate child.

"Matters could have been worse."

"Oh, really?"

"At least she received a civil send-off. Others are not as fortunate, given away to local contractors who use the bodies to help extend the wharf on South Street."

Hard to imagine greed could take one to such a low place, Duncan thought.

Drinks and food arrived to provide a welcomed pause. Duncan picked at the pastry-covered meat, unable to activate his hunger. Mr. Ogden spied the heaviness in his friend's expression and attempted to engage him with a different topic.

"What are your plans now?"

No response.

A nudge broke Duncan out of his stagnation. "Sorry. What did you say?"

"Your plans?"

"Oh, ah, I'm an ironworker and machinist by trade. Hope to find something along the waterfront," and he deflected any further talk on his part by inquiring as to Mr. Ogden's future.

"Well, I was forced to resign my position as chief steward."

"How'd that come about?" Duncan said, having difficulty concentrating.

"The first mate reported me to the captain for absconding with supplies from first-class."

No response.

"I argued, saying that food and water often went untouched and could be better used in the hold. But the captain was not convinced and asked for my resignation. Or be courtmartialed."

Duncan pretended to listen and said, "Now what?"

Mr. Ogden explained that back in Liverpool he was a member of the International Order of Odd Fellows (IOOF). "Victoria Lodge, No. 448," he said to clarify. "Blacks are not allowed entrance into any of the fraternities here in America. I aim to fix that."

No response.

"Are you all right?" Mr. Ogden said as he studied the glazed-over look attached to Duncan's face.

"Please forgive me," Duncan said. "I'm afraid I'm not very good company."

"No need to explain," Mr. Ogden said. "Perhaps we could do this another time."

"Perhaps."

"I'll leave you with your thoughts then," and Mr. Ogden rose, put on his derby and turned to leave.

"Wait."

Mr. Ogden pivoted back around. Duncan surrendered a thank you, saying that he appreciated everything that the steward tried to do for Lizzy and the infant. "And for myself as well."

"Of course." Mr. Ogden tipped the brim of his hat, wished Duncan all the best and exited.

Duncan followed the retreat of the man, grateful to have come across such a person. Alex sipped his coffee, staring out the window, oblivious to two women who were descending the steps from the rooms above the tavern. They were gathering their dresses, talking along the way. One was a blue-eyed beauty with auburn hair and a pleasant smile. She ceased the interchange with her companion long enough to catch the stoic, almost lost expression upon the nearby patron. She stopped in front of his line of vision, but he never wavered as if he could see through her to the outside and beyond.

"Are you there?" the blue-eyed one said. "Sir?" and she mimed a hello with the fluttering of her hand.

Duncan blinked to refocus, sat ramrod and said, "Please forgive me. It's been a bit of a day."

"I can see that," the blue-eyed beauty said. "Would you like to join us? A whiskey can smooth out the edges."

"Awfully kind of you but I should probably—"

"Nonsense. We won't have it," and she turned to the lady astride and added, "Isn't that right, Fanny?"

"It most certainly is."

Alex Duncan rose and joined the ladies at a larger table overlooking the avenue. "Name's Alex Duncan. Pleasure to make your acquaintance, ladies."

"No acquaintance has been made, sir," the blue-eyed one said. "Certainly not any pleasure."

"Once again I find myself apologizing. Like I said, it's been a bit of a—"

"Just putting on the fun," the blue-eyed one said. "Relax. It's okay."

"Of course." Duncan, sensing he was backsliding, added, "You have a brogue about you, madam. If I was a betting man, I'd say you were from the southern part of Scotland. Near the English border."

"You possess a keen ear, Mr. Duncan," and she extended her hand in an offering. "It's Miss Ann Holliday. I was born in northern Ireland but inherited my parents' tongue from Annandale."

He took her hand, saying, "I was given birth in Strabane."

"Ah, yes. I understand they are mostly dirt farmers in that part of the Emerald Isle," Miss Holliday said.

He skirted the topic of his family's poverty and said, "Like you, my parents emigrated from Scotland, from the flatlands," and he forced a grin, relieved he had voiced a complete sentence without the need for another apology.

"You can release your hand, Mr. Duncan," Miss Holliday said, playing with his infatuation.

"Yes, of course," and he withdrew his hold, feeling clumsy. Again.

A soft smile began to form on Ann Holliday's countenance before she pivoted to introduced her associate. "This is my sister, Frances Holliday. Her friends address her as Fanny. You may acknowledge her as Miss Holliday."

The younger sister was a freckled, ferret-faced woman, jimberjawed with a beak for a nose. She sat stiff with a pointy chin in the manner secured at a finishing school.

He started to offer his hand but thought better of it and delivered a polite nod instead. "What circumstance finds two stunning ladies such as yourselves in New York?"

Frances Holliday flexed her expression at the stranger's hackneyed phrasing and motioned to her sister as if she should take this one.

"Mr. Duncan, you'll not get into our knickers with such boyish approaches," Ann Holliday said. "No doubt it served you well in Strabane but it will not do along Pearl Street."

"Such a pity," he said. "Perhaps I should take my *boyish* manners somewhere more befitting a man of my upbringing, perhaps along the waterfront."

"You speak your mind," Ann Holliday said. "A refreshing approach, indeed."

"Happy to accommodate."

The conversation flowed as easily as the whiskies. The combination served as an elixir for his woes of earlier. His lament over Lizzy and the infant began to fade with the introduction of a variety of topics, ranging from concert hall music to native uprisings to politics. The dialogue was robust and easy. Not wanting to seem too eager, Alex Duncan thanked the ladies for an enchanting afternoon and said goodbye.

A smile grew upon Ann Holliday's face as she studied his backside. "Possesses a decent arse, wouldn't you agree, sister?"

"It'll do until a better one comes along, I suppose."

Chapter Five

Through the summer of 1840 Alexander Duncan worked various jobs but none that suited his skills. Though shipbuilding was on the rise due to the increase in trans-Atlantic traffic, positions were mainly distributed to the Irish who were willing to work for less. Didn't matter if they lacked the expertise, profit trumped workmanship.

Duncan wasn't going to wallow in poverty. He could have stayed in Ireland and done that. No, he was going to take advantage of his internship at the Strabane foundry and start anew.

He entered the offices of Grinnell, Minturn & Co., which had acquired a fleet of more than fifty ships. With Quaker roots, they held a keen interest in aiding the depressed of Ireland, uping their voyages to Liverpool by twofold per week. Again, Duncan rejected a job offer of less than a dollar per day and trudged back to his quarters.

The porky landlord at Brother Delong's followed Duncan up the stairs, berating him for unpaid rent, demanding he clear out by the end of the day. "And don't be giving out this address to any of your peaheaded Scottish friends."

Duncan packed his valise with a curse on his lips. The past four months revealed little in the way of salvation. His mind whirled with thoughts of the pit he had found himself in; his wallet containing barely enough to purchase a single biscuit.

With heavy legs he shuffled from the waterfront and came upon the hustle of the Financial District. He stepped blindly onto a busy street where the nags of a milk wagon reared their heads with a protest. Duncan blinked away his wanderings as an expletive flew his way.

He released a clump of oxygen before noticing the name of the cross street. On a hunch, he veered down Pearl Street until arriving at Fraunces Tavern. The one image that had brightened these past weeks for him was the face of the Scottish lass he met in May. Couldn't get her out of his mind. The endless sky-blue eyes, the bold ginger hair, the spark in her countenance, the curves—ah, the curves. A man could get lost in those arcs and never want for rescue.

He entered, passed the framed tooth of George Washington and peeked into the dining room. Empty.

Must not be open, he thought. *Oh, well. Worth a chance*, and he exited.

Probably for the best. What would he say? What would he have to offer? A lady of Ann Holliday's breeding would wait for no man, let alone one who brought the East River with him, reeking of sweat and pauperism.

He crossed Fifth Avenue, which divided Manhattan, and entered the genteel sector of the city. Well-dressed men in tophats escorted ladies in ankle-length dresses, which took second place to the concoctions nesting upon their heads where feathers of birds arranged themselves in a wide assortment of positions and colors.

Miss Holliday would look splendid in such an outfit, he mused as the corner of his mouth rose with delight. Such simple notions, however, would have to suffice for entertainment, as that was all he could afford.

Lower Broadway found him marveling at the avenue's breadth and length. Handsome shops, neat awnings and ornamental buildings added glitter to the treelined sidewalks.

Greek revival homes, brownstones and carriage houses introduced Duncan to the type of neighborhood he had read about in the *Galway Daily* and the *London Times*. The palaces encircled Gramery Park with its flower beds, fountain and crushed stone paths.

Duncan approached and saw gentlemen and ladies sitting at benches. An itch pushed him forward. If he could be among such people, even if for a brief moment, it might satisfy a craving to be someone else, to pretend that such surroundings could be part of who he might become. He went to lift the latch on the park's gate but it wouldn't open. A posted sign nearby read: FOR PRIVATE USE ONLY.

Fecking langers. Piss on ya.

The opulent dwellings degenerated into apartment-houses and tenements where the traffic and industries of the East River reached him. He drifted through the alleys of the Fourth Ward and came upon a string of warehouses butting up against each other. Shutters covered windows. Soot smeared brick facades. The gloomness had become part and parcel of the place where he felt most comfortable.

A man, wearing a white collar and black robe, stood outside a brothel, preaching, drawing in a collection of rag-tags. "Don't be swayed, my friends, by the machinations of Satan," the priest shouted to the group. "The flesh of a woman is short-lived next to the eternal love of God."

A man with a goatee and a floating eye exited through a pair of wingbat doors. "You here again to disparage the good name of my establishment?"

"Your sinful practices will not go unnoticed," the priest retorted. "Relent and repent before the eyes of the Lord or He shall wreak doom upon you and your house of evil."

Alex Duncan pushed his way forward for a better look. He loved the show. It was honest and real. No pretensions. Just the stripped-down, bare bones of everyday life.

"We're gonna settle this once and for all," the owner of the whorehouse said before motioning to a confederate who pinched a number of rat carcasses from a burlap sack and started flinging them at the priest.

Others wanted in on the fun and in short order a pack of pointy snouts flew through the mist to find their target. The priest stood his ground, singing a biblical hymn.

The whistles of coppers corrupted the air as paddy wagons soon arrived to clear away the bunch. Men in blue waved batons as they formed a v-shaped wedge, bulling their way through the throng.

From behind a pile of coal, Duncan gathered in the scene. Everyone scattered to different alleys, several tossing the last of the vermin and a tune along the way. With the ebbing of the ballyhoo, he continued along the waterfront not knowing his destination or purpose until arriving at the Cunard Line at the foot of Stanton Street on the East River. A man with a full beard and a pipe was tying off a lighter.

He noticed the valise in the stranger's grip and said, "Would ya be lookin' to leave these shores?"

"Sure, why not?" the stranger said.

"Well, then," the bearded one said. "Come aboard, lad. We be in need of a hand or two."

"Where are you headed?" the stranger asked.

"Does it matter?" the bearded one said.

The stranger hesitated, thought about it and said, "Suppose not," and introduced himself. "Name is Alexander Duncan."

"Don't need a name, just a body," and the bearded one led Duncan aboard the lighter, which made its way to a three-masted vessel.

* * *

The *Patrick Henry* cruised down the Atlantic seashore, rounded the Florida Keys and headed into the Gulf of Mexico, mooring in New Orleans. Through the thicket of masts, Duncan glimpsed the ensigns of untold number of nations fluttering in the breeze while men stacked bales and crates on the crowded dockside.

He stepped down the gangplank and into a medley of sounds. A musical blur of languages engulfed him—French, Spanish, Italian and Portuguese. The smells came varied and pungent—the tang of sassafras, the aroma of bacon fat and the roasting of flour into roux. As he stepped away from the area, the fragrances of jasmine and magnolias took over. And the women. Oh my, the women. Wafts of perfume rose up from their complexions, which varied from honey to pecan to ebony. It didn't matter if the ladies were outfitted in expensive silk or simple calico, they were ornamented with more care and style than any single woman he had ever witnessed.

But the most distinct pleasantry was the town's job market.

Whether it was the French Quarter or the Garden District or the Central Business District, ironworkers were in high demand. Each day he read the local newspapers, full of prospects. From one interview to the next, he strolled through the streets of the Big Easy until procuring an office job along the wharf.

Creole Cottages, Italianates and Victorians boasted balconies, doors and windows adorned with iron fastenings. It was a city where he could establish a bank account, lay the foundation for a new life.

Out of habit he started perusing New York's *Morning Herald,* which mentioned the arrival of clippers and packet ships from Londonderry, Belfast and Liverpool. His brother might be registered on the passenger list. While Alex and Sam were never close, they were family. Friends were hard to come by in New Orleans. Perhaps a relative could help fill the void.

In the absence of kin, he grew to depend upon images of Ann Holliday for companionship. The curves of her frame haunted him. She was with him night and day to the point he could no longer concentrate on whatever task was at hand. In September of '43 he wrote to the boarding lodge on Pearl St. in New York. Several weeks later he received a response from Samuel Fraunces, the proprietor of the inn, who surrendered a new address for the lady in question.

Alex Duncan and Ann Holliday began a correspondence that was both mutual and endearing. For the next fourteen months they wrote to each other, each letter more compelling than the previous. He may have exaggerated his financial success, but what harm could that do? Without reason to prolong things further, he travelled to New York and proposed. Ann Jane Holliday accepted his invitation in matrimony on the single condition that her sister Fanny be allowed to live with them.

On August 5, 1844 they married. Since Mr. Duncan had to return to New Orleans for business, the couple honeymooned along the way with Fanny in tow. While privacy was at a premium, the newlyweds made the best of it.

Upon arriving in New Orleans, everyone settled into a handsome townhouse with claret-colored brick, tall shuttered doors and a narrow verandah trimmed with iron lace. The carriage house behind was cramped but well provisioned with two stalls and room for a carriage.

Nine months and three weeks later, Jeannie Duncan was born into the world, followed by sister Rebecca in '46 and brother Sammy Alexander two years later. Alex didn't have much time for the children as he was busy satisfying his wife's desire for the finer things in life. He often worked seventy-hour weeks, coming home exhausted with no strength to oblige Ann's bedroom demands. The times darkened with news from abroad that his da had passed away of dropsy and that his mum died soon afterwards, most likely of a broken heart.

* * *

"Alexander, get that," Ann yelled to her husband with the bang of the doorknocker.

"I'm busy," Alex said as he poured over paperwork in his study.

Another knock.

"I'm busy as well, d-e-a-r," and she dragged out the word to make her point.

Alex closed a ledger and headed for the door where an unexpected surprise awaited.

"*Tabhair amach*," Alex said in Gaelic to the visitor. "You're giving out the stink. Better get in here and take a bath."

"See you still have your charm about you," Sam Duncan said.

Alex wrapped his arms around his brother. "It's been a while. Eight years?" Alex guessed as he withdrew a step.

"Believe so."

"Well, it's taken you long enough to catch up."

"I was delayed, you shite in a bucket," Sam retorted.

"Brought some of da along, did you?" Alex said, recognizing the cutthroat phrase his father often used. "Come, meet the family," and Alex latched onto Sam's bags and led him into the parlor.

During the next few days, picnics and leisurely walks were

coupled with laughter and tales of the old country. Sam told of their parents' wake at Nathaniel Bosworth's place, of how Alex's former manager had provided enough ale to drown the melancholy of most souls. While such rites were usually held at the home of the deceased, this was not the case for Samuel and Lucinda Duncan. The British had confiscated their land due to lack of production. The potato famine had taken hold of the entire country with people like the Duncans finding themselves at the local almshouse.

"If you had stayed behind, perhaps things might have turned out differently," Sam said.

"Can't beat back the will of God," Alex answered. "It was only a matter of time before death came calling. You knew that."

"I knew such an event would not come around for a while. Years of emptying bed pans, cleaning sores, spoon-feeding and dressing mum and da."

"You're here now," Alex said. "That's all that—"

"Nearly a decade of my life wasted away while you built a family and a future for yourself."

After the wrangling, the brothers agreed upon a ceasefire, promising each other never to experience the poverty that took their parents. Though their vows were sincere, they could not agree on which road to take. Alex was quite content in New Orleans but Sam yearned for the opportunities out west.

Two events happened within a month of each other in 1848 to support Sam's desire: on January 24th, James Marshall discovered gold; on February 2nd, the Treaty of Guadalupe Hidalgo was signed, ceding Alta California and other territories to the U.S.

Sam itched to be more than a mere *tattie-hoker*. He was set to leave for San Francisco when an accidental thrill delayed him. Frances Holliday had captured his desires. While he had held such lust in check, he couldn't resist the woman. He soon was allowed to address her as "Fanny" and took a keen interest in her easy smile and engaging conversation, though her ferret-face and beak-like nose took some getting used to.

The nights in New Orleans grew sultry. The heat drove

many to Antoine's on St. Louis Street for a Sazerac on the rocks. Cocktails would ramp up passions, coaxing Fanny and Sam upstairs. The tryst was to be a one-time fling of foolishness.

But the weeks eased forward with each Saturday delivering the pair to Antoine's for a Sazerac and a trip to the third floor where room 302 had been reserved for them. The heat dissolved but not their longing as the months wore on. What was once excused as flummadiddle had swelled into a severe violation of the *Book of Confessions*, the cornerstone for the Scottish Presbyterian Church.

With one last hoorah—if such hunger can be reduced to that—the pair decided that their Christmas gift to each other would be to separate. While Fanny desired matrimony, Sam did not. Better to part as friends than tied to each other in eternal regret. A final drink at Antoine's sealed the agreement, and Sam Duncan departed for California.

In the ensuing days, Fanny's despair grew. She received support from her sister to function on most days. While her affair with Sam was kept from prying eyes, her baby-bump was not. Alex was furious with his brother and urged Fanny to contact him and appraise him of the situation.

A relationship based on pity, however, would not stand the test of time. She would raise the child on her own. In August of the following year, a baby boy entered the fold. Fanny christened the child Samuel Montgomery Duncan Junior. Alex, however, didn't think the tyke should be burdened with such a title.

There was only one recourse to take according to Ann. Her husband would not be allowed to put on the poor mouth and do nothing, leaving his sister-in-law defiled and forgotten.

* * *

Dressed in a gray-pinstriped suit, Alex Duncan kissed his two youngest children on the forehead before eyeing his oldest, Jeannie. "Be a good girl and help your mum."

"You're silly, daddy," and the five-year-old sprinted toward the parlor to play with her dollhouse. Alex looked at his wife, saying that he would write as soon as he got settled. "Shouldn't be more than a few months," and he lifted his carpet bag.

"Don't dilly-dally. There will be bills enough to pay as well as improvements to make."

"Of course, dear." He could charm the freckles off a barmaid, but his wife was another matter altogether. With a quiet face, he brought her close.

She felt a hard object and retreated a step. "What's this?" and she tapped the butt of a revolver poking outward from his waistband.

"It's a short-barreled Slocum. Five-shot, .32 caliber with a little kick due to—"

"Just bring your brother back to my sister and her newborn."

Chapter Six

In May of 1850, the *Falcon* of the Pacific Mail Steamship Company docked in New Orleans with twenty-nine passengers on board, mostly government employees and missionaries bound for California. Berths were available for one hundred more souls. Alex Duncan scanned the crowd and estimated there was twice that number waiting to embark for the trip to Chagres, Panama.

A stiffness latched onto the throng. Scrappy men eyed the persons on either side. The look of desperation varied but their purpose was the same: get to the gold fields before the next fellow.

Men stormed up the gangplank over the protest of Captain Notestein. The crew rushed to the scene with whatever makeshift weapons lay nearby. Duncan's expression tightened and he placed a hand on his pistol, pressing forward, caught up in the rush. The stampede crashed into a wall of raised axe handles and knuckles. Spittle hooked onto the barks of determined men.

The captain's pleas for calm fell below the din. With the situation about to unravel, the first mate fired off a round. The space went silent.

Captain Notestein shaped his palms into a megaphone and yelled, "All unauthorized persons must remove themselves from the gangplank. Immediately. A lottery will decide which of you may seek passage."

"Already had the lottery," an unkept man bellowed. "Guess what? We're all winners."

The tangle returned and the captain pressed down the air, asking for order, but his quivering manner betrayed him and the disgruntled multitude felt emboldened, refusing to debark. The first mate started to unsheathe his sword but the captain laid a hand on the sailor's intent and returned his gaze upon the mob, saying that provisions would be provided to accommodate everyone.

With that entreaty, the *Falcon* readied for departure, adding hammocks in the storage hold, in the blubber compartments. Bedrolls covered the top deck, appearing like a quilt of mismatched pieces. No crack or cranny spared.

When the steamship arrived in Panama six days later, it wasn't able to anchor near shore due to reefs and sand bars. Duncan and the others were forced to pay natives to shuttle them between the *Falcon* and the town of Chagres.

Gold fever inhabited several of the crew as well who abandoned the ship alongside the passengers. Additional vessels began to arrive from distant shores, emptying hordes of fortune hunters. The place swelled with impatience as men clamored for transportation to Las Cruces, forty-five miles upstream along the Chagres River.

Duncan shouldered his way through the throng, his demands evaporating amidst the jangle of likeminded men. There was a difference between him and most others, however. He wasn't interested in the riches of the Sierras, wanting nothing more than to avoid the ire of his family.

Within the bobbing and weaving of heads, Duncan spotted a native with an almond complexion, holding a pistol to a couple of bungo crewmen, gesturing for them to remain seated. Duncan toted his carpet bag to the scene where he overheard the man speaking in Spanish, acting the part of *el jefe*. Duncan knew enough of the language to understand that an argument of some manner was underway. *El jefe* had refused his crew's request for rest, saying that the vessel was required to make the return trip immediately.

Duncan nudged *el jefe* and jangled a bag of coins. The man weighed the collection in his hand before returning a grin.

* * *

Duncan tossed a centipede overboard and took a seat under a canopy along with five other travelers as the racket from shore waned within the wake of the bungo. Duncan discarded his jacket and vest and dipped his ascot in the algae-green water before wrapping the damp tie around his neck. Everything and everybody dripped with moisture as the jungle came alive. Violet-capped hummingbirds, golden greenlets and orange-crowned orioles flew overhead with their songs while a troop of red-crested tamarins hooted along the bank.

Swaths of palms, Kapok and mango trees straddled both sides of the river. Prongs and ferns and branches hung over the water's edge while pinholes of light sifted downward.

Frogs posed on a giant leaf unawares of a snake that crept up the tree trunk. Duncan wondered what other lethal creatures worked these waters. He had no further to look than the length of the bungo where scruffy-faced characters sat in silence, each guarding their speech and goods with deadly stares. Alex felt for the handle of his Slocum as if to make sure it was still there.

As the day began to close, thousands of bats jetted from the folded leaves of trees and zig-zagged across the sky, taking their fill on mosquitos and such. Have at it, boys, Duncan thought. Everyone else is.

El jefe steered the bungo past Punta Bahia and De Lesseps Island and pulled into Bohio, a bush hamlet of two hundred natives where a crude outdoor market bustled with activity. Duncan weaved his way between dried-up old ladies, vendors and gringos. Pack mules advanced along the thoroughfare, bent under the weight of cocoa beans, squash, corn, yucca and other goods. His curiosity piqued with all the hurly-burly and he took his time meandering through the crowd.

The Spanish tongue filled the air as traders showcased their produce, lauding its quality in hopes of bartering for certain needs. Nearby, a different form of speech spilled from lean-tos as Chinamen haggled with passersby.

The three hotels were overflowing with signs posted on the entrance, which read: *NO HAY HABITACIONES LIBRES.* Duncan continued his search for accommodations, walking past huts, all of which rented hammocks. After probing much of the town, he found available quarters with a family of six who were more than happy to share their one-room abode in exchange for two hundred pesos. While the price was exorbitant, Duncan considered himself lucky to find a place to rest his weary bones.

All sat cross-legged on the dirt floor and helped themselves to a bowl of *sancocho*. The mother possessed a mole-flecked face but it didn't detract from her pleasant countenance as she served hearty portions of sweet plantains and white rice with the soup.

Duncan excused himself after dinner and went to find some solitude outside where he settled upon a stump. His quiet was soon interrupted by the family's four children who ranged in age from three to nine. They sat in front of him with folded hands as might an audience waiting to be entertained. Duncan exhaled, hand-brushed his scalp and surrendered to the silent demands.

He picked his pocket watch from his waistcoat and dangled it from its chain. Eight eyeballs traced its arc, mesmerized by the light bouncing off the gold casing. The act reached a climax as Duncan snapped open the timepiece to unveil a miniature picture on the left and a clock on the right.

Oohs and aahs rose alongside toothy smiles.

A stringy-haired boy pointed to the portrait of the man and woman. "*Quiénes son?*" the boy asked.

"*Mi madre y mi padre,*" Duncan answered with what little Spanish had come his way the previous two weeks.

A lengthy dialogue ensued involving several language flubs by Duncan. So much so that Duncan tried to apologize. "*Estoy...*" and his mind stalled until a vague recollection came to him. "*Estoy embarazado,*" he said, proud of his effort.

Giggles and untamed chortles filled the space. Two fell sideways to the ground with their laughter.

"*Que?*" Duncan asked.

The stringy-haired one corrected the gringo, telling him that he most likely wasn't *embarazado,* pregnant. Perhaps *embarrassed* but not pregnant. Duncan excused himself, saying that that was enough. He got up and went inside for the night, only to be followed by the quartet that marched in step with him.

Duncan stopped and turned around to the flock. "Don't you have somewhere to go?" he said before switching it up: *"¿No have el dóndo to el vamoose?"*

"No," said Stringy Hair.

Duncan tossed his socks, pants and shirt over a bamboo chair and slipped into a hammock with nothing on but a pair of long johns. He went to lower the mosquito netting when he spotted the four kids sitting on the floor, staring at him.

"El caliento and el tiredo," Duncan said as he swished the back of his hand. "Go away."

The gringo rolled over with his fatigue, showing his backside, feeling the heat from playful eyes.

* * *

The bungo pushed past Isla Chicha. The day's first light squeezed through the foliage while an armadillo retreated into the bush. By ten a.m. the heat had arrived in full force. Duncan began to shed a layer of clothing when he spotted a ring of men waving and shouting from the far bank. He relayed his finding to *el jefe* who ordered his crew to row toward the uproar.

A group of gringos babbled away. Sentences jumbled over each another, but it was clear enough that the jungle had had its way with them.

One fellow, wearing chin whiskers and a derby, pulled a pistol from his shoulder holster. "We're coming aboard. Make way."

"Habitación para un solo. Room for only one," *el jefe* answered.

"I can fix that," and the one with the chin whiskers slid his weapon to a square-shouldered passenger who owned a receding hairline. "Get off."

"You need to work on your greeting," Duncan said. "The barrel of a gun does not induce charm."

"Shut your Irish gob and move," the intruder said, motioning with his weapon toward the shore.

"First, I don't care much for the Irish reference as my mouth is of Scottish descent," Duncan retorted before slipping back his waistcoat to reveal the handle of his Slocum. "Secondly, as any langer can plainly see, there are five of us who are equipped to challenge your request," and he gestured toward his fellow passengers who showcased their revolvers as well.

Without warning, a shot rang out and the jungle went berserk. Screaming and screeching accompanied jagged movements from nearby.

The intruder gazed downward, past his weapon to his pantleg where a rivulet of crimson ran thick and dark. He fell to his knees, pupils dilated with shock.

A swirl of smoke spilled from the weapon of *el jefe* as he repeated his instructions, that there was room for one additional passenger. That was all. "*No más que eso.*"

A caiman darted across the water toward the injured one. Others latched onto him and retreated to the safety of the bush. One, however, lagged behind. A young squirt, no older than fourteen with a pinched face, hopped aboard and extended his hand, which held several coins.

The bungo boss counted the currency before shaking his head, saying, "One thousand pesos."

"That's...that's," and the squirt's words stumbled with the math.

"Fifty dollars," Duncan clarified from astern.

"Why that's over three times the goin' rate," the lad said. "Plus, there be just three days remainin' to the trip. Blackmail, that's what this be," and he folded his arms in defiance.

El jefe snickered at the *cajones* of the young man before motioning back to the bank, back to where the caiman was picking up a scent. Duncan sympathized with the lad, recalling his own youthful days when adventure occupied every thought.

"Here," Duncan said as he passed a small bag to *el jefe*. "This should cover any shortage."

"Thanks, mister," the lad said as he took a seat next to his benefactor.

"What's your name?" Duncan asked.

"Billy Fraser."

"Headed to San Francisco?" Duncan asked.

"Not exactly. More like Cholula. Mexico. I've got an uncle there who—"

"Your itinerary has changed. You can work off your debt when we arrive in California. Okay with you?"

"What?"

"I'll accept that as a *yes*."

* * *

Another few days passed before they reached Las Cruces. *El jefe* turned the boat around without so much as a goodbye while the passengers parted in different directions.

Duncan hired mules to carry him and the kid for the remaining eighteen miles to Panama City. Along the way exchanges were made to fill the hours.

"Where are you from, Billy Fraser?" Alex Duncan asked.

"Missouri, for the most part."

"Slave country, is it?"

"Some counties, yes. Some counties, not. Reckon it be as confused as any place."

"Confusion does seem to be the theme of the day."

A few miles down the road an enterprise of some note was underway. Rails and ties were being unloaded from flatcars. Duncan wondered how deep into the jungle the line would extend. Had he known in advance, a delay of a year might have been the proper action but that would not have sat well with his wife or sister-in-law. Both were anxious for him to locate Sam and return to New Orleans. Too bad family had to count for something.

Further along the tracks, gringos on horseback were throwing obscenities at a clutch of workers, using names like "chink" and *"ching chong."*

One of the white men took a whip to an Oriental who bent under the beating. He straightened to show his pride. Perhaps back in China he was someone of distinction. Perhaps a civic leader or a business owner or a teacher.

Duncan guessed that tragedies had engulfed the man, forcing him to leave his loved ones, only to come to such a place to endure the wrath of inferior men.

* * *

Hotel rooms were overbooked as well as the dirt floors of slum shanties. With the day closing fast and their bodies eager for food and rest, Duncan and the kid settled into a large tent district outside the city walls.

"Best we use my shelter seein' as how you didn't pack one," Billy said.

"Fine by me," Duncan said as he sat down his valise.

"A thousand pesos," Billy said. "That'd be the goin' rate for shelter in these parts."

"Done some figuring, have you?" Duncan said.

"Believe I have."

"Christ on a bike," Duncan whispered to no one in particular.

"Pardon?"

"No mind. I'll pay your blood money."

"Good answer," Billy said in a mocking voice.

Chapter Seven

Two weeks passed as the kid and the Ulster Scot waited for transportation in Panama City. Nerves frayed. Patience dwindled. By the time the *California* dropped anchor, five hundred angry souls were at the dock. With more passengers demanding to board than berths available, Duncan sensed the situation could turn ugly as it had back in New Orleans. Same pissed-off men. Same toxic environment.

In the hall of the Pacific Mail Steamship Company a ticket agent proceeded to allow those with "Through Passage" to board. Duncan grew upset with himself for his lack of foresight. *Should've booked ahead*, he thought.

Rumors dashed through the crowd that a number of the passengers were Peruvians. Complaints showered the ticket agent, exclaiming more or less that U.S. citizens had priority on Yankee ships.

The steamship line was able to pacify the gringos by persuading the Peruvians to triple up in state rooms, promoting a compromise of two Americans for each foreigner on board. But Duncan was not among the lucky ones.

This was becoming an all too familiar trend, one that Duncan was growing tired of with each passing day. He and Billy Fraser approached a man who appeared to be gripping an official voucher as if guarding the Crown Jewels.

"Need some cash?" Duncan asked as he pinched the sleeve of the stranger.

The man threw a frown to the grip, saying, "Need some space is what I need," the stranger said in a gruff manner as he pulled away.

"Give you a thousand dollars for two tickets."

"You touched or somethin'?" the stranger said.

"Most likely," Duncan answered. "The offer is good for the next thirty seconds," and he showed a wad of greenbacks.

* * *

The *California* steamed out of Panama on May 31, 1850 with 365 passengers, 165 more than what she was designed for. While at sea, a stoker hid the whereabouts of a stowaway from officers. Upon the discovery of the fare-dodger, his accomplice was soon found out as well. The captain fined the stoker and berated him in front of the rest of the crew as well as the travelers. Duncan watched the spectacle, which had the obvious intent of making an example of the man. The tactic backfired.

Some of the crew revolted, refusing to carry out their assigned tasks. The captain was forced to dock at Mazatlán and resolve the matter with the dismissal of several employees. There was no shortage of men willing to work their way to San Francisco, but the delay put a dent into the ship's provisions. With the gold rush in full swing, supplies were hard to come by, whether it be fresh water or food or coal.

Within a couple of days of the incident, the *California* ran out of fuel. An emergency was declared and the captain ordered the collection of combustible materials. Billy Fraser's complaint regarding the removal of his cot went unheeded. Duncan knew from his crossing of the Atlantic that one's relationship with the crew was crucial and told the kid to shut his yap.

"You own no reason to fuss," Duncan persisted.

"And you ain't nothin' but an old flapdoodle."

"Not too late to throw your arse back in the jungle with the caimans and such."

But Duncan soon yielded to the same frustration when his cot found the woodpile as well. Tables, chairs and large sections of the deck joined the parade to the boiler. By the time all passed through the Golden Gate on June 23, 1850, not a stick was left untouched. The journey had been uncomfortable and full of the unexpected, but at least the comforts of civilization would soon be close at hand. Or so it was thought.

The *California* eased past chiseled cliffs. Piledrivers whined with the strain of beefing up a seawall while in the background tents and goats dotted Telegraph Hill atop of which stood a semaphore.

The steamship rounded the last bend and the close-set buildings of San Francisco came into view. As the vessel put into port, Duncan couldn't count the number of craft jockeying for moorings. Hundreds of ships bobbed and shifted as crews flung curses one to the other.

The *California* docked at Clark's Wharf at the foot of Broadway near Yerba Buena Cove. Lines flew to shore where hands secured the ship to bollards.

The language of eager men and the grind of carriage wheels rose up from the city. Fetid scents joined the bustle with the assault of pitch, cooking grease, sweat and dung.

With the kid in tow, Duncan disembarked from the vessel, delighted to avoid the costly lighterage that went with mooring offshore. His wallet was in need of a transfusion what with the constant bribes doled out along the journey.

A forest of masts dominated the harbor. Duncan surmised that the rumors were true, that crews had mutinied and skipped to the gold fields.

They sloshed through the mudflats, climbed a series of wooden steps and entered the Apollo Saloon. The tavern was constructed from the ruins of a two-masted schooner, which had its stern removed for easy access.

A pair of empty stools beckoned and they sat, Duncan bringing his carpetbag to his lap, advising the kid to do the same. "Wouldn't trust any of these knackers," Duncan said. "My guess is they'd rob the drawers straight off that scrawny frame of yours if a profit be in it."

"My frame happens to be just fine, thank you," and to prove his point the kid nodded to a pair of thinly clad women who dangled inviting grins his way.

"Those smiles come with a price. You do know that, eh?"

A bartender with a sour demeanor arrived, saving the lad from further embarrassment. "What'll it be?"

They ordered the house specialty, pisco punch brandy,

before the barkeep retreated without another word.

They tanked up, enjoying the flirtation of whores and the tunes from a lively piano when, without warning, a discordant sound intruded. A sapskull was chattering to his whiskey and rye, slurring his phrases. The grunting drew Duncan's attention and he looked sideways to spot the man pissing himself, putting out the stink as urine ran down his pantleg to a copper gutter.

"Time we left," Duncan said to the kid.

"*Time* we had another drink," and Billy gestured to the bartender.

"Stay," Duncan said as he gathered his carpetbag. "No matter to me," and he tossed a couple of gold pieces toward his empty glass.

"Need to loosen the purse strings on that tight Irish arse of yours," and the kid followed his benefactor out the door.

They passed a warehouse and a string of adobe cottages wrapped in bullock skins. On either side of Broadway's dirt promenade, two- and three-story clapboards with false fronts crowded each other. Further up the road, additional structures were underway. The clatter of hammers and saws and such spilled onto the thoroughfare.

"A man could find work easy enough in this place," Billy said.

No response.

"Is that what you're here for, to start some sort of business?" Billy asked.

"I'm here to locate my brother and bring him back to New Orleans."

"Seems you're passin' on an opportunity just for the sake of a relative. Hardly makes any sense."

"If you were acquainted with my wife, it would make perfectly good sense. And by the way, it *is* your business. Or at least I intend to make it so."

"Don't follow."

"There's a job waiting for you," Duncan said. "One that'll pay off your debt."

* * *

Just three years earlier, the city was known as Yerba Buena under the Mexican regime, but now the place deserved a name worthy of its rising popularity. The moniker "San Francisco" was stolen from the town of St. Francis, which settled on "Benicia" as its new label. As if it had a choice. Not ethics or laws or regulations had any bearing on the shift. Thievery was at the heart and soul of Bagdad by the Bay. Always was. Always would be.

Duncan had no problem with the ways of his most recent address. In fact, it endeared him even closer to the city, which reminded him of the uncouth nature of his birthplace back in Ireland. One could carve out a small fortune for himself in such a topsy-turvy location. Law and order took a backseat to personal gain. Chaos was a good thing.

In order to pay for his lodging and other expenses, Alex set up shop on Clay Street where he continued with his specialty of making iron doors and shutters. As it turned out, this was for the best as it soon became apparent that his brother would not be located without some effort. Billy Fraser scoured the city for the next two months but always returned empty-handed.

Alex began to fear that perhaps his younger sibling had been shanghaied to appease some captain's mandate to field a crew, or worst yet, that Sam had been done in by one of the many roving bands of thugs inhabiting the city.

East of Kearny Street was known as Sydney Town, home to the Sydney Ducks whose chief form of entertainment was the harassment of anyone from the United Kingdom. No distinction made between Brits or Irish or Scots. Everyone fair game.

In late July Billy tripped across information relating to Sam Duncan's whereabouts. Word had it that he was co-owner of a lumber mill along the Sonoma coast. Alex dispatched the lad immediately, paying his passage aboard a lumber schooner.

After three weeks with no word, Alex was about to surrender the kid to the way of other greedy souls. Then one afternoon, Billy entered the business of DUNCAN WINDOW and SHUTTER REPAIR.

"Found your brother," the kid said as he gummed a wad of tobacco while slumping into a wingback chair, plopping the heel of his boot onto a mahogany desk.

Duncan glared at the indiscretion, silent.

"What? Ain't ya gonna say somethin'? A hello might be in order."

Duncan's stone expression caught the kid's attention and the lad removed his boot from the desk and sat up.

"And take that God-awful weed out of your mouth," Duncan said.

The kid searched for a receptacle as his employer rifled off a series of questions. With no solution close at hand, Billy swallowed his chew.

"Where is he?" Duncan asked.

"Where's who?"

"My brother, you eejit, the guy we've been chasing after these last several months."

"I ain't no *ejit*," Billy said. "And just to refresh your Irish noggin, it ain't *we* who been chasin' after your runaway brother. It been *me* and me alone."

"Christ on a bike," Duncan said.

"Never was partial to Sunday school but to my recollection Jesus never rode no bike."

"My brother?" Duncan said to refresh the topic at hand.

"Started Blumedale Sawmill Company. With a Joshua Hendry fella. Somewhere between Bloomfield and Freestone. In western Sonoma County," Billy answered.

No response.

"No way your brother's returnin' to Orleans," the kid added. "Can't blame him. Ain't gonna let go of a money-maker for a woman. Even if she did have his prodigy."

The air grew thick with the news. "Your debt has been paid," Alex said before returning his eyes to a ledger.

"If'n it was my brother, I'd be searchin' for him myself, not leavin' it up to another."

Billy Fraser pivoted and rolled thru the exit with a snort, to find his place in life. It wasn't that Duncan didn't appreciate the kid's efforts. It was more of an unwillingness to admit that perhaps the lad was right, that more of a personal effort was called for.

Alex had mailed the latest news of his brother to his wife, but it had been months without a reply. In October of 1851 a vessel was spotted entering the Gate. Homesick argonauts scampered to the foot of Telegraph Hill to get a better look at the position of the semaphore's two arms. Cheers bolted up with the news that the ship was a Pacific Mailer.

Duncan sped toward the post office near Portsmouth Square in hopes of obtaining a place near the head of the line. To his dismay, scores of others held onto the same notion.

Hours later in his room above his shop, Alex opened a letter bearing his wife's return address. In no uncertain terms, she wrote of her disappointment as well as that of her sister. Fanny loved Sam beyond any safe accounting and desired for him to return "home" to New Orleans where his child longed for a father's embrace.

In closing, Ann Duncan reminded her husband that he too was a father, and she listed the names of their three children in case their identities had escaped his memory.

Alex let the correspondence droop to his lap. What was he to do? If he returned to Louisiana, he would lose the makings of an up-and-coming business. If he stayed, he would further enflame the fury of his wife and sister-in-law.

* * *

A team of eight draft horses struggled with their load down Clay Street. A two-story clapboard teetered atop a flatbed while a man with square-shoulders and thinning hair walked ahead to clear a path.

Alex Duncan shooed away an on-coming milk wagon, directing it to the next lane. Pedestrians gawked at the unusual sight. It was the first such endeavor in the city's history. Moving his business six blocks down Sansome Street would bring him closer to the heart of the Financial District. Money was to be had. No time to waste.

Everyone wanted in on the act. And like Alex Duncan, many learned that it wasn't necessary to journey to the Sierras to bring dreams to fruition. Ship lines made a hefty profit smuggling convicts to needy employers back east. Street gangs bathed in riches via extortion and gambling. Others traversed the city streets, selling picks, axes and pans for $15 each, a 750% markup. Men went to war over the procurement of tens of thousands of bird eggs from the Farallon Islands while "professional" ladies soon crowded the brothels along Pacific Street.

There was plenty of competition to be wary of, but for a man like Duncan it would not be a deterrent as he never took kindly to the notion of defeat. He was already battle-proven, having endured the hardships of Ireland as well as surviving the crossing of an ocean and an isthmus. Then in the afternoon of '54 a different kind of challenge arrived, one far more powerful than those of yesteryear.

"Hello, dear," a female sounded from the shop's entrance.

The familiar voice stunned Alex. His composure abandoned him as he tried to latch onto a proper greeting.

"Nice to see you," he said with an awkward grin.

"*Nice to see you?*" Ann repeated. "Is that all you have to say after a two-year absence?"

Three heads peeked from behind her gown.

"And who might these be?" Duncan asked.

"They might be your children," Ann said in a matter-of-fact tone.

The trio of tots ignored the request of the stranger to come closer and drifted further behind the protection of their mother's hem.

"It's okay," he said. "I won't bite," and he stretched out his arms in a welcome.

Jeannie, Rebecca and Sammy Alexander gazed upward to their mum as if asking if the man might be capable of such an act. Ann Duncan nudged her flock forward, saying that the man most likely was harmless.

"That is correct, isn't it, *dear*?" she said to her husband, emphasizing the last word in a theatrical voice.

He went to embrace his children when a second woman appeared in the doorway with a tyke of her own.

"Hello," Alex said. "It's good to—"

"Save it for someone who gives a rat's arse," Fanny Holliday said. "Where's your brother?"

"Getting right to it, are we?" Alex said.

Fanny and Ann Holliday shared many similarities as sisters. They both possessed a no-nonsense flair with an attitude to match. The difference was that one owned the title of "Mrs." while the other did not.

Fanny drummed the toe of her shoe upon the planked floor, folding her arms. Her expression stiff with expectation.

"Ah, yes, well," Duncan said, rubbing his hands together. "Sam is…Sam is making his fortune. For you and yours," and he gestured to the wee one attached to her hand.

"His name is *Samuel*," Fanny corrected. "Samuel Montgomery Duncan Junior, christened after the person who implanted me with his seed."

"Yes, I'm quite aware of the boy's name as well as the circumstances regarding his conception," Alex said. "By the way, interesting spin on the whole love-making thing. Not sure I'd phrase it quite—"

"Dear," Ann interrupted, "please give my sister the information she seeks."

"Yes, all right then," he said. "Last I heard Sam moved his lumber mill from Bloomfield to Salt Point further up the coast. Still in business with a Mr. Joshua Hendry."

"Since I cannot expect you to do right by your sister-in-law, I have journeyed to this god-awful place with a plan. Do you understand my meaning?" Ann said.

"I'm sure I do not."

Chapter Eight

Twin Orlov trotters pulled a four-seat carriage down Sansom Street. The animals stood fifteen hands high wearing regal white coats and muscular builds. How the Russian steeds landed in San Francisco was beyond Duncan's comprehension. No accounting for the power of silver, he guessed.

Alex looked smart in his tailor-made wool suit with white shirt, detachable collar, cuff links and chainwatch. Ann and Fanny didn't possess the same flair for clothes, appearing drab in brown, full length dresses. Feathered hats and gloves, however, helped spice up the affair while the four children wore scarves to protect them from the biting fog.

Alex decided not to sell his shop in case his wife's scheme fell to ruin. He understood well enough that a handsome profit could be realized in the timber industry but balked at the idea that he and his brother could make such a joint affair work. Differences had mounted. Bitterness had seeped in.

The horses pushed on until reaching Clark's Wharf near the foot of Broadway where everyone disembarked. Ann stepped to the ticket window of McLane Shipping Co. and presented a packet of travel vouchers while Alex tended to Fanny and the youngsters.

"Going to Salt Point, I see," the agent said who spoke out of the side of his mouth, a block of chew ballooning a cheek.

"Yes," Ann answered. "I was told that an additional dollar per person would procure premiere cabins."

"Absolutely correct, ma'am," and the agent, with a sweep of his arm, pointed to a poster of an ocean liner gracing the wall, saying, "The *Excel* is comparable to this grand vessel. You'll not be disappointed."

The agent stamped the vouchers and directed all to Pier 3 while a rivulet of muddy juice ran down his chin. "Have a wonderful voyage, ma'am."

With tickets in hand, the Duncans gathered at the dock. A pair of steamer tugs soon arrived, nudging an insignificant schooner to the wharf. A swarthy-looking creature stepped ashore and proceeded to check the destination tags on pieces of luggage. Toots and gurgles and all sorts of noises leaked from the man as he hefted a trunk to his shoulders.

"Excuse me, sir, but what do you think you are doing?" a woman in a feathered hat called out.

He looked to the woman and excused himself, saying, "Been cursed with active bowels, ma'am. Family hand-me-down, I'm afraid."

"I was referring to the luggage, sir," the woman repeated. "What are you doing with our luggage?'

"You be goin' up north? To Salt Point?"

"Yes."

"Then you be our passengers. Time to board."

"There must be some mistake," Ann said. "I booked passage for us aboard a luxury liner, which this...this bucket certainly is not."

"Couldn't agree more, ma'am," Swarthyman said. "The *Excel's* never been confused with luxury. That be for sure," and off he went.

Ann stared at her husband, "Say something."

Alex followed her pointy finger to the back of the sailor and yelled, "Wait one moment," and he hurried to the fellow. The pair exchanged a few words before Alex returned.

"Well?" Ann said.

"Evidently, the tickets are non-refundable."

Ann's expression pressed into a frown.

"Perhaps this was a poor idea," Alex persisted. "Perhaps we should return home, dear?"

"*Home*, dear, is where the heart is," and Ann lifted her dress with the cliché along with a renewed determination, directing all toward the gangplank.

The *Excel* was a two-masted schooner with plenty of room

for a six-man crew and a dozen passengers. Its cargo on this day included five tons of coal, which were stored in the keel as ballast. In the hold were a piano, chewing tobacco, wood stoves, hoarhound candy and other items for the lumber mills up and down the coast. All in all, a light load.

George Morgan did not don the white uniform of an ocean liner's captain. What he lacked in presentation he more than made up for with a working-man's smile, genuine to the core. He welcomed the family with a handshake for each. Junior accepted the greeting with glee while Ann's sprats busied themselves with an examination of each other's belly buttons.

With the introductions put aside, the Duncans passed the helm and a lifeboat to the far end of the companionway where two cabins clustered together. The rooms were outfitted in similar fashion, each no bigger than a rope locker with a mustiness that consumed a Morris Chair, a desk and bunkbeds. Dingy-gray was the décor of choice with the exception of a band of light, which staged a fleet of dancing mites.

Ann untied her feathered hat and placed it with care upon the desk. It was a black silk number with a box-pleated band, ribbon and polka-dots. The headdress reminded her of high society back in New York, of those years filled with promise and the lure of proper suitors. Oh, well. *Se la vie*, as they say.

No sooner had they gotten underway when the youngest, six-year-old Rebecca, crooned that she had to pee, which triggered similar urges from her brother and sister. The troop clamored to the head where Rebecca worked her way onto the toilet seat. The tot's fleshy rearend squeaked with every movement, causing giggles to erupt from her siblings.

"That will be quite enough," Ann said.

Yuks and tee-hees, however, continued to escape between fingers, which were pressed against young lips.

"Children, behave yourselves," and the mother released a defeated gasp as if the world was coming to an end.

* * *

Outside the Gate, the *Excel* nosed through an onslaught of

swells. Sails bellied up against the gust, the mainbrace creaking and groaning. With the light cargo, she ran unwieldy as she tacked into the northerner.

With fright in her eyes, Fanny brought Junior to her sister's cabin where an unsteady feeling filled the space. Ann cautioned all to anchor themselves to the bunkbeds. The youngest of the clan, however, seemed intrigued with the commotion and went to the porthole to see for himself.

The five-year-old's head drifted back around to his uncle who was standing nearby.

"Nothing to set your knickers ablaze," Uncle Alex said with a half-smile. "Understand?"

Ann overheard the brief sermon and said, "There is no need to add an inferno to the scene, let alone someone's knickers."

"No scene. No inferno." But the damage was done and Alex returned his attention to Junior.

"You'll be meeting your father for the first time tomorrow," Uncle Alex said. "How do you feel about that?"

The boy kept his vision on the storm and shrugged, talking over his shoulder. "My mum's more excited than I am."

"Why do you think that is?"

"She needs him more than I do."

The boy's self-reliant, Uncle Alex thought. More than he could say about his own.

The storm continued its howling, each blow stronger than the last. Passengers stumbled to the poop deck where they unloaded their discomfort. Others retreated to the galley and gathered around the woodstove, but the scent of burning pork drove them back to their cabins.

The freeboard was well above the waterline, the vessel riding high and loose. Three of the four crew members, garbed in slickers and gaiters, scrambled across the deck and climbed Jacob's ladder to unfurl the sails.

Alex Duncan made his way to the helm. "Got a bit of a breeze picking up, it appears," he said to Captain Morgan.

The captain spied the look on the passenger's expression and said, "Your Irish fancy will be safe enough."

"I'm not Irish," Duncan yelled over the angry tempest.

"What?"

"I'm not...," and as Duncan started to repeat himself, a crack from above seized the moment.

The jibboom snapped, cascading to the deck. The topsail of the foremast blew like a cat with its tail on fire. The second mate was able to untangle the mess, allowing the *Excel* to stay on course.

Almost fifteen hours and fifty-five miles out of San Francisco, the schooner arrived at its first destination, a dead calm welcoming it. The Bodega Township had grown from a few nomadic natives to a thriving community of some 250 souls, mostly by way of Canada and northern Europe.

Just four years prior in 1850 the brig *Frolic,* with trade goods from China, washed ashore at this very spot. Salvagers flocked to the site only to discover that a Pomo tribe had disemboweled the ship to its core. Instead of returning home empty-handed, however, the would-be-salvagers brought back something of great value—news of virgin forests ripe for the plucking.

Alex Duncan scanned the landscape through a spyglass. Redwoods dotted the ridges in the distance while rows of potatoes carpeted the sloping meadows in the foreground.

He began to hyperventilate. His palms went clammy. It was as if the starchy, earthy scent of the taters had raced across the bay to invade his senses. Death seeped through every pore. Images of his home back in Ireland flitted across his mindscape, of a black malignancy coursing its way through leafy stalks.

The arrival of a fogbank served as an elixir. Duncan started to come around when a voice brought him from one misery to another.

"What is the matter with you?" Ann said, her fingers nagging at his coat sleeve.

He lowered the spyglass and said, "Nothing. I'm...I'm fine."

And they stood there, side by side. One blinking away the past. The other longing for the future.

The *Excel* dropped anchor in six fathoms of water on the leeward side of Bodega Head. Crewmen scurried about, readying the ship for unloading. As there was no merchandise top deck, a wench began to lift goods from the hole. Lightermen from shore used sweeps to oar a thirty-foot barge alongside the *Excel*. The process of transferring the cargo from the schooner to the barge was tedious and slow, but the calm waters aided the cause without incident.

If his wife's ambitious plans were to succeed, Alex thought he ought to introduce himself to his potential neighbors and suggested that Ann stay behind and watch over the brood.

"I'll only be gone as long as it takes to receive a handshake or two," Alex said. "Be back before you can say *Christ on a bike*."

"You'll do no such thing," Ann retorted. "There'll be no side jaunts or gallivanting. I know you. A visit to a saloon or a whorehouse is your true intention, of that I am certain. You are but a man and corrupt in the ways of the devil, Mr. Duncan."

"Such corruption, dear, is beyond my means as this financial venture of yours will most likely empty my pockets."

Ann's untethered hat flew from her head and went overboard. Her eyes went wide with rage, saying, "See what you've done," and she stomped from the deck toward her quarters.

Alex dismissed the accusation, crunching up his forehead in puzzlement, and returned his attention to the activity underway. The barge had returned to shore where oarsmen and lighters began to unload coal and several other products. Such a delivery became the event of each month, celebrated by the residents who had made their way to Doran Beach.

The assembly was a fine blend of occidentals and indigenous people. It was pleasant to witness those of different origins rubbing elbows together, enjoying the arrival of the simple necessities of life. Mail, canvas coats and gun powder were doled out to various whites while several of the natives took an interest in the sacks of tobacco and candy.

Duncan adjusted the spyglass and noticed women wearing embroidered shawls while more than a few of the men donned silk sashes and handkerchiefs. He wondered if these enchantments were salvaged from the brig *Frolic*, her goods from the Orient lifted by the local Indians not long ago. If that was the case, it was obvious to Duncan that this was a place of sharing and peaceful coexistence.

Alex's eye followed Captain Morgan who stopped to talk with an older gentleman, perhaps in his sixties, donning a gray mane and a soft countenance. Alongside stood a beauty, endowed with a hazel-colored complexion and black curls, which fell beyond her shoulders.

Alex guessed the couple to be Mr. and Mrs. Smith. According to several accounts, the man had introduced the state to the tuber as well as being the first to convert a mill to steam power. This received favor from the Mexican government, which awarded him the generous land grant of Rancho Bodega. His wife would be Manuela. Of Peruvian descent.

She must be forty years younger than her husband, Alex thought. He wondered about their story. How such an odd pairing had made its way to these shores.

The activity at Doran Beach was winding down. Captain Morgan and his crew had completed the unloading and were taking on precut lumber and crates of potatoes while the locals were scattering in different directions with their wares.

The *Excel* would soon be underway. Alex put away the spyglass and swilled whiskey from his flask to fuel him for the unwanted reunion to come.

Chapter Nine

The *Excel* tacked through the northerner while Junior and his uncle went topside to scan the coastal scene. A couple of goats stood on the ledge of a forty-foot rock, which appeared to be an islet unto itself. Nephew and uncle shared twin looks at the curious sight, wondering how in God's good name those critters arrived there.

Sand dunes extended north from the granite outcrop to the mouth of a river, which poured silt into the Pacific. Uncle Alex saw the questions mounting in his nephew's expression and said, "It's not always this muddy or violent. Most likely due to the winter storms."

"What's it called?" the nephew asked.

"Supposedly, the Spaniards called it the Rio Grande, but I don't give much credence to that since there's a stream down Texas way by the same name. The Russians later called it Slavyanka, after some woman or other. Today we just call it the Russian River."

"Russians?" the nephew said in surprise.

"They left about ten or twelve years ago. Built Fort Ross a bit further up the coast, named after another woman. So the story goes."

"Women seem to get a lot of attention, don't they?"

Uncle Alex nodded, hoping that would suffice as an answer since the truth would take a life-time to explain.

"Look!" Junior exclaimed as he pointed to a pod of blue-gray mammals resting on a sand spit.

The uncle brushed the boy's hair. "They're harbor seals. The rookery provides a safe place to give birth and rear their young."

A pup lifted its doggy head and released a racket. "Sounds not unlike the bark of your Auntie Ann when she doesn't get her way," Uncle Alex said.

The nephew grinned a broad grin. "You're funny."

The *Excel* skipped over the waters, beating hard into the gust, giving a wide berth to a three-mile stretch of cliffs that seemed to disappear into the clouds.

If Stephen Smith's Bodega was considered an outpost, then what would one call this formidable piece of land? No wonder the area had remained isolated for centuries.

After another nine miles, the schooner passed under a broken citadel plopped on a meadow atop a bluff. Junior assumed that it was the fort mentioned earlier. He cupped his hands over his eyes and took in the activity. Stick figures busied themselves, appearing to paint the outer walls white, which Junior noticed matched the color of a house and a barn not too distant away. In the background, smoke rose from a rolling pasture. Since the burn did not seem to produce any panic of sorts, the boy figured all was as it should be.

Next came an A-frame structure, which stood at the front edge of a timberline near an escarpment. Single lengths of boards slid down an apron chute to a vessel moored in a cove. Men piled wood high on the deck, not much freeboard showing.

"Ship will tip over," exclaimed the youngster.

"If the lumber is not stacked just right, the vessel could turn turtle or perhaps—"

Captain Morgan apologized for the interruption and told Mr. Duncan that he should gather his clan. "Have everyone ready for debarkation."

Alex and his nephew headed to their cabins while the *Excel* sailed past Stillwater Cove and Walsh Landing. Rocks jutted up from the sea as if thrown there once upon by an angry god. Hull-chewing masses.

Gerstle Cove was little more than a hundred yards wide and bordered by cliffs. Bishop pines clung to the bluffs while orange, purple and pink succulents decorated the cracks and gullies of the U-shaped "doghole", aptly named for there was barely enough space for a dog to turn around in.

The Duncans gathered in a single cabin as the ship headed toward the inlet. The hurried footsteps and unnerving chatter above told everyone that this would not be any ordinary docking.

At Salt Point Head the jib and mainsail were hauled and furled while the topsails were used to provide minimum power. The captain steered leeward of the promontory and into the cove. Sailors reefed the remaining sheets while a skiff was lowered over the side with two men aboard. One snatched onto the hawser line and secured it to a buoy. The ship's bow swung around as might a lure on a fishing line caught in a current.

The three Duncan children squawked. Ann stared at Alex as if saying, *what the hell?* It wasn't until two additional lines were attached to different buoys that the matriarch of the family sighed a relief.

"Perhaps we should have come by stage, dear," Ann said in a sarcastic tone.

"Travelling by ship was your idea, remember, d-e-a-r," and Alex drew out the word in a theatrical way. "Besides, no roads have been built to this part of the country. Welcome to the frontier."

"Well, the worst is over, I suppose," Ann said.

"Wouldn't be so sure," Alex responded.

Ann ignored the claim and immersed herself with the task at hand. She searched for her feathered hat before remembering it was no longer amongst her things and threw her husband a familiar look. With disdain etched upon her expression, she gathered her children and stepped into the companionway along with Fanny and her son. The sisters spouted nothings regarding the ordeal of the mooring process, one complaint outdoing the next.

Alex fumbled with the valises while Junior offered a hand. "Well, thank you," and the uncle leaned into his nephew and whispered, "I think you're going to enjoy this next part."

The Duncans made their way to the foredeck where Captain Morgan was overseeing the final disposition of the vessel. With the bow facing the Pacific, the ship could better handle the swells. It would pitch but not roll. Passengers and cargo would be transported via a sling-carrier, which was attached to a cable that stretched from a floating marker beyond the ship's foredeck to a drum at the top of the cliff.

Captain Morgan nodded to Mr. Duncan who took his meaning and turned to his wife and sister-in-law.

"Ladies, after you," Alex said as he made a sweeping gesture toward the conveyance.

Ann looked at the carrier, at her husband, back to the carrier. "Are you out of your Irish mind?"

"Let me remind you, my dear, that Irish is not my—"

"I am not getting on that thing," Ann said. "Nor is Fanny or the children. And that is that, *dear*."

Captain Morgan gathered in the tiff and said that he was on a schedule. "What'll be, Mr. Duncan?"

"Anyone care to join me?" Alex said to the brood.

Over his mum's objections, Junior volunteered and hurried to his uncle's side. The pair stepped aboard the carrier, which was held steady by deckhands. A counterweight dropped from the tower toward the beach, easing the carrier and its two passengers upward. Uncle and nephew peered below and waved, swaying in the breeze some fifty feet above the water.

"Ma'am," the captain said to Ann Duncan, "If you and yours not be going ashore, I'll ask ya to return to your cabins as the crew needs to unload the cargo."

"Well," Ann exclaimed in a huff, "if a five-year-old and a dimwit Irishman can do it, we certainly can," and she looked to her sister and her three children for verification, but none was there.

* * *

At opposite ends of a Federal-style building, stone hearths delivered warmth to a barren room. Pocket shutters were drawn tight to assist in warding off the cold. The adults sat at a table while the children scurried about, except for Junior who was building a house of cards in the corner.

"It's good to see you," Fanny Holliday said to Sam Montgomery Duncan.

"Yes, well," Sam said, fumbling over his words. "I trust you had a safe journey."

Fanny nodded before requesting her son to join them. "Junior, come say hello to your father."

The lad lifted his vision from his endeavor, rose and stepped forward. "Nice to meet you, sir," Junior said, extending his hand.

"Likewise," and the father accepted the offering, saying, "You've become quite the little man, haven't you?"

"Not little, almost six," and Junior dashed back to his stack of cards.

"Please, forgive him," Fanny said. "This is all so new."

"Enough with the niceties," Ann interjected in a large voice. "Let's talk business, shall we?" and she threw a stare at her husband as if to say that it was his turn.

"Let me begin by saying that—"

"No beginnings, no speeches. Just get to it," Ann said in a matter-of-fact tone.

"Of course," Alex answered before surrendering his attention to Joshua Hendry. "Sir, I am prepared to buy your interest in the mill. My wife also reminds me that the offer arrives at above market value."

Hendry absorbed the information while Sam Duncan doubted the offer's legitimacy, saying that Alex possessed no such funds. "Joshua and I have built this with our own sweat, starting with the mill at Bloomfield. Now you waltz in here and believe you can shift all that with a handshake and the value of the clothes on your back? You never cease to amaze me, brother."

"I've procured a line of credit on my San Francisco business," Alex answered.

"A business which no doubt has a line of debtors spilling out the door," Sam said.

"You're giving out the stink with your blather, little brother."

"And you're nothing but a weasel running its crack across the countryside."

The debate swelled from a business proposition to a litany

of old itches. Each blamed the other for the family demise back in Ireland. Fanny and Ann jumped in, trying to lower the temperature. Words, however, continued to run over each other while the Duncan children, thinking that a game of sorts was in the making, skipped around the table shouting gibberish, mimicking the voices of the adults.

"How much?" Hendry said over the caterwauling.

Brothers and spouses ceased arguing in mid-sentence. Eyes shifted in rhythm to Hendry as if choreographed for a stage play.

"What?" Ann said amidst the sudden explosion of quiet.

"How much for my interest?" Hendry repeated.

Alex ran over the numbers while Sam pleaded with his associate not to submit. "We've come too far to capitulate to the whims of someone who hung his family out to dry, who now seeks to deepen his own pockets from the toil of others."

The bickering began anew when Ann slammed the flat of her hands upon the table. "There'll be no more squabbling today. All parties will accept the deal or I'll bring holy hell upon the lot of you. Understood?"

No response.

"Oh, and one more thing," Ann said, glowering into the eyes of Sam Duncan. "You are to marry my sister," and she paused as if daring the man to submit a rejection. When none rose, she reached for a lamp and marched to her room as if to announce the meeting had come to a close.

* * *

Vows were exchanged at a small gathering at the Fort Ross chapel. Sam Duncan promised—under pressure from all concerned—to cherish Fanny Holliday and son Junior for the remainder of their days. There was no denying that Sam Duncan received the short end of the bargain: a marriage he was trying to run away from and a business relationship he wanted no part of.

Though passionate lovers back in New Orleans, it took some time for Sam and Fanny to reacquaint themselves with the subtleties of the bedroom. The honeymoon was cut short due to business obligations, which was fine with the groom. While a spark still remained, it was dimly lit.

With Joshua Hendry no longer a business partner and family members nudging into every crevice of his personal life, Sam felt boxed in. The mill at Salt Point was his creation and the world be damn if he'd let his sister-in-law or brother get the upper hand.

"It doesn't matter if we're equals on some piece of paper," Sam said to Alex, "I still own the land." The younger sibling had purchased 5500 acres of the German Rancho, which included Salt Point. "You'll follow my lead and my lead alone. Understood?"

"Understood, little brother," Alex answered.

"And don't call me *little brother*. You can refer to me as Sam, or Mr. Duncan if you must."

A hefty pause weighed upon the moment as they stepped toward the sawmill, which was inland a mile and at the top of Big Gulch Creek.

"Where'd you get the steam engine?" Alex asked as he poured over the heart of the mill.

"Bought it from a couple of Benicia carpenters who hauled it down from a Sierra gold mine," Sam said. "Produces about 5000 board feet a day."

"Stephen Smith's mill at Bodega puts out 12,000 board feet."

"What're you trying to say?"

Alex peered deeper into the engine, fiddling with this thingamajig and that. "Might be able to rebuild it. Beef it up a bit. But draw your own conclusions, *Mr. Duncan*, seeing as how you're the boss and all."

Sam didn't respond, refusing to admit that perhaps his brother might be more than just a shite in a bucket. After all, Alex was an iron worker and a machinist. Had to count for something.

They continued touring the mill, walking past a camp of timber tramps, which consisted mostly of sods from the Emerald Isle. The irony was not lost on either brother. At one time they were underfoot of their Irish neighbors back in Strabane. Now they were at the top of the rung, dolling out directives and salaries to men who were once the scorn of every breathing Scot.

The brothers walked at a leisurely pace, each feeling out the intentions of the other. Sam said he had hired gatekeepers. "They ride the boarders. Prevent squatters from settling on the land."

Alex had heard of such men who, in truth, enjoyed nothing better than to administer a good thumping now and then. "Sounds as if you've acquired your own brand of vigilante, right here in beautiful Salt Point," Alex said with a smirk, enjoying himself.

No response.

"Maybe you could learn something from Stephen Smith at Bodega," Alex persisted. "Whites, Indians, even squatters…they somehow have figured out how to coexist. One happy family."

Sam Duncan lengthened his silence, thinking that his sibling was all balls. One fat flummadiddle.

Chapter Ten

During the next couple of years, Alex and Sam did their duty for family and business. Alex enlarged the steam engine, enabling the mill to increase by twofold its previous output of lumber. Furthermore, the brothers formed an uneasy alliance to promote a new product—the manufacture of sandstone from a nearby outcropping, which would cobble the streets of a fast-growing San Francisco.

On the home front, they each attached a much-needed extra bedroom to their individual abodes. This was done prior to the coming of a trio of Duncans. Alex and Ann introduced sons Hugh and Alexander to the world in 1857. Not to be outdone, Sam and Fanny brought forth Lucinda, named after the matriarch of the clan. Even in affairs of the heart, it appeared that there existed an aura of competition between the brothers.

While the sexual proclivity of the Duncans seemed to ripen, there remained inconsistencies in other areas. Deer and elk provided sustenance on most days, but wheat and other products were hard to grow in the uncertain climate. Tea, sugar and spices were often absent as well.

Ann and Fanny struggled with what they had, which encouraged the wrath of their husbands. Alex complained about the use of burnt corn as a substitute for coffee, putting his bowels in disarray. "Living on nothing but flour and coffee is corking me up," he would say.

His whining soon overlapped from the dining table to the bedroom. Ann grew tired of his fussing and took to the habit of wearing a flannel gown and bonnet to bed. She played the spinster while he referred to her—in hushed tones—as a "muddled hen".

* * *

The fathers loaded the kids into the bed of a wagon while the wives presented a united front, protesting the trip. It had been three years since Fanny and Sam were joined in "blissful" matrimony at the Fort Ross chapel. While the ride was a mere twelve miles from Salt Point, the path was rutted with unknowns.

"One trip along this god-forbidden coast is sufficient for any lifetime," Ann said, cradling newborn Alexander in her arms. "The only good that can come of this nonsense is a bunioned arse."

"It'll be good for your constitution, dear," Alex said as he boosted her into the transport with a gentle shove upon her buttocks.

"That's not my *constitution*, dear," and she slapped his hand away.

Alex pinched up his collar at his wife's phrasing while she retreated into the far corner of the wagon and wrapped a horsehide blanket around herself and infants Hugh and Alexander.

* * *

A pair of bays whinnied as they trotted along a trail shaped long before. Children bounced to and fro while mothers worried that a violent attack of the heaves might come their way at any moment. But the uneven ride soon took on an aura of its own as the kids vied with each other to see who could jostle the highest. Admonishments from Ann and Fanny ceased the frolic. As an alternative, the children settled down and took to the landscape for entertainment.

The mist diminished to a froth before the sun decided to make a showing. Sparkles of light winked from the roving Pacific while the scent of salt and the whoosh of waves came ashore. Blooms of color burst from wildflowers blanketing the cliffs, which were honeycombed with sandstone pockets. The sight stimulated the kids' imaginations. What creatures lived within these crannies and fractures? Were they particular to Salt

Point or from some distant land of fantasy?

While the children surrendered to their daydreaming, the conversation up front turned somber. "The Kashaya at Fort Ross, they receive fair treatment from Benitz?" Alex asked.

"Earn a monthly wage of eight dollars as well as room and board," Sam answered.

"And how did they come into his possession?"

"Many were purchased at auction."

"Auction?"

Sam went on to explain that the California legislature had passed a bill permitting the auctioning off of any Indian after his or her arrest. A simple complaint of smoking or spitting in public would be reason enough for detainment and subsequent servitude.

"The Kashaya at Fort Ross are apprentices until adulthood," Sam added.

"*Apprentices*?" Alex repeated. "You mean *slaves*, don't you?"

No response.

"Is it true you can buy an Indian for a pittance?" Alex said. "Most likely much less than the eight hundred dollars those Southern boys are paying for African chattel."

"Your head is full of mince pie."

"And your bum is out the window."

Sam exhaled a clump of oxygen. "You wanna listen or you just wanna piss in the wind?"

Alex calmed himself and gestured for his brother to continue.

"Whites have been kidnapping tribal children in order to come into some easy money. They sneak up on a rancheria, kill the bucks, pick out the best-looking squaws, ravish them and make off with the young ones."

To prove his point Sam said that seven years previous the 1st Dragoons U.S. Cavalry attacked a group of Pomo on Bonopoti Island at Clear Lake, killing four hundred adults while kidnapping the juveniles for the auction block. The event became known as the Bloody Island Massacre. He went on, adding that during the following year, whites in Mendocino and

Humboldt Counties killed over a thousand Yuki.

Enough with the flummadiddle, Alex thought. "I think you forget, *little brother*, that we were similar outcasts at one time, used as nothing better than pawns by the redcoats against those northern Irish Paddies."

"You haven't been listening, have you?" Sam said in a raised voice. "The Kashaya are safe with Benitz."

* * *

The redwood forest drooped to the edge of knobby promontories. The sun hid behind the veil of branches as shadows melded together to form a stark and bleak land.

Ghouls and monsters returned to slink within the imaginations of the children. Fright took hold at the sound of twigs giving way under the weight of some creature. An elk lifted its head, sniffed the air and pranced deeper into the woods. Youthful eyes darted back and forth with a sense of relief until a second intrusion returned chaos to fragile minds. A flock of quail shot up from the nearby brush while a scrub jay shrieked a warning. The young released their hold on one another as the wagon exited the darkness and slipped under a lacy finger of fog hugging a meadow.

After another two miles, the wagons cut onto a path, which led to a community of some reckoning. Sam Duncan steered the bays past a row of cabins and pulled to a hitching post. Alex hopped from his perch and secured the horses while Ann and Fanny corralled the kids.

As Alex walked toward the fort, a sensation hit him—as it often did—and he looked back over his shoulder toward the east. An unusual number of horsemen rode the ridge. They appeared as shadowy cutouts, backlit by the rising sun. The show of force puzzled Alex.

Something's on the tenterhooks, he thought, as tension floated on the breeze. He brought his vision back around, taking in the sights ahead when the entrance to twin semi-subterranean structures caught his eye. Nearby, a scene between natives and whites started to unfold. Hands flitted about. Voices rose. Long guns rested at the ready.

Alex didn't know what to make of it and fell quiet as the Duncan clan passed through the stockade gate and into the parade grounds. Neither of the blockhouses remained from the Russian-occupied days, their canons having gone silent. Still standing were the manager's two-story house, clerks' quarters, artisans' workshops, barracks and a chapel where Fanny and Sam had exchanged vows.

Sam Duncan introduced the new owner of Fort Ross to his sibling. William Benitz owned a robust physique with a serious expression attached.

"Nice to make your acquaintance, sir," Benitz said, extending a greeting to Alex Duncan.

"Thank you for having me and my family," Alex said, accepting the handshake. "Although I must confess, the purpose of our visit has been rather vague, as I believe was my brother's intent."

"Not to worry," Benitz answered. "All will be made clear shortly. But first, allow me to present a few of our distinguished guests."

The Duncan brothers made the rounds, drifting from one huddle to the next. Sheriff A.C. Bledsoe came first, a black Stetson sitting atop his head. He looked somewhat perturbed as if he'd rather be someplace else.

Next came Tyler Curtis with his bride, Manuela. Alex recalled the news of their marriage, as it was *the* event along the coast during the previous year. She was the former and much younger wife of Bodega owner Stephen Smith who had passed away recently. Rumors circulated that Tyler Curtis had wedded the widow for more than just her beauty.

Something about the man bothered Alex Duncan. It was more than the fact that Curtis seemed out of rhythm with the landscape, parading around like some peacock with his ascot and top hat. What it was, exactly, Duncan couldn't decipher. One thing was for certain—he never cared much for dandies. Too much fluff. And Tyler Curtis was all of that.

With the summoning of the church bells, some three hundred people took their seats. The chapel served as a macabre background to a makeshift stage where William Benitz waited for the humming to settle. With all eyes upon him, he nodded to an armed man by the gate. A dozen horsemen escorted hundreds of Indians into the parade grounds, lining them up at the rear of the assembly.

Alex Duncan witnessed the fixed expressions aboard the faces of the Kashaya as they filed in, each showing angst and irritation. He slid his vision to the horsemen who reminded him of the shadowy figures from earlier.

Christ on a bike. This can't be good, Duncan thought before pivoting back around and returning his attention to the stage.

"We are gathered here today to ensure that civility is not forgotten in these parts." Benitz's voice didn't carry the rigor of someone who believed in the statement. He paused to take in the look of Sheriff Bledsoe, his hesitation only confirming the suspicions of some.

"While the proper authorities would rather settle this manner at the courthouse in faraway Santa Rosa," Benitz added, "I believe the good citizens of the Salt Point and Ocean Townships have a right to clarity, to witness justice for themselves."

With that declaration, Benitz gestured to a hefty man standing next to an iron-hinged door with bars across its portal. Three natives stumbled forth, ankles and hands chained. A noose ran from one man's neck to the next and onto the third. The butt of a whip nudged them up a flight of steps and onto the stage.

In front of the platform, a man scurried about, toting a camera box on a tripod, testing one angle and another, his gray mane tagging along for the ride. Another person, perhaps twenty with a bloated face and prematurely bald, ran his mouth at the person. Alex thought it strange that such a young thing should be spouting orders to someone twice his age.

The assistant with the camera box dipped his head under a billowing black shroud before reappearing again, motioning for the trio to inch further to the left. The prisoners didn't take his meaning until another with bloated cheeks and bald came closer and pulled on the ankle chains of the Indians, moving them sideways. He surrendered a thumbs up as if thanking the natives in assisting with their final farewell.

Alex Duncan thought the gesture crude and started to rise when a tug on his coat sleeve told him to do otherwise. "Behave yourself," Sam said.

Alex jerked away from his brother's hold and stepped forward to the young squirt with the bloated cheeks.

"Take your fecking camera and shove it up your fecking arse," Alex said as he squared up to the man, clutching onto his arm.

"I'll do no such thing," the bloated-cheek one responded. "And release your hand from me or I shall have to render it unfit for wiping that Irish ass of yours."

"I'm not Irish!" Alex said before realizing his raised voice had gathered in the look of William Benitz.

The host emitted a theatrical cough before gesturing for Alex Duncan to retake his seat. The Scot spied the uneasiness growing upon the expressions of others and retreated into the shadows. His scorn, however, did not abate as he fixed his gaze upon the photographer.

Benitz returned his attention to the throng, dismissing the ballyhoo with a snicker. "Irish—you would think they'd appreciate a decent hanging. Who knew?"

"Now, where was I?" Benitz said before a remembrance snatched onto him. In a preacher's voice he said to the prisoners, "Have we not lived in harmony? Have my wife and I not provided for you? With all that his sacred and holy, why have you sought to repay us in this manner?"

The prisoners remained silent, their eyes held steady upon family and fellow tribal members, upon the god Katsu.

"Very well. As you wish," and Benitz cleared his throat and said, "You are hereby sentenced to hang for the theft of cattle by the power vested in me as proprietor and keeper of Fort Ross."

Before the Kashaya could pray to the gods above, the deed was done. A flash of powder from the photographer's light told all that history was in the making.

A chant, steeped in pain and sorrow, rose up:

Journey To Duncans Mills

"The sun sets at night, and the stars shun the day,
But glory remains when the light fades away.
Begin, ye tormentors, your threats are in vain,
For the coyote shall never complain."

Chapter Eleven

A week later Alex rose early, wrapped himself in a blanket and built a fire. The madrone crackled with the aid of last night's coals and he settled into his favorite chair to read the *Sonoma County Journal*, Petaluma's four-page weekly. An editorial by Thomas L. Thompson caught his eye. It was a rather extensive article, accompanied by a photograph of three Indians hanging from nooses.

The piece supported the action of William Benitz, saying that the theft of cattle violated the Act for the Government and Protection of Indians:

> "The Kashaya must be kept in line otherwise they threaten the established order of civilization. The disrespect they displayed toward their employer is no better than that of many Southern niggers."

Duncan let the newspaper drop to his lap and peered into the flames. Racist eejit, he thought.

Sam entered without knocking, went to his brother and said, "See you got the *Journal*."

Alex answered with a question. "Who's this fella, Thomas Thompson?"

"Who?"

"Thompson, editor of the paper."

"You mean the bald-headed kid whom you had words with at Fort Ross?" Sam said.

"Aye, that's the one," Alex said.

"The one with whom you managed to smear our good name

in front of all those people?" Sam persisted.

"Aye, that's him," Alex said, playing the game.

"Do you have any idea how your actions embarrassed me? The family? The business?" Sam said.

"Such embarrassment has most likely been documented before the event," Alex said. "Now get on with it," and he raised his hands in anticipation.

Sam expelled a load of oxygen, realized the hopelessness of rehabilitating his brother and said, "He is the offspring of former Virginia Congressman Robert Thompson. The boy and his daddy showed up in '53. Bought the *Journal* with family money while the son appointed himself editor at age seventeen. Why?"

"Thought it a bit insensitive to be yanking the chains of prisoners for the pleasure of a prettier pose. Too much ego on the eejit, if you ask me," Alex persisted.

"Thomas Thompson just wants to make a name for himself," Sam said. "The newspaper business is a cutthroat affair. Can't blame the lad."

"Sure I can," Alex said. "And I intend to do so at every opportunity. Same thing goes for Benitz."

"Listen, William Benitz is decent folk," Sam said. "He was squeezed into a corner. Sheriff Bledsoe desired to take the cattle thieves to—"

"Who's to know if they were cattle thieves or not?" Alex interrupted. "Nobody fences off their property. Cattle don't know one boundary from the next. 'Sides, what if those Kashaya did slaughter a cow or two? Some are down to eating bark and grass. So, I'm told."

Another load of oxygen fell from Sam. "As I was saying, Sheriff Bledsoe desired to cart the prisoners off to Santa Rosa and have them stand trial, but the locals wanted justice without delay."

"This Act for the Protection of Indians is nothing more than another flummadiddle," Alex said. "People with influence have abused the law for years. They pay the bail of an Indian at auction, purchase the fellow for servitude and, if things don't go the way of one's liking, hang him."

"Hey, big brother, I didn't write the law. No reason for us to be at each other like bucking goats."

Alex's expression tightened

"A lie is often halfway around the globe before the truth can get its boots on," Sam argued. "Be careful what you say, big brother," and he fetched a mug of coffee and exited without another word.

Alex thumbed through the newspaper, blind to the printed words, thoughts running amok.

The flapping of pages snapped him out of his wanderings. His eyes fell upon the continuing story of the Fort Ross incident with editor Thomas Thompson mentioning the luminaries in attendance. The Duncans were listed along with others including Tyler Curtis and his bride, Manuela.

Alex didn't know how he felt about being highlighted within the same breath as this Curtis fellow. The guy struck Alex as just another sapskull, similar to those profiteers who raped his homeland.

Time would tell but there were already indications that Tyler Curtis was positioning himself to take advantage of his wife's new inheritance, a windfall she received after the death of her late husband, Stephen Smith. Bodega Bay would be up for grabs.

* * *

Manuela Smith Curtis fed the fire with blocks of peat from the marsh near Bodega Bay. Thoughts of recent days weighed on her. She lost herself in the hypnotic flickering of flames. While her bed often remained cold when married to a man forty years older than her, she missed his acts of kindness. Stephen Smith often spoiled her with gowns and feathered hats. He attended to her health as well, providing Marshall's catholicon for diseases of the womb as well as Graefenberg's sarsaparilla for purifying the blood. But it was his treatment of Indians and squatters on the rancheria that proved his mettle. He was generous with trades, exchanging fair amounts of beef and clothing for a pittance of labor. His passing was untimely for most, but not all.

With limited English-speaking skills and an innate fear of being exported as a foreigner, Manuela would make her second marriage work. Though Tyler Curtis owned a silver tongue, he possessed other qualities that were endearing. He was young, ambitious and well-connected. The arrangement would do. It had to. She was not about to go back to her former life as a Peruvian potato farmer. Not today. Not ever.

* * *

"I've secured the land rights of my dear wife, God bless her Spanish naivety," Curtis said to an officer.

"I don't desire to hear the particulars of your marital doings, sir." Lieutenant Edward Dillon was a twenty-five-year-old with a soft complexion who commanded the 1st Dragoon Cavalry unit.

"I've petitioned the Probate Court of California to sell parcels of Rancho Bodega, a landmass upward of 37,000 acres," Curtis boasted.

"I am here at the request of Governor Johnson," the officer said, sticking to the business at hand as he opened a leather pouch and picked a vellum envelope from within.

Curtis received the document and perused it, chattering away. "And those three simpletons, whom Manuela refers to as her children, won't be an issue," he persisted, his eyes trolling down the page, his mouth running ahead.

"Sir, can we get on with it?" the officer said in an impatient tone.

"You see, I've acquired guardianship over the trio. Clever, don't you think?" and he returned the parchment.

"Sir, my men are waiting."

"Bodega is nothing better than an unruly land with country pumpkins and savages as caretakers. I shall slice it into bits and return to civilization with a handsome profit."

"Sir!"

"You know what the problem is with this land of the Pomo? There are Pomos on it."

* * *

Bullwhips and rifles persuaded the natives to fall in a ragged line. Barefoot children of the Southern Pomo and Miwok tribes clung to the sides of parents while others assisted with the elderly and the weary. Belongings were meager, wrapped in blankets and slung over shoulders. The "protected ones" eased from the shores of the bay and headed north along the coast.

The natives had been told that the relocation was for their own good, that life on the reservation would ensure the survival of their species. Most of Sonoma County had been spoken for. Land grant owners from the Mexican era, as well as squatters from around the globe, had claimed the area for themselves. It was the white man's right, his destiny.

Tyler Curtis bade farewell to the nuisance, or at least that was his take on the people. Most of the settlers, however, bore no ill-will toward the Indian. At least while Bodega was under Stephen Smith's control. But he was dead and gone. Curtis was in charge now.

The collection made their way through potato patches and wheat fields and pastures. Short horns and stock sheep bedded down behind outcroppings to shrink from the onshore gusts. The shelters of squatters came next, telling of poverty but possessing a sense of will about them.

The rain slipped sideways, stinging flesh. Soldiers cinched up their ponchos and showed their backs to the Pacific. The terrain grew sloppy. Bits of earth splashed up the frames of those on foot. A young one began to whimper. The father—who wore a red bandana around his forehead—brought his daughter close, not so much to comfort her as to shield her cries from a sour-faced soldier on a nearby mount. The disturbance annoyed him. Not bad enough he was called out on such a day but to put up with a gnawer was beyond his grade pay.

A whip cracked the air just before the blow landed. The father's back fell in pain, his daughter's tears morphed from sadness to fear. The howl of the wind prevented any exchange of words and Sourface pointed up the trail, as if to say "keep moving". The father nodded his understanding and whispered something in his native tongue to his child.

The two-mile trek to Salmon Creek proved unremarkable despite the efforts of the weather and Sourface. The slope of the land was gentle to the edge of the bluffs where the storm had stirred the waves into a lather, which crested over a string of boulders.

Barges, laden with agricultural produce, made their way down the creek to the ocean where lighters waited to carry bales of hay, wheat and potatoes to schooners anchored offshore. The sight had become a familiar one to the natives, a constant reminder of who ruled the land.

Three more Southern Pomo villages were rounded up along the way and herded north with the rest of the bunch. Silence was the order of the day as they were raised to accept their fate as the coyotes and the god Katsu saw fit.

Black steeds flicked their ears forward and nickered, pressing those on foot into a tight pack as all hit the stream. Mallards tumbled out of the brush and took flight. If the Indians owned the skill to swim, fine. If not, so be it.

Further up the track they headed east, climbing hairpin switchbacks some eight hundred feet into the ether. Mounts churned through the mud, laboring, nostrils heaving. The muscular beasts plunged and fretted as they twisted and sidestepped in an effort to take the windborne rain on their flanks. Nor were the humans spared. Bones froze under the onslaught. The entire world seemed to be drowning.

The one-mile ascent proved too much for an elderly woman who drooped to the earth along the edge of Marshall Gulch. She sat there, gazing upwards through the downpour, chanting to Katsu as her fellow tribal members passed by, nodding their goodbyes.

The terrain leveled out and they quickened their step through a series of open rollers where grasses heaved to and fro. The tempest had increased such that not even Lieutenant Dillon could corral the wherewithal to appreciate the topography that was not unlike the majestic highlands of his native Scotland.

The open range gave way to a dense forest, which buried the group in a ragged descent into a valley where the angry sky reappeared. Cattle inched their way across green pastures. Hand plows and a silo straddled the outer edge of the field.

The father with the red bandana did not recognize a piece of machinery, which appeared as an iron ogress with steel claws. Nor did he recall a name affixed to a wooden arched entrance, which read COLEMAN HILL RANCH. Why should he? So many foreign monikers. So difficult to pronounce or make sense of. Other farms and ranches came and went, the land dotted with blood and power.

Legs began to cramp as Pomos and Miwoks exited the farmland and made a second ascent. Sugarloaf Mountain was 1150 feet above sea level, testing the most ardent souls.

They crested the ridge where a flock of wild turkeys bade hello with gobbles and clucks. The greeting, however, went unnoticed as all wound through ferns and thorny undergrowth. The uneven ground dug into bare feet while blackberry bushes jabbed at shirts and pants. Pleas rose up for rest.

"*Sihputay, sihputay*," a Pomo said to a soldier, miming the act of drinking, pointing to a nearby creek.

Sourface obliged and booted the Indian down the hillock to the stream below. The trooper shared the incident with another, chuckling, enjoying a bit of humor to pack away the growing monotony.

The crisp edge of winter continued to needle faces as they dropped from a saddle to a spit of level land. A third and final ascent came quickly after which a laguna and a great plain stretched before them.

The red-bandana father remembered when herds of elk and pronghorn antelope visited the wetlands, when his tribe fashioned canoes, shelters, ropes and baskets from the nearby tule and willow and sedge. Stumps now stood as tombstones to a once thriving oak forest, forgotten. Gone were the flocks of mallards, a record 6,200 shot in one day by a single hunter.

The pair slogged behind, the father sweating and trembling, most likely from the onset of saddleback fever. He peeled himself from the marsh and edged crablike to solid ground where dribbles of rain settled in the wrinkled folds of his clothing. His breath grew heavy as he peered down upon his only surviving child, her brown eyes blinking with the what-ifs.

Sourface rode to the scene, the brass buttons on his gray coat gleaming, his collar rising stiff. He studied the Indian's condition and opened his head with a scattergun. Sourface holstered his weapon, pulled on the reins and moved to the next worry, leaving the child to weep over the crimson-stained chest of her father.

Pastures gave way to a swelling settlement and before long they arrived on the outskirts of a town in the making. A thicket of some twenty homes rested on the edge of Santa Rosa. Common structures, they reminded Lieutenant Dillon of the squatters' cabins he witnessed back in Bodega. The weatherboarding was of split redwood with shake roofs, smoke spilling from chimneys. While rudimentary, the shanty-style homes formed the foundation for greater things to come. After all, they fortified the lives of a robust race of people, of the same hardy colonial stock that followed the trail from those states aligned with the secession-thinking South. This particular was so common that the county was often referred to as "The State of Missouri". These settlers brought their old ways with them to forge a new beginning, a beginning with no stains attached, a beginning pure and white.

Santa Rosans thought so much of their town that they were positive it would be a better seat for the county headquarters than Sonoma. An election in 1854 confirmed such but that wasn't enough for these rebellious types. Not wanting to wait for the slow transference of power, a band of citizens rode to Sonoma and stole the courthouse records and transplanted them to Santa Rosa. These were people to be reckoned with, come hell, high water or the law.

A hundred buildings and some thirty businesses lined the thoroughfare. Men stood quiet in their three-piece suits while ladies clutched onto strings of tykes who chawed on licorice sticks. At the foot of Fourth Street, the town square featured a five-story architectural beauty.

Lieutenant Dillon followed its Grego-Roman lines to the top of a domed cornice where the lady of justice held a scale. Upon closer examination, the soldier spied an oddity. A patch covered the eyes of the goddess. He wondered which version held the truth—the one with eyes opened or the blindfolded one.

The natives used arms and shoulders to wall-off incoming projectiles. Vegetables and stones replaced the rain of earlier as the contingency trudged past the town's lone restaurant, blacksmith shops, a large livery stable and private residences. At the Santa Rosa House, the fumes of bad whiskey and the clamor of southern-style revelry mingled with the aroma of cheap cigars.

Curiosities began to infiltrate the mind of the twenty-five-year-old officer. Lieutenant Dillon had witnessed firsthand the collective misery of the natives. While this was his first field commission, the last fifteen hours had made an impression upon him. He would have plenty of time to resolve any conflicts as 135 miles remained until they would reach the Round Valley Reservation.

Chapter Twelve

"Where's the newspaper?" Alex Duncan barked as he bolted into the house.

"Does the word privacy hold any water with you?" Sam said.

"The *Journal*. Where is it?" Alex didn't wait for a response and headed toward a wicker basket.

"Do you mind?" Sam said in a spurt.

"Got it," Alex said, holding up the periodical.

A frustrated Sam shrugged.

Alex remained standing as he rifled through the Petaluma paper. If there was anyone who would gloat on the mishaps of the less fortunate, it would be editor Thomas L. Thompson.

"Nothing. Nod a word," Alex exclaimed as he perused the last page. "Christ on a bike," and he crumpled the weekly into a ball and tossed it into the fireplace.

"Just to let you know, I've had little chance to read the news," Sam said. "If that means anything to you."

Alex slumped into a chair. "It's almost as if the press has already laid to rest the Indian, wiped his existence from the annals of history."

"What are you blathering on about? What *existence*? What *history*?"

Alex directed a stubby finger at his sibling, saying, "Exactly. You have proved my point, little brother."

"You give out the poor mouth with little definition in your speech," Sam said. "Speak your mind clearly."

"One would think that such an event would be worthy of at least a syllable or two," and Alex expounded to prove his point. "Some local natives are labeling it *The Death March.*

Apparently, more than one elderly person was left by the side of the trail to wither away. A child drowned while crossing Salmon Creek. A man's head went missing in front of his daughter."

"Quite the misfortune," Sam said in a nonchalant tone.

"*Misfortune?*" Alex repeated. "I'd say it was a tad bit more than that."

"There is little we can do. Besides, more than a few of the citizenry agree that the time of the Indian has gone the way of other inferior races. Personally, I would dare to go further and say that the expenditure of our tax dollar on the construction of a reservation is foolishness, not to mention the funds required for its maintenance and security. Why should we play wet nurse to a horde of savages?"

Christ on a bike! Alex stormed through the exit, crossing his arms over his chest against the bite of the onshore wind. The cold, however, didn't penetrate his body, which was fueled by his anger, his face growing flush.

Bawdy epithets flew from his mouth, cussing out his brother, editor Thompson and the world in general. "May the cat eat you all and may the devil eat the cat."

To his thinking, he was surrounded by eejits who deserved a double dose of the devil's lip. It was an expression that once described his life back in Strabane but seemed more fitting now than ever.

"What're you doing?" Junior said to his uncle.

Alex Duncan spun around and said, "Cursing. I find it good for the soul. Pushes out all sorts of toxins."

"You and my father fighting again?" Junior asked.

"A soused hog's face, that one."

"He says the same of you."

"He does, does he?"

"It appears you're *a shite in a bucket* as well, whatever that's supposed to mean."

* * *

The winter had purged itself of its maladies and went

dormant. Cattle and sheep gnawed their way across sunny pastures while blacktail deer and elk feasted on berry bushes. Most critters heralded the arrival of spring. But for some, it did little to sooth nagging resentments.

Alex rose early from a fitful sleep and slipped into his trousers, careful not to wake Ann or their newborn, William, who occupied the space between them. The breech birth nearly stole his spouse from him as the midwife did not own the skills necessary for a caesarian delivery. The fact that William entered the world butt first might have been a statement of some truth. Life didn't seem to have much to offer. Be that as it may, a newborn had come into their lives. While it was Alex's duty to love the child, its addition to the conjugal bed did little to promote marital bliss.

The male loins can often go their own way. An occasional poke would be nice. He had had offers from some of the millworkers to rendezvous up at the Gualala whorehouse where the women were famous for owning light skirts. As a substitute, he became enamored with a regular pull on the cork.

He hoisted his suspenders over his shoulders and tiptoed through the exit. By design, Junior was waiting for him behind the men's outhouse.

"My father will flip upside down if he catches me," Junior said to his uncle.

"Doubt he could handle such an undertaking but it might be best if we keep our lips sealed on the matter."

Junior's face grew tight before releasing the periodical. "Don't leave it lying around."

"You can be sure of that, lad," Uncle Alex said. "Now off with ya."

Junior sped back to his cabin while his uncle took a seat upon the wooden thrown. On the front page of the *Sonoma County Journal* a story told of the doings of a Walter Jarboe. He was a fifty-year-old born in Kentucky who served in the Mexican-American War.

Editor Thomas Thompson went on to say how Jarboe grew restless and volunteered to bring civilization to the West Coast:

"Mr. Jarboe represents what is best in mankind with his unwavering response to the lingering crisis in our area. When presented with the official blessing of Governor Johnson, Mr. Jarboe was quoted as saying, 'However cruel it may be, nothing short of extermination will suffice to rid the country of the Indian.'"

Alex let fly a curse when a knock sounded on the outhouse door. "Go away. I'll not be interrupted while entertaining a fit."

Junior worried that all was not right and asked if his uncle required assistance. "Should I fetch father?"

"Your father and his kind are the reason for my condition. Now leave me be."

"There's some goings-on back at the cabin," Junior said. "Might want to finish with your fit and have a looksee."

* * *

Sam and Fanny Duncan shielded their children from the strangers who appeared as wild as unbroken horses with manes in matted tatters, eyes large and glazed over.

The lone adult pinched his fingers together, bringing them to his lips, miming the act of eating. He looked sideways to a pair of young ones and repeated the gesture as if to include them with his plea. "*Ma?a ?dawa.n?*"

"Clear off," Sam said in a firm voice. "Shoo," and he waved a hand at them as if encountering a stray dog.

Alex arrived with a complaint. "Can't a man host his morning business in peace?"

"These people showed up unannounced, asking for assistance," Fanny interjected. "Sam was kind enough to show them the road. We don't want their trouble here."

"Probably Yuki. From up north," Alex said before returning his attention to the Indian, pointing to him, asking his name.

The stranger understood and said, "Elsu," and he laid his hand on his chest and repeated, "Elsu."

Elsu motioned to the girls beside him, saying, "*Bumuci.du?*

?ahqha dawa.n?"

"Must be his daughters," Alex said. "Most likely hungry, I suspect."

Fanny carried on, saying that the Indians needed to leave. Sam agreed and began a litany of reasons, saying that the troubles of the Yuki belonged to them alone.

"Probably on the run," Alex guessed. "Word is that Walter Jarboe and his band slaughtered upward of three hundred of their tribe near Gualala, drove another four hundred east to the Round Valley Reservation."

"Sad story but not our concern," Sam insisted.

"We have to do something, right?" Alex said.

"This Jarboe bloke means business," Sam said. "Supposedly he has fifty mercenaries at his beckon call, armed with government issued weapons and the backing of the governor."

No response.

"'Fraid you got your tatties over the side on this one, big brother," Sam added.

* * *

Ann heated some leftover stew and served the three Yuki. Her act of generosity surprised Alex.

He started to pass a jug to Elsu when Ann snatched it mid-transfer. "The poor man doesn't need any of your John Barleycorn," and she stored it next to a sack of grain.

"Just trying to be neighborly," Alex said.

"They are not neighbors," Ann said. "They have no neighborhood. They are refugees."

"Eh, I suppose that'd be the truth of it. Thank you, Mrs. Duncan for that reminder," and Alex showed a playful smile.

"You're welcome, Mr. Duncan," and Ann began to pour another helping when Junior busted through the entrance.

"Horsemen spotted coming this way," Junior said, panting.

The uncle patted the boy on the head. "We best get to it then."

Elsu and his daughters gathered their things, exited and

headed toward the bluff while Ann hurried to erase any signs of their visit.

The rumble came to them along with the ascent of plumes of dust. *Forty strong, maybe fifty*, Alex guessed. He stood in front of his cabin with his drink, hoping his trembling hand did not betray him.

The troupe approached fast as if on urgent business. Steeds came to a sudden stop, hoofs pushing up needles and woodchips and all manner of chaff.

Alex Duncan fanned away the intrusion, coughing. "That'd be quite the entrance," he said. "Though I prefer something with a bit less bluster."

Sam Duncan and the heads of the other households joined the gathering, the children and women remaining behind locked doors. The hoopla snagged onto the curiosity of a few millworkers as well who crossed the open pasture with whatever devices might serve as weapons.

A man loosened the reins, inched his spurs into the flanks of his horse and moved forward. He wore a chin beard. No mustache. A permanent scowl sat high above a sizeable paunch.

"I'm Captain Walter Jarboe, Commander of the Eel River Rangers."

"I'm Alex Duncan and this is my brother Sam. We're the owners of the Salt Point Mill," and he took a pull on his jug.

Sam stepped in front of his sibling, demanding to know the meaning of the person's presence, but Alex wouldn't let him steal the show and said, "Those outfits don't appear to be government issued," he said, eyeing the black three-quarter-length dusters with matching trousers and hats.

Jarboe squinted to better judge the person before him, drawing his carbine from its scabbard. "How 'bout this?" and the barrel squared up to meet Alex Duncan. "This government-issued enough for ya?"

"Impressive," Alex said. "Remington, I believe."

"I doubt you'd put on such a grin if ya knew who I was," and he looked back over his shoulder to a compatriot and said, "C.B., read one of those clippings."

A toothy smile popped from a lopsided fellow who

delighted in the prospect of seeing his outfit's name in print. "This here's from Petaluma's *Journal*," and C.B. cleared his throat with a theatrical gesture. "'The Eel River Rangers, led by Captain Walter Jarboe along with—'"

"*Captain Walter Jarboe*," the chin-whiskered commander repeated with bravado. "That'd be me," he said, staring down the Duncans.

"Wait, captain," C.B. said. "I ain't hardly finished," and the toothy one returned the clipping to his vision: "'The Eel River Rangers, led by Captain Walter Jarboe along with C.B. Carter and other notables, have bravely taken on the task of corralling the remaining Yuki and other hostiles from the territory.'"

C.B. lowered the clipping and raised his eyes to his captain, saying, "Sure is a mighty sight seein' one's name in the paper."

"Boastings of this nature are typically reserved for kings and such," Alex Duncan said. "I don't suppose you're a king now, are you, Mr. Jarboe?"

"It's *Captain* Jarboe, and I'll not be tested any further by the likes of some no-count civilian."

"But you own no such disdain when that civilian is the one who keeps you in purse, correct?" Alex Duncan said.

Jarboe wouldn't bite. It had become common knowledge that an uppity-up by the name of Serranus Hastings was financing the doings of the Eel River Rangers. No doubt Hastings had accumulated many favors from Sacramento, having served as the state's chief justice as well as attorney general.

Without another word, Jarboe signaled to his second-in-command to search the premises. C.B. Carter scattered the Rangers in different directions. A unit rode uphill and across the pasture to the sawmill, another inspected the bunkhouse while a third group went to the area along the bluff.

C.B. Carter and a couple of riders came to the donkey engine and took a gander over the side of the cliff. A cable ran to a moored schooner below in the cove. Sailors stacked lumber onto the deck of the vessel. Nothing suspicious met the Rangers' once-over and they retired to their commander's side.

Jarboe's expression strained with disappointment. "Search

the family quarters," he said in a burst.

"You'll do no such thing," Alex said.

Jarboe ignored the petition, turned to his second-in-command and motioned toward the cabins.

The Eel River boys banged their way into the domains of the Duncans. Fanny corralled her young ones, throwing condemnations along the way. Chairs were brushed aside. Beds turned upside down. Armoires, cubbyholes and cabinets disturbed.

C.B. Carter exited the second house on the tail end of a broom, which was in the hands of Ann Duncan. "Get your cockeyed arse outta my house," and she took another swat at the Ranger.

Jarboe broke his silence with Alex Duncan, saying, "That's a fearsome woman ya be attached to."

"You can have her if she's to your liking. Comes with seven young ones...Package deal, all or nothing. Give a good rate for the bunch."

"What kind of man would sell off his own kin?"

"Don't hold any firm notion on the subject, but I'm of the understanding that it's a popular concept nowadays, that is the buying and selling of human beings," and another pull.

"I know your meanin'," Jarboe answered. "Nevertheless, I'm not in the market for jawin' women or bawlin' shavers, even if they are white."

Alex surveyed the activity, grew serious and said, "I'll be asking you to leave now and if you refuse, well..." and he motioned to a second wave of timber tramps who had descended from the mill. Axes, sledges, knives, cooking pans and other instruments were raised with gusto.

* * *

The residents of Salt Point fixed their stares on the Eel River Rangers as they returned the way they came. It wasn't until the rumble of horses' hoofs waned in the distance that everyone went back to work without a word as if the occurrence was an everyday affair.

A trio made their way from the edge of the bluff. Sam Duncan studied the natives, saying to his brother, "You hid the Yuki onboard the schooner?"

"Thought it a bit of genius, if I do say," and Alex took another pull on his whiskey.

"Your foolishness will one day be the ruin of this family," Sam said before collaring Junior and marching away.

* * *

During the next few months of 1858, the campaign against the Indians raged along the north coast. With the financial backing of Serranus Hastings and the state, Captain Walter Jarboe continued preying upon the Yuki people in Mendocino County. Local governments also continued their support, paying bounties for the scalps and horses of Native Americans. For the Yuki who survived the Remingtons of the Eel River Rangers, a new life awaited at the Round Valley Reservation, a life absent of freedom and filled with rival tribes.

Chapter Thirteen

Junior tapped on the outhouse door, receiving the same response as every other Monday.

"You got it, lad?" a baritone voice asked from inside.

"You won't be any too happy," Junior said before passing a newspaper through the slit of the opened portal.

Junior returned to his shelter while his uncle rifled through Petaluma's *Journal*. Again, not a word regarding Jarboe's war on the Yuki people nor state-sponsored roundups to the reservation.

Eejits and knackers. Each and everyone.

Duncan rose with his angst from the throne, buttoned up his pants and shoved open the door, slamming it into another.

"Damn all to hell," a squirt said from the other side. "Ya busted my nose."

There was something about the pinched-faced fella that appeared familiar and Duncan lifted the lad's hand from his face. "Well, I'll be. It's you, isn't it?"

"Figured I'd run into ya 'fore too long. Held no notion it'd be on the wrong side of an outhouse door." His face corkscrewed in pain.

Duncan told him not to move and cracked the nose back into place.

"Damn!" The lad blinked the moisture from his eyes, paused to regain his bearings and wiggled his nose in a test. "Well, I'll be. If that ain't the darndest thing. How'd ya do that?"

"Last time I saw you was in my office down San Francisco way," Duncan said. "What brings you to Salt Point, Billy Fraser?"

"It's *William* Fraser," the lad corrected. "Seemed as if I'd suffered enough to own an adult name of sorts."

"William it is," Duncan said. "So, where have your sufferings taken you these past nine years?"

"Tried a bit of gold diggin', near the headwaters of the Sacramento," Fraser said. "By the time I got there, it was pretty much cleaned out. Just filings and flecks and such. Not enough to purchase a poke. Then I wandered into Santa Rosa, seein' as how the town was gettin' busier than piglets on a sow's tits."

"And?"

"And after realizin' there were too many of my kind there, I remembered your brother doin' right by himself and so here I am."

"You said that Santa Rosa wasn't to your liking," Duncan said. "One would think that mingling with your fellow Missourians would bring back a bit of home."

Fraser patted his nose, all the while talking: "Too many of the wrong kind of Missourians there. Those fools are hell bent on bringing the South to Santa Rosa."

A remembrance looped through Duncan's mind. An article by Thompson of Petaluma's *Journal* described Sonoma County as "The State of Missouri", saying that the usage of the term had grown to become the area's unofficial title.

"You can bed with the other single men up at the mill," Duncan said.

"I ain't a free man no more. Hitched up with a woman who had my child. Has plenty of hips to her. She'll do, I suppose."

"Where are they staying?" Duncan

"Down in Ocean Township near Bodega Bay. Bunch of us are fixin' to settle the land there."

"You ever have an occasion to run into a dandy by the name of Tyler Curtis? Likes to run his mouth."

"Everyone's familiar with the man, seeing as how he drove off the Indians from the land and all. Most had no quarrel with the natives, but I'm of the opinion that now there might be more land for me and mine."

"You sure about that?"

"'bout what?"

"About having more land."

William Fraser ransacked his brain to decipher Duncan's meaning but offered little more than a shrug. Duncan spied the blankness aboard Fraser's countenance and led the lad to a nearby shed. They stepped inside where Duncan rummaged through a stack of newspapers.

He wetted his fingers and turned the pages of the March, 1858 edition. "Read this," and he creased the paper into a proper fold and handed it to the lad.

Fraser studied his vision over the editorial, coughed a nervous cough and returned it to Duncan. "Do ya mind?"

Duncan, recalling the lad's inability to read, recited the article aloud:

> "'Administrator's Sale. NOTICE is hereby given, that pursuant to an order of the Honorable Probate Court of Sonoma County, the undersigned will offer for sale at Public Auction portions of the Bodega Rancho. TYLER CURTIS. Adm'r of the estate of Stephen Smith.'"

Fraser shook his head as if still in the dark.

"Your beloved Curtis is selling the land from under your feet," Alex said to clarify.

"He's got no right."

"He seems to think differently."

No response.

"Don't act so surprised," Duncan said. "Curtis is a bona fide knacker. No denying. He married the widow Manuela Smith for one purpose. To gain access to her dead husband's holdings."

No response.

"Now that the Indian is gone," Alex said, "only one problem remains."

No response.

"Your arse is halfway out the door, Mr. *William* Fraser."

* * *

While keeping the conversation to a minimum, the brothers mounted a couple of steeds and rode across the open pasture to the sawmill at Big Gulch Creek and beyond.

"Heard you hired on a new hand," Sam said in rhythm with his prancing bay.

"William Fraser is his name," Alex said. "Hails from Missouri. Met him while crossing the isthmus. Down Panama way."

"Can't afford him," Sam said. "Not with the recession and the state of things."

"He's the lad that found you hiding out near Bloomfield. At your first mill. Shouldn't you do him a favor for returning you to the family?" and Alex released a smirk.

"Should send him to the far side of hell for exposing my whereabouts, is what I should do," Sam said.

Each month the ride grew longer. Not just because of the festering tension between the siblings but also due to the decrease in available timber. Stumps served as grave markers for the woodland that no longer was. The Duncans maneuvered through the wasteland until reaching the most recent tree line, which inched eastward with persistence. The remaining redwoods awaited the executioner's cut, standing tall and proud. Alex tried to imagine the many battles these monoliths had endured since the birth of Christianity only to accept an uninvited fate at the hands of a feller's three-foot tool.

The trees crowded each other in their competition for sunlight. Acres lay buried in shade except those few hours near noon when a beam darted downward to put a spotlight on Mother Earth.

To map the course to the timber tramps' campsite, Alex and Sam relied upon the faint indications of north perceptible on the mossy side of trees. As they drew closer to their destination, the workings of axes cried out, guiding them forward.

They surveyed their holdings for the next two hours, doing an accounting along the way. Numbers came and went, as was the way of businessmen. In the end, there was no way around it. Timber was running short in these hills.

* * *

Fourteen-foot-length logs were positioned, each in turn, onto a conveyor belt and drawn to the mill's mule saw. Steel teeth stood perpendicular and cut each section in half, a manageable size for the circular saws to come. Slabs of lumber soon made their way along another carriage until exiting the plant. Once placed onto a railcar, the timber was hauled by a gang of six horses along tracks to the cove.

Cut pieces of wood were attached to the sling-carrier at the top of the bluff and lowered down the cable to a waiting schooner. The two-masted *Coquette,* captained by Andrew Griffiths, was moored below, having arrived late after battling stiff headwinds during its twenty-five-hour journey from San Francisco.

A freakish summer storm was on the way. Just a matter of hours. Time was wound tight.

The Duncan brothers paced near the donkey engine high above Gerstle Cove. The recession and the shortage of redwoods in the area had taken a financial hit on the mill. They could little afford any further setbacks. Had to get this schooner loaded and on its way.

Crewmen released the lumber from the sling-carrier and began stacking it on the deck. Captain Griffiths howled orders, his voice breaking amidst the driving winds. Sailors fought to stay afoot as the vessel bobbed up and down within the gusts. With a shallow keel, balance was critical. The correct distribution of timber proved a challenge as a northerner made its introduction.

Green water slopped over the deck. The captain ordered the release of the cable. He thought about hoisting the sails, taking what lumber he could and seeking the safety of the open sea. But it was too late.

The foremast cracked and began its descent, taking with it lines and spars and sheets. A tangled mess covered the deck as the surf erupted. The eighty-foot vessel jostled about like driftwood until breaking its mooring lines. The gale threw the schooner into the churning cauldron. Fear occupied the looks of captain and crew alike, many down to one knee, clenching onto whatever handholds presented themselves. A series of wicked breakers raised their hoary heads, picked up the ship and flung her beyond the drift line to the sands.

There were no fatalities, merely bumps and frazzled dispositions. Nine men—three at a time—rode the travelling carrier to safety where they boarded a railcar and made their way to the mill's bunkhouse while the captain enjoyed a meal at Sam Duncan's place.

The conversation soon turned to the calamity at hand, Captain Griffiths saying that a guard should be posted to oversee the cargo and the wreckage. Though the *Coquette* was broken apart, thieves and salvagers would pick the site clean until all that was left were seagull turds and a dislodged plank or two. With that detail discussed, words were bandied regarding the impact of such a loss and the state of affairs in general.

"As if we needed further maladies upon our shores, there are rumors of civil war close at hand," Sam Duncan added.

"Might not be so bad," the captain said. "Wars are good for the economy."

"I suppose you might be correct in your thinking," Sam said. "Wars require ships, which require lumber to build them."

"Might just lift us out of this damn recession," the captain added.

Sam nodded in agreement while brother Alex sat in silence, wondering where the dialogue was headed. He had long ago made a habit of pulling back his opinions until he understood the position of others.

"One way to ensure trouble," the captain continued as he forked a slice of game meat, "is to elect that coon-lover from Illinois. He'll rile up the neck hairs of those Democrats, sure as comes Sunday."

"You'd be pro-slavery, is that the truth of it?" Alex said.

"I be a businessman, is what I be," the captain said. "Long as the county sides with the southerners, so does my purse."

"Money and greed before morality?" Alex said in a bitter tongue.

"It doesn't make it right," the captain argued, "but it does make it so."

* * *

The cargo of the *Coquette* found its way into the possession of others one night when the guard was overtaken by surprise. Some believed it was the work of the local natives. Others that professional salvagers had a hand in it.

Alex fixed his stare on a blank wall, taking pulls on his whiskey, his mind running amok with possibilities until a prospect settled in the forefront of his thinking. "Bet it was that Tyler Curtis from Bodega. He seems the sort to attempt a stunt like this."

"There are times when you pinch too much salt on your stories," Ann said as she arranged her face. She placed a pair of tweezers upon the vanity, turned to him and said, "Liquor will do that to a man, dear."

Another pull.

* * *

"We have to talk," Sam said to his sibling. "Better not speak out in the air," and he gestured toward the office.

Sam locked the door behind him and drew the curtains. "We've been surviving on the tip of a gnat's hair," and he started to pace the room. "We not only loss a significant load of lumber with the thievery of the *Coquette* but also the contract since it contained a deadline for delivery."

"Time to relocate," Alex offered.

"With the lease of new land near the Russian Gulch, we might be able to rebound," Sam said as he travelled across the floor.

He had recently entered into an agreement with Winfield Wright whose Buckhorn Ranch stretched along the coast from Russian Gulch to three miles south of the Russian River.

"The river could provide a method to transport logs from the hinterland," Alex added.

"But the mouth provides little in the way of a safe harbor."

"And the sandbars render the river unnavigable."

"Would have to build the mill close to Bodega Bay where safe anchorage exists."

"That's the Ocean Township, of which that knacker Tyler Curtis is the major landholder," Alex added. "You do know that, right?"

Chapter Fourteen

A lighter brought the Duncans ashore at Bodega Bay where Tyler Curtis put on a congenial face, wearing a frock coat, ascot and top hat.

Alex's countenance grew tight, wary of the dandy's smooth style while Sam presented himself as the peddler that he truly was. The trio boarded a wagon and rode to a two-story, white clapboard with blue shutters. The entrance featured a winding staircase, which separated the living room from the parlor.

A handsome woman with shy manners and olive skin surrendered a curtsy to the guests. *"Bienvenido, seniors."*

"Gracias, señora," Alex said, remembering his last visit when he wrongly addressed her as *Señorita* Smith. But now she owned a new name. One that many said was thrust upon her by an opportunist of grand proportions.

"Por favor," and Manuela Curtis motioned toward the sitting room.

Smoke meandered from the cigars of well-heeled men. They rose with the appearance of the Duncans and introduced themselves. Alex flinched at the sight of a young bald person with whom he had a verbal confrontation at the Fort Ross hangings.

"Still the proprietor of Petaluma's *Journal?*" Alex asked.

"Yes," Thompson answered, "but we have much bigger game in our sights."

"*We?*" Alex said, fishing for details.

Tyler Curtis intercepted the potential fallout and completed the introductions. Accompanying the newspaper publisher was his father, Robert Augustine Thompson, former U.S. representative from Virginia. Father and son owned little in common. The old man displayed confidence, a full head of hair and a lean physique, unlike his insecure, balding progeny. Also in attendance was Serranus Hastings, the former state supreme court justice, attorney general and benefactor of the Eel River Rangers.

This was fast becoming a perplexing encounter. What was the reason for such an assemblage of power? Alex wondered.

"Let us sit," Tyler Curtis said before snapping his fingers at his wife who sped from the room as if the act had been rehearsed a thousand times.

She returned shortly with a tray laden with glasses of pisco punch. Alex recalled it from his early days in San Francisco. Though it had been only nine years, it felt as if a lifetime had passed.

Curtis went on to explain how the refreshment was once Peru's shining star, his wife's birthplace. "But like all things, time is the only constant. Nowadays the drink is imported from Chili while Manuela's native land is buried in cotton. Change is inevitable, my friends. We should embrace it."

"That is why my brother and I have come to seek your blessing," Sam said while Alex cringed at the use of the term.

The sanctimonious fool doesn't deserve a seat next to such a holy word, Alex thought. *Blessed be his arse* is more like it.

Sam continued, saying how the current recession had indeed affected his family's mill, how the redwood forest had run its course near Salt Point. "I've leased land near the Russian River. There is, however, no suitable anchorage there and we were wondering if you could see your way to—"

"Mr. Duncan, please," Tyler Curtis said. "You embarrass yourself."

"Afraid I don't follow," Sam said.

"Yeah, me neither," Alex added in a terse voice.

Curtis looked to Hastings and the Thompsons who returned playful smiles as if some hidden meaning hovered over all.

Alex caught the exchange. "What? Am I missing something here?"

Curtis returned his attention to the Duncans, saying that the Ocean Township had been struggling with "outsiders" for quite some time, that Smith—his wife's former husband and one-time owner of Bodega—played nursemaid to savages and squatters alike. "And so you see we have very little interest in entertaining additional trouble."

Alex climbed halfway out of his seat before his brother could calm him. "We are not trouble, Mr. Curtis," Sam argued. "We are businessmen seeking to establish a mill on the southside of the Russian River with the possibility of attaining an easement across your land to a safe port at Bodega Bay."

"And can you vouch for your employees?" Curtis asked "Do you pretend to assert that they are bona fide as well?"

"No," Alex injected. "Not all. Some are English. Others Irish. You know how they can be, eh?" and he gathered in the irritated faces of the bunch before returning his look to Curtis. "In fact, there is a decent chance that one of your fellow countrymen might have had a hand in the stealing of our cargo from the wrecked *Coquette*. Ring any bells, Mr. Curtis?"

"What are you implying, sir?" Curtis said.

"Gentlemen," old man Thompson said from the other side of the parlor. "Enough with the dickering. Let's speak plainly for the hour is waning and I've a warm breast waiting for me." The former congressman rose and put a hand on the shoulder of his son. "We have ambitious plans for Thomas whom many Democrats see as a viable candidate for political office."

Serranus Hastings vouched for the lad with a nod and a verbal "Here, here."

Alex Duncan hesitated. "I fail to see what your son's political goals have to do with—"

"Please," and Sam gestured again for his brother to lower his tone.

"As I was saying," old man Thompson said, "my son possesses potential but he requires a proper platform from which to launch himself."

"Petaluma's *Journal* does not allow him to do that," Curtis volunteered. "Santa Rosa's *Sonoma Democrat*, however, has a much larger circulation. The boy simply needs financial backing to move forward."

"Are you suggesting," Alex said, "that in order to obtain our easement, we must toss money at the feet of this racist lunatic?" and he steered his chin toward the younger Thompson.

"Feet. Hands. It makes no difference," Serranus Hastings interjected. "So long as it comes the boy's way," and he rolled a cigar between his lips.

But the twenty-year-old Thomas Thompson was not as cavalier regarding the accusation and came out of his chair with a glare. "Mr. Duncan, I take umbrage regarding your disparaging remarks toward my character."

"Good," Alex said as he felt for his Slocum.

Old man Thompson intervened to calm his son and in a persuasive voice said, "Mr. Duncan, there is a reason why the Santa Rosa periodical is titled *Sonoma Democrat*. It wishes to be the spokesperson for the county's citizens, of which the majority identify with the Democratic Party and the South. My son merely intends to elevate its potential."

"And I intend to have no further dealings with cutpurses, bawds and pro-slavery eejits." Alex rose for the final time, released his hold on his weapon and, without so much as a *good day*, exited.

Thomas Thompson turned to Sam Duncan and said, "Will your brother be a problem?"

"He *is* the problem," Sam corrected. "Takes after his da, a little too strongheaded for his own good. Nothing that can't be fixed," and he feigned a grin.

* * *

Though half asleep, he could sense the presence of someone else. With a troubling feeling, he blinked, opened a single eye and caught the silhouette of a man standing over him. "What the hell?" Sam said in a burst as he shot up from his bed.

"Shhh, relax your crack or you'll wake your wife," Alex said, a finger to his lips to emphasize his point.

"*I'll* wake my wife? *You're* the arse who broke into my house and—"

Alex hushed him again and gestured to the exit. Sam slipped his legs from under the blankets and tiptoed to the coatrack where he put on his jacket before exiting into the darkness.

"This better be good," Sam said as he stuffed his hands into his coat pockets.

"Thomas Thompson's da is head of the State Land Commission," Alex said.

"I'm going back to bed," Sam said and started back toward his house.

Alex snatched onto the arm of his sibling. "I'm thinking that Robert Thompson made a deal with Curtis and Hastings. *Quid pro quo*. The land claims of both are approved in exchange for their support of the old man's kid and his bid to purchase the *Sonoma Democrat*."

"You've gone a bit off course with this one," Sam said.

"And wouldn't it be grand if those racist eejits could get the Duncan brothers to join the parade," Alex added.

"And maybe you're all balls," Sam retorted. "Maybe you can't see the truth if it crawled up your arse."

"Nothing's gonna crawl up my arse," Alex said. "I tell you that for free."

"Listen," Sam said, pressing the air down with his palms, "we need that easement across Curtis's land. Without that, the future is doomed."

Alex examined his brother's distance as a notion came into being. "Wait just a second here. Curtis and Hastings knew in advance that their land claims would be ratified. That's why they felt cozy with running the Indians off to the Round Valley Reservation."

Alex furrowed his brow, thinking hard. Sam remained silent, edgy. The truth was closing in.

"But what does Curtis say regarding those squatters at Bodega?" Alex said, his attention returning to the icy façade aboard his brother.

"In the end, it's all about survival," Sam blurted.

"What does that mean?"

"It means that squatters across the county are starting to mobilize," Sam said. "A bunch camped in Cyrus Alexander's fields near Santa Rosa and burned his barn to the ground. Further north in Healdsburg, a curfew has been declared."

"And you're of the mind that these squatters would interfere with our intentions south of the Russian River, is that it?"

A nod.

Alex studied his sibling's expression. "Is my little brother fixing to do something stupid?"

"Me?" Sam said. "Lord no. I'll leave that to those who can afford stupidity."

* * *

Alex Duncan walked up to the mill and sought out William Fraser. "You seen this?" and he passed the *Journal* to the lad.

Fraser didn't reach for the newspaper, surrendering a frustrated shrug as if to say they'd been through this before. "Aye, right," Duncan said and drew the *Journal* closer and read aloud:

> "'Opposition to the Democratic Party in Sonoma County is composed of Old Line Whigs, Petaluma Republicans, and a few of a secret league called Settlers...'"

Duncan's concentration pulled away and settled upon the lad. "*Settlers*," Duncan repeated. "Would Thompson and his newspaper be referring to you and your squatter-friends?"

No response.

"*Secret league*, eh?"

"What concern is it of yours?"

Duncan flipped the page to the editorial section where a Geyserville settler set the scene in a letter to Thomas Thompson:

> "'The quiet that has universally reigned in our village is gone and a reign of terror has been established instead. Armed men, mounted, are constantly charging through our streets. Martial law has been proclaimed.'"

Duncan's vision rose from the article. "Thompson is placing the blame for the lawlessness in the county on this Settlers League."

"Ya expect us to sit by while others try to steal our land, is that it?"

"You have to know that this is only the beginning," and Duncan held the *Journal* high in a theatrical gesture.

"We'll be ready for whatever they throw our way."

"People like Thomas Thompson and his old man lay hold of the power," Duncan said. "You haven't a chance in Hades."

Chapter Fifteen

Through his political connections, Tyler Curtis obtained in March of 1859 a writ of ejectment by default against the squatters who occupied his Bodega Rancho. The lawsuit named fifty-eight defendants, ranging in wealth from the likes of James Coleman, a prosperous dairy rancher, to William Fraser, a struggling timber tramp.

* * *

"You people are gonna have to vacate this land," Sheriff A.C. Bledsoe said, a black Stetson sitting atop his head.

"Don't reckon we will," William Fraser said, standing alongside twenty other souls.

"You sassin' the law, boy?" Sheriff Bledsoe said.

"Figure the law could use a good sass now and then," Fraser said.

"Got here a paper authorizing me to kick your scrawny ass outta here," and he picked a legal document from his coat pocket.

"I was told that that Curtis fella might try somethin' like this," William Fraser said.

"Told by whom?"

"Told by none-of-yer-fecking-business, that's who."

"Leave now and we won't make any arrests."

"Says you and six others by my count," Fraser said, glancing at each of the deputies in turn. "Don't see as how you own enough manpower to haul all of us in."

"Do it one-at-a-time if that's what's called for."

"Sounds like a waste of tax dollars, if ya ask me."

* * *

Potrero Point lay on the eastside of a promontory near Mission Bay. Blue collar types occupied this desolate spit of San Francisco, the isolation suiting its Irish residents. The area grew to be known as Dogpatch, a title which many a Paddy not only identified with but embraced.

A dandy, wearing a frock coat and silk top hat, emptied from a carriage in front of the recently constructed PG&E plant. His attire and confident gait told workers nearby that he was not one of them. A crowd built to overflowing as a sea of scrappy boots hid most of Pennsylvania Avenue from view.

"My name is Tyler Curtis," the dandy said over the murmurs. "I hale from the Ocean Township community of Bodega."

"State your business or be off with ya," a man said in a heavy brogue. His tangled hair drooped down to his collar with burnsides inching along his cheeks to a ragged mustache.

"I'll pay each man fifty dollars—in coin, not scrip—to join me on an adventure along the north coast."

"Would there be any bashing involved in such an adventure?" the one with the burnsides shouted.

"Guaranteed," Curtis answered.

* * *

Forty-eight armed ruffians boarded lighters, which ferried them from San Francisco's embarcadero to a seventy-foot, two-masted vessel. The *Kate Hayes* pulled up anchor and announced its departure with the shrill of its whistle. Black soot trailed behind as it headed due north toward San Pablo Bay where it nosed into the Petaluma River.

The river's muddy hue seemed to run parallel with the mood onboard. Picnickers and other civic-minded passengers cringed from the bands of thugs. The Irish of Dogpatch relished the malice they carried. Some fingered the curls of young lasses who cowered into the arms of their parents. Others liberated the possessions of travelers. Pocket watches, earrings, necklaces and a pair of riding boots found the palms of mercenaries. Nor was the cargo in the hold immune to such travesties as the looting ramped up in proportion to the amount of whiskey swilled. Bales of spices, tin goods and textiles found their way overboard for the benefit of a laugh or two.

The side-wheeler pushed upstream through tidal marshes. The voyage grew tedious and the Irish took on an air of boredom. Tyler Curtis was thankful when the six-hour voyage came to its end. He could now give more purpose to the enterprise as he marched his militia off the *Kate Hayes* at Haystack Landing. The unit bypassed the busyness of downtown Petaluma and made its way north and into the countryside where a stagecoach depot and inn beckoned.

Curtis desired to avoid the Washoe House for fear that booze might lure the men from their mission. The one with the burnsides objected, saying that a break was in order. Curtis, knowing the band had travelled but a mere four miles from the dock, urged them onward.

Sobriety began to settle in alongside a resurgence of the doldrums. Curtis drove them hard for the next twenty-five miles. Dust filled the void where laughter and marauding once were until coming upon the one-room Watson schoolhouse and the outpost of Valley Ford. Canteens were filled with the promise of food and drink just two miles further north.

"Ain't hardly enough," Burnsides called out.

Curtis took his meaning and began dispensing out five-dollar gold pieces, assurances provided that ten times that amount awaited upon completion of their task. This seemed to pacify the group, which started up again in earnest.

The rag-tag band arrived at the Curtis ranch with nightfall in full view. Manuela and servants did their best to please the appetites of the men, but the stock of venison and potatoes soon gave way to turnips and cabbage. Rumblings morphed into complaints.

Tyler Curtis snapped his fingers at his Peruvian wife who, in turn, gestured to the handmaids. The ladies returned, rolling casks of whiskey into the parlor. Men shouldered each other to the front of the line where they filled mugs to the brim.

The liquor soon took control and all surrendered to sleep. Every room downstairs contained the weary as well as each step of the staircase. One head piled atop another.

The next morning, Manuela rose early to perform her chores. Without warning, a conspiracy of ravens sounded a warning from outside. She abandoned her mop and bucket and tiptoed over snorting hulks to the window.

The day's first light muscled its way through the fog. There was movement within the mist. Hard to ascertain its identity. Perhaps the breeze was kicking up the heather. Perhaps a critter was making its way home.

More movement. More objects.

Parts of human forms squeezed through the soup. One after another. Manuela counted near a hundred. At least eighty. She recognized some. James Coleman and William Fraser for starters. Most of them she had known since the days of her first husband, Stephen Smith, when there existed a state of peaceful coexistence. But now these men carried rifles, pistols and pitchforks.

Manuela scurried upstairs, not caring if her feet found a limb or two along the way. Indecipherable groans and other complaints followed her as she sped to the master bedroom.

"*Despierta, tonto. Despierta!*" Manuela shouted as she shook the shoulder of her spouse. But the fool didn't stir.

She retreated downstairs, retrieved the bucket. Its contents sloshed onto bodies as she retraced her steps up the staircase. More complaints.

Water cascaded onto Tyler Curtis's frame. "What in the name of suffering Jesus?"

"*Hombres armados afuera! Ándale! Ándale!*" and Manuela gestured downstairs. To the outside.

"I'm coming," Curtis said as he rubbed the sleep from his eyes.

But he didn't move fast enough for his wife and she repeated her demand. "*Ándale! Ándale!*"

He slipped into his pants and shirt and reached for his ascot when Manuela slapped his hand, saying, "*No hay tiempo! Hombres armados!*" and she yanked him toward the exit.

Tyler Curtis stood barefoot, shivering on the front steps of his house. His angst toward Manuela for not allowing him more time to properly dress was replaced by curiosity.

"What are you men doing here?" Curtis said as he scanned figures half-concealed behind the misty curtain.

A man stepped forward, taking the lead. "Dismiss your thugs and send them back to Frisco. They are not wanted here."

Curtis squinted to better discern the man's features. "James Coleman? Is that you?"

"It has been for some time now."

Curtis took another study of the throng, stalling, gathering intel. They were armed and ready for a fight, that much was certain. But how had they come to know of Curtis's army, let alone its intent? A question for later as the present moment was shrinking.

No use in bluffing, Curtis thought and said, "You and your fellow squatters have no right to this land. I command the entire lot of you to gather your things and depart. You have twenty-four hours. If there is anyone who dares remain, he will be shot on sight."

"You stole Bodega from Stephen Smith," James Coleman said. "You've taken his widow for your own and molded her to fit your wishes."

"My personal life is none of your—"

"We know this land grab of yours is a sham," Coleman added.

Bluster and shouts of affirmation filled the air. One young man raised his Peacemaker and yelled above the rattle, saying that he for one would not listen to the whims of the State Land Commission.

"Maybe ya hold Thomas Thompson and his father in the palm of your hand," the young man started, "but many of these Mexican land grants aren't worth the crack of my ass."

More bluster.

Curtis recalled the upstart's name—William Fraser, a timber tramp employed by the Duncans. But how did such a person come by information regarding the connection between the Land Commission and Bodega? Curious.

"You are outarmed and outmanned," Curtis argued. "Go home and pack."

"*You* are the one on the short end of both," Coleman corrected. "By my count, there are but forty-eight men at your disposal. We have almost twice that number."

It was then that Curtis realized that not only had the squatters received ample warning but that they were well prepared as well. He tightened his expression and retreated to his house without another word. Once inside, he ordered Manuela to fix several pots of coffee before stepping from lump to lump, putting his toe into the backside of hungover men. More moans. More complaints.

Burnsides demanded whiskey. A comrade followed suit and soon a chorus rose up with the same request.

The cacophony irked Curtis. "Sober up or you'll not receive a penny more."

The men of Dogpatch did as told for it was important that a profit be made. After all, they had taken leave from their jobs in San Francisco. Returning without additional coin in hand would be an embarrassment.

* * *

The skies turned gray as the sun retreated before the gloom. Full of doubt, the day lingered on with the mercenaries readying themselves for a fight. The prospect of a skirmish brightened moods. It was one of the few happenings that could stand up to the disappointment of no drink.

Manuela and the servants dashed to each man, dispensing materials. Cotton patches were wrapped around prime brushes and soaked with hog lard, all the better to erase dirt and grime from the chamber. Next, buckets of .58 caliber bullets were distributed.

The Irish thugs felt confident. Why shouldn't they? The Model 1855 was Remington's latest product, deadly over 1000 yards distance. It wasn't often that the men of Dogpatch found themselves aligned with government-issued weapons. A gift from Robert Thompson and the boys at the state capital.

They stood by the windows, anxious for battle. Burnsides argued to ignore Curtis's command to stand down, that they must rush the enemy and teach them a lesson. But again, Curtis reminded them of who was boss, which wasn't necessarily him but the gold pieces to come.

Splashes of light ebbed behind the fogbank as the day travelled westward. Guns rested against sills. Rumps found the wooden floor. Apathy settled into a pool of discontent. Grumblings started to rise anew.

Tyler Curtis peeked outside. The squatters had made camp. Cooking fires dotted the land. Men with torches lined the perimeter.

* * *

Before the morning sun broke through the fog, the squatters took up their positions. Again. The same nothings reappeared for the entirety of the second day. On the third day, the squatters' numbers swelled to over three hundred while the attitude of the mercenaries began to shrink away like a spider on a spit.

The deadline for vacating the area had come and gone. Not only had the squatters rejected the eviction notice but the last forty-eight hours had served to bolster a determination previously unfamiliar to the men. No milksops here.

Curtis recognized the gumption that had become part of the group, a bunch he once described as weak and bendable. With this realization plus the fact that his own men were teetering on the edge of mutiny, Curtis approached the squatters with a proposition.

James Coleman, William Fraser and others stepped forward at the sight of Curtis. No longer did he appear barefoot and without proper attire. Before them pranced the smooth-talking dandy they had come to know and disrespect. An ironed frock coat, ascot and silk top hat reinforced the notion that this man was never one of them.

"There is no reason for such foolishness," Curtis said.

"To our eyes this is anything but foolish," Coleman said.

Rumblings. Murmurings.

"We all have work to do. Let's put this misunderstanding behind us, shall we?" Curtis said.

"Don't know what you're banging on about," Coleman said, "but sure as a cart is to a horse, there's more attached to those words spilling from your mouth than you be letting on."

William Fraser agreed. "You're bringin' up my breakfast with your claptrap," and he paused for theatrical effect. "How dead do ya think we are? We ain't like those rummy Irishmen, so thick in the head they can't see your story beyond those silver coins of yours."

A brew of cheers and ballyhoos darted upwards.

It was about then that a man wearing a black Stetson along with six other horsemen arrived out of the rising dew. Sheriff Bledsoe pulled on the reins and, without dismounting, said, "Curtis, you've committed a gross outrage with the bringing of an armed body in violation of law and good order, and for purposes which cannot be recognized or tolerated."

"Sheriff, you are misinformed and unnecessarily excited," Curtis retorted. "Not a shot has been fired. Nor shall it. God's honest truth."

"And which god would that be?" William Fraser cried out. "The one flyin' out of your holy arse?"

The growing rant engulfed the sheriff who stared down Curtis and said, "You'll deal with this straight away. I trust I make myself clear on this point, sir."

Curtis hesitated, gnawing on his lip, before returning his attention to the squatters, "I'll lease the land back to you at half the rent of equitable holdings. What say you?"

"Those henchmen," and Coleman gestured toward the house, "are to return to Petaluma and book passage for Frisco. Immediately."

Curtis stretched his ascot with his fingers, edgy, taking in the look of the sheriff. "My thought as well."

"Of course, it was," William Frazer added in a wry tone.

Journey To Duncans Mills

* * *

"Word is out," Tyler Curtis said in a half-convincing voice to his men. "Additional forces have arrived to boost the ranks of the squatters. We're outnumbered seven-to-one."

"A fair fight it is then," Burnsides said with a nod.

"Afraid it's time to pack it in, boys," Curtis argued.

"We didn't come all this way just to lie down like a bunch of wonder-hussies," Burnsides said, emboldened by the rising support of his fellow Irishmen.

His back against the wall, Curtis relented, saying that they would receive forty dollars in gold coin as promised upon their return to San Francisco. Burnsides threw out a smirk, declaring that the money owed would be paid upfront.

"Including fees for food and passage," Burnsides added as he held out his hand in expectation.

* * *

The mercenaries, each in turn, emptied the Curtis house and dropped their weapons to the ground. A timber tramp approached one of the goons, kicked him in the bum and told him to skedaddle. The man, his cheeks adorned with burnsides, squared-off before putting his fists away with the glare of the sheriff.

The troop began the twenty-seven-mile trek back to Petaluma with gold pieces in pockets and discontent on faces. The coinage eased the disappointment of retreat, but each man's soul festered with the loss of battle promised. Not a single punch was had. It was a legacy best forgotten, never to be passed down.

To ensure the arrival of the band, dozens of armed squatters escorted the bunch the length of the march. The tale of the mercenaries' defeat reached Petaluma in advance. Citizens poured out of alleyways and storefronts to view the display. Businesses came to a halt. The procession down Main Street eclipsed into a parade with the firing off of cannons as the thugs of Dogpatch boarded a vessel at Haystack Landing for San

Francisco.

A son and his father exited the offices of the *Sonoma County Journal*. The pair eyed the scene with a wary look. The timeline for bringing the "truth" to the county would have to be moved up.

Chapter Sixteen

Viewed from seaward, stretches of the Sonoma Coast held an inhospitable perspective. For mariners, it was not a spectacle of beauty but rather a portrait of ferocity. The lone points of refuge being the dogholes, which were nothing more than pocket-sized indentations. While not holding enough water to fill one's bucket, they did provide a bit of security from angry seas.

The two-masted *Excel* tacked into the narrows of Gerstle Cove. The surf crested and broke over rocks before disappearing within the trough while foam nipped at the heels of the schooner.

The vessel moored under the ninety-foot cliff and for the next three days loaded cargo. Bridle chains, conveyor belts, circular saws, furniture, food stuffs, cooking wares and more made their way down the cable. Next came a parade of critters. The limbs of oxen, horses, cattle, pigs and other livestock dangled free from double-leather slings as they, each in turn, brayed or neighed or snorted their way from the pasture above to the deck pens below.

With twenty tons of cargo secured onboard, the Duncans followed suit. The scene reminded Ann of the day she procured tickets aboard the very same boat nearly nine years previous. Though the *Excel* was not the ocean liner she had been promised at the time, it was, nevertheless, a means to an end.

The Duncan families took separate quarters with Ann objecting, saying that her horde deserved the larger cabin as they outnumbered her sister's brood. "We're holding onto seven tykes while they're less than half that number," she said to her husband.

"Perhaps if you hadn't been so free with your skirt back in the day, we wouldn't be owning such an edge over your sister and my brother in that department," Alex said.

"I'll have you know that my skirt is no longer any of your affair," and she retreated to a corner and placed her brown velour hat gently on the seat of a wing-back chair.

"See you still have a fondness for ungodly large headdresses," he said in a half-hearted attempt to swing the conversation back to a bit of normalcy.

"And don't you go throwing this one overboard, Mr. Duncan."

"Right," and he picked a flask from his coat pocket.

* * *

Captain Morgan gave the order through a miniature microphone to weigh anchor and unmoor the vessel. A sailor released the hawser line from a forward buoy while another tended to the aft lines.

"Off tacks and sheets. Reef the top sails," the captain yelled.

The jib halyards were tightened to take the luff out of the forward sheets. The nose of the *Excel* inched its way from the cove and past the point. The captain called for the reset of the topsails to divert the wind to the leeward side. The helm went hard to port.

"Wind is backing," confirmed a crewman nearby.

The captain put the ship into a broad reach and the *Excel* began running downwind. "Prepare mainsail to haul," the captain yelled from the wheel.

With the sails set, the crew saw to other tasks, inspecting cables for the animal pens and double-checking the distribution of cargo in the hold. Cordage was coiled while trusses and tackles were stored. With duties behind them for the moment, sailors eased over a fire rising from a drum and enjoyed a cup of coffee.

Alex approached the cabin of his brother and let himself in. "Anyone care to supper?"

Fanny threw a shawl over her bare arms. "You have the

manners of an arse," she said in a spurt. "Your parents should not have released you so soon from Strabane prior to teaching you how to knock before entering."

"Arses are not known for their manners. Or lack of, for that matter," Alex corrected.

Fanny surrendered a puzzled expression and threw her hands up. "What in the name of our Lord is that intended to mean?"

"*Arses*," Alex repeated. "Known more for their attitude, such as stubbornness or obstinance, not manners."

"May your fall to Hades be slow and painful," and Fanny led all out the door and down the companionway toward the galley.

Salt pork, creamed codfish and cabbage made the rounds. Ann stayed in her cabin as she was feeling under the weather, leaving ten children and three adults to fend for themselves while Alex celebrated her absence with another swill from his flask.

The conversation bounced from Alex Duncan's uncouth ways to the undercooked pork to the increased yaw motion of the schooner. Within the whirlwind of words, Alex lifted the Petaluma *Journal* from his coat pocket.

"Your Mr. Tyler Curtis is quite the bluster," Alex said to his brother, pointing to an item on page three.

Curious, Sam brought the periodical close where the last paragraph of the article caught his attention:

> "...It was never intended that they (men employed from San Francisco) should assist the sheriff in driving the settlers from the ranch. They were to occupy the places made vacant and when the number is taken into consideration, the force will not, I think, appear sufficiently formidable to justify apprehensions that a general war against the settlers was intended."

Sam lowered the paper and looked at Alex. "What are you expecting me to say?"

"I'm expecting you to say that Curtis's attempt to mollify the anger of the locals is fecking claptrap, that the article is a pitiful example of a knacker putting on the poor mouth. That's what I expect you to say, little brother."

Sam stood by the words of Curtis, attesting to every man's right to avail himself of the 1st Amendment. Alex countered, arguing that such flummadiddle wasn't worth the paper it was printed on.

"And I'll tell you another," Alex persisted. "Only an editor of Thomas Thompson's low-lying character would support this flimsy excuse of an explanation. Those Irish Paddies of Dogpatch were nothing but thugs bent on a blow or two."

"This is not the place for such talk," Sam said in a low voice, catching the disapproving eye of his spouse.

"Thomas Thompson. His old man. Tyler Curtis. Serranus Hastings. They're all in this together, the lot of 'em," Alex said. "Mark my meaning—no good can come from such an alliance."

Sam fell quiet with the words of his brother, mulling over a future partnership with the likes of such men.

With the steady glare of Fanny hovering over him, Alex decided to depart. He retrieved the *Journal*, wrapped a slab of creamed codfish and rose from the table.

He made his way to the quarterdeck for a smoke. It was another nasty habit he had added to his repertoire. One thing he found to his liking was that neither a cigarette nor a whiskey talked back. At least not right away.

It was during this break that he overheard the captain ordering the unfurling of extra sheets to take advantage of a following wind. Men hauled up a topsail and a jib. With no freeboard, however, the *Excel* ran heavy. Tough to make up time with a full cargo no matter how much sail was used.

Slow going, Alex thought. Eight strikes of the ship's bell came to him, indicating that it had been four hours since they weighed anchor at Salt Point.

With the echo of the clanging still riding the breeze, a couple of crewmen rushed up from the forecastle and relieved a pair of mates, one of whom bummed a cigarette off Duncan. With a sniff of the Philip Morris, the sailor nodded a thank you and went below.

The new watch began trimming the sails and keeping a lookout. Alex's vision was trailing the activity when a brown velour hat appeared in the background.

Alex flicked his cigarette to the deck, put away the newspaper and stepped toward his wife. "You should be in your quarters."

"Needed...a bit...of air," Ann said in spurts, her skin pasty and drained.

"Brought you something to eat," and he unwrapped the creamed codfish.

Ann cringed at the sight. Her cheeks ballooned. She pressed her fingers against her mouth and sped to the gunwale where the contents of her stomach made their way to the Pacific.

"Is it something I said?" Without a response, he began to nibble on the fish. He ate while talking, saying that the sauce hadn't turned yet, that it still possessed a milky vibrance. But with each description another eruption rained overboard.

With a glimpse of his wife's hat flying from her head, a vague remembrance came to him of a similar event. Not one to tarry within the cortex of the mishmash that was sure to come, he licked his fingers and made for his cabin.

* * *

Without warning, a cry came from the first mate. "Fire! Fire!"

From the lazarette, smoke twirled upward. Captain Morgan was aware of the placement of several oil drums in the immediate vicinity and ordered a venting along the quarterdeck. Men grabbed axes and began hacking away. The Duncan women and children were escorted to the foredeck while Alex and Sam joined a water brigade. Voices piled atop one another as a trio of crewmen rigged boom tackles to ready a lifeboat for evacuation. Two sailors stocked the dinghy with blankets and provisions while the third hung a red lantern at its crosstrees.

Smoke continued to flow despite the brigade's efforts. Alex caught the concern aboard his brother's face. With no words to console his younger sibling, Alex returned to his task and passed another bucket forward.

The first mate wrapped a wet rag about his torso and slipped down through the hatch and into the unknown. He coughed and gagged and staggered about, feeling his way among blocks, cordage and fenders until locating the source of the problem. Several men answered his call for help and scurried below with more water buckets and sacks of flour from the galley to smother the flareup.

Smoldering sheets blackened the lazarette and damaged the skipper's quarters above, but the blaze did not reach the oil drums, which sat in about three feet of seawater. The first mate fanned away a last spiral of murk and picked a singed cigarette from atop a pile of canvas.

Who was responsible for the incident remained a mystery. It was doubtful that any of the crew was responsible as none could afford the Philip Morris brand discovered by the first mate.

The Duncans returned to their cabins as the mop-up job continued. Handpumps were manned. Bulkheads examined. Cargo inspected.

* * *

The *Excel* limped to the leeward side of Bodega Point and dropped anchor. With evening fast approaching, the Duncans disembarked into lighters while a winch began the task of off-loading critters from deck pens onto barges.

After landing ashore at Doran Beach, the Duncans boarded a couple of wagons and headed north. The sunset put a crimson touch upon the Curtis mansion, which one of the transports steered toward. The other contained Alex and Ann and their brood, which continued further up the coast.

An invitation had been extended to all to bed down with the Curtis clan until such time as the completion of the Duncans' new homes. Fanny and Sam were most pleased to accept while Alex refused, saying that he wouldn't set foot in a place that housed such a knacker as Tyler Curtis.

"So, I and the kids have to suffer because of your silly pride, is that it?" Ann said, the color back in her cheeks.

"It is so," Alex said in a matter-of-fact tone.

"And don't go thinking that my mind's gone to mush," Ann continued. "I've not forgotten that once again you are responsible for the loss of my hat. A gold piece should soon find my purse, if you get my meaning, Mr. Duncan."

No response.

Her complaints jumped from one subject to the next. "I see you've taken up smoking. Filthy habit."

No response.

The notion sparked an inkling and she said, "Did you have anything to do with that inferno aboard the *Excel?*"

Silence occupied the space until they arrived at the home of William Fraser who greeted all before introducing his family. "And this is my wife, Rose, and our child, Nathan."

The two-year-old cooed within the arms of its mother who owned a pair of ample hips. "Nice to meet everyone," Rose said before gesturing to her abode, saying that a tureen of hot chocolate awaited.

Seven children hopped from the wagon with chirps of joy and dashed toward the structure, squeezing past the entrance and into the dust-mite-filled confines. The two-bedroom cabin was considered luxurious by squatters' rights, but the expectation that it could accommodate a household of twelve was a generous opinion at best.

At supper Rose served up beef hash and boiled potatoes, which were met with few objections except for that of Ann whose feigned compliance showed her growing disdain for the starchy tuber. Her disposition changed little with the introduction of dessert.

Alex thought he might have a bit of fun and said, "Perhaps tomorrow I can arrange for creamed codfish to make its way to the table. You'd like that, wouldn't you, dear?"

"You can be a right cheeky bastard, Mr. Duncan," she said.

"I do my best, Mrs. Duncan," and he surrendered a wry grin.

Chapter Seventeen

Santa Rosa in 1860 was a bulging town with two churches, a school, nine dry goods stores, two hotels, one butcher shop, two livery stables and an assortment of other businesses along with seventy-four residences and a population of four hundred. It was where Thomas L. Thompson needed to be, at least according to his father. The old man was pulling the strings, pushing his son toward a political career.

The pair sat at the bar of the Santa Rosa Hotel, which was the gathering place for healthy exchanges of whiskey and thoughts. The white clapboard enjoyed a balcony on the second floor where lodgers took quarters. On the ground level, the structure housed a restaurant, saloon, post office and a Wells Fargo station.

The father raised his whiskey and offered a toast. "*Carpe diem*, son. Seize the day."

"Thank you, father," and the bloated-face, twenty-year-old swilled his drink, droplets roosting on his chin whiskers.

Tyler Curtis and Serranus Hastings stepped into the saloon, gathered the attention of the Thompsons and gestured to a table in the corner. The quartet sat, drinking and toasting, toasting and drinking. Boastings of past achievements spilled from tongues, proud of themselves.

"The *Sonoma Democrat* can now truly live up to its name," Tyler Curtis said.

It was money from the Democratic Party as well as from the Deep South that enabled the purchase of the *Sonoma Democrat* by the Thompsons.

"And more support is pouring in everyday from our Confederate friends," old man Thompson added before taking a pull on his cigar.

"Petaluma was never the right fit for us," the younger Thompson said.

Curtis and Hastings nodded an accord, agreeing with the statement. Yankees had fouled the place with their anti-slavery sentiments. Santa Rosa would be more to their liking, stocked with believers of the cause. The new editor of the *Democrat* would ensure that Sonoma County lived up to its new billing as the State of Missouri by throwing its weight against Lincoln.

"I was surprised to see that that upstart from Illinois obtained the Republican Party's nomination," Curtis offered.

"I'd have bet a poke that Lincoln didn't own the chance of a nigger on the run," the younger Thompson added. "My head is in perpetual agitation. Can't wrap my thoughts around—"

Old man Thompson barged in, keeping the conversation on target, saying that the turmoil within their own party was the roadblock, not Lincoln. "Stephen Douglas lost my support and that of other Democrats at the Baltimore convention with his soft-pedaling on slavery."

"But I heard you and others did what was necessary, correct?" Serranus Hastings asked.

"We did," the old man answered. "Myself and a group of electors walked out and nominated Kentuckian John C. Breckinridge as our candidate, a conservative hard-liner."

"He'll aid us in our efforts to keep the county aligned with the South," Curtis added. "We should all be thankful the area hasn't added a single Negro to the census. It was trouble enough putting those damn Indians in their place. Don't own the finances to wage another war."

"Can't trust the census," the younger Thompson said. "Rumor has it that a darkie is holding up at the Duncans."

* * *

Alex touted a plan for building a sawmill at Bodega Corner (Bridgehaven), one mile upstream from the mouth of the Russian River. "In addition, the stream can be used to transport logs."

Sam disagreed, saying that such a site would be prone to flooding, that the mill should be constructed on the bluff overlooking Goat Rock, high and dry.

With his persuasive personality, Alex had his way and Duncansville was established. None were too surprised by the turn of events, least of all Sam. But the constant battles with his brother were trying. Despite their differences, a bunkhouse, cookhouse and a general store soon rose with some dignity. In short order an engine, boilers and saws were installed in the shell of the mill plant.

While Fanny, Sam and their three kids were in no hurry to leave the comforts of the Curtis mansion, Ann Duncan mutated into a tired being, bored with the crowded conditions of the Fraser cabin. With this reminder, her husband pressed the millers to complete their new home in the quick of summer.

* * *

A lanky Negro, wearing wire-rim specs and a barber's apron, dusted off the salon chair. The shop was nibbled out from the rear of the general store, inconspicuous and cozy. It had quickly grown into a gathering place where people would come and sit and listen to the news of the day.

Charles Franklin Sloan appreciated the work and aimed to demonstrate such to Alex Duncan with the availability of various periodicals. Armed with a razor-sharp wit and a keen recall for goings-on, you could say that Charles Franklin Sloan and Alex Duncan were destined to be friends.

"Latest paper, Mr. Duncan. Yes, sir," Charles Sloan said as he handed over the *Sonoma Democrat.*

"It's *Alex*. Call me Alex. Please."

"Yes, sir, Mr. Alex. No problem at all."

"Just *Alex*," Duncan said with a nod.

"Interestin' article on the front page," and a finger crooked to the spot.

Duncan read the title: "The World is Governed Too Much". Paragraphs followed, confirming editor Thomas Thompson's fight for states' rights and opposing the election of Abraham

Lincoln.

"Don't pay any mind to this rag," Duncan said. "Not a whit of truth to it."

"Might be sound to have a grasp on the devil's words. Get a jump on him if need be," Sloan suggested.

A white hair cloth looped across the lap of Duncan while his eyes glanced around the space. Artifacts from around the globe were on display.

"Quite the collection," Alex said.

"More be comin'," Sloan answered as he drew a straightedge up and down a strop.

"Did a bit of traveling, did you?"

"The travelin' comes to me."

"Don't follow."

"People sit in that chair and have a desire to share their stories. Even leave a memento now and then."

Alex's eyes wandered the shelves. "Peculiar doll there," and Alex pointed with his chin to a double-faced figurine.

"Quit your movin'," and the barber steadied the chin of his patron.

"What's the story on that?"

"Liberator Doll. Displayed at the windows of abolitionists on the underground railroad. White-face side meant all was clear. Black-face side signaled trouble."

"You know the history behind each of these?" Alex asked as he scanned the legion of objects.

"Weepin' mother of Jesus. Hold still."

* * *

The next three weeks saw much progress as the plant was enclosed, a horse stable was completed and the framework went up for a pair of two-story homes. The Duncan brothers were pleased with the quality of the work, which showed the skillset of several new hires. Hostlers and blacksmiths from Ireland, axe men from Norway, mechanics from Germany, carpenters from Denmark—it was a potpourri of nationalities and talents.

Alex had placed William Fraser and the other married men

in the mill so they could remain close to family. The unattached bedded down at the bunkhouse, which soon adopted the scent of whiskey and the sins of gambling.

Sam and Alex stood near the little muley saw, discussing the short-term plans for the mill. They both agreed—a rare occurrence, indeed—that a basecamp needed to be established near the timberline of their newly acquired property. With the recent purchase of land from the German Rancho, the brothers could harvest trees from near the coast at Russian Gulch to several miles inland, 3500 acres in all. They also were of the same mind when it came to the use of the Russian River. Though unnavigable, it would serve as a handy waterway for transporting logs from the forests to the plant. On one point, however, they continued to hold very different opinions.

"Little brother," Alex started in a testy voice, "are you steadfast in your thinking of introducing a dock at Doran Beach?"

"I am," Sam said. "Bodega Point will shield vessels from the northern winds. If we run a quay three hundred feet out into the bay, the depth should be sufficient to accommodate any size schooner. In addition, we'd no longer have to deal with the hazards which dogholes present."

"The area is within the boundaries of the Bodega Rancho, lest you have forgotten," Alex said.

The muley saw started up and Sam motioned toward the exit. Walking side-by-side, Sam said, "If your concern lies with Tyler Curtis, I've secured the necessary easement rights."

"Did you retain all ten fingers upon the shaking of hands on such a deal?"

No response.

"Can't trust that knacker any further than you can toss your own arse," Alex persisted.

"We have no other options. The coves in these parts roil with rip tides and boulders the size of locomotives. Too dangerous," and Sam began to walk away.

"You're as stubborn as an old muddled hen," Alex said to the backside of his brother.

"A muddled hen is safe enough from a fox with no teeth,"

Sam said over his shoulder.

So, I've lost my bite, eh? Alex thought before taking a nip from his flask.

* * *

The days went by as advancements were made on Duncansville. Axe men worked eastward, clearcutting the area, hauling felled logs to the river where the current acted as a beltway to the mill downstream. The Duncan ladies began furnishing their new homes, which were bookends of one another, each two-story boxes with chimneys on opposing sides. Simple, straightforward and utilitarian in the old federal style. Plans were in the mix for a hotel, which would accommodate a modest saloon. With the assurance of both whiskey and coin, the Duncan brothers could hold onto a proper labor force.

However, Ann put her proverbial boot down when it came to a whorehouse. To her mind, such an institution would tempt not only the souls of the single men but the married ones as well. Though Ann's skirt was no longer a shared commodity, she saw no reason why another's should feel the warmth of her husband's touch.

A rail system wound its way from the flats of Bodega Corner and up a half-mile switchback to bluffs, which stood seventy feet or higher above the Pacific. The intent was to have horse-drawn railcars travel another six miles to Bodega Bay where a dock would be built.

The Duncan siblings continued to tarry as to the whereabouts of the final destination. But one thing was clear—whatever had to be done, had to be done on the short side of time. Logs were arriving at the mill. Stacks of cut lumber lay at the foot of the tracks.

"Running low on currency," Sam said as he stood looking out at Goat Rock in the distance.

"The recession may be in full bloom," Alex said, "but San Francisco can't expand fast enough. Time to cash in."

* * *

During his spare time, Alex surveyed the coastline seeking an alternative to a port within Tyler Curtis's domain. His search brought him to every recess and nook, every alcove and cranny. Wherever he went, however, sandbars or rocks or surging seas caused his mind to fill with frustration.

It was during one of these excursions that his focus prevented him from noticing the neighing of approaching horses from behind. "Mr. Alex Duncan, is that you?" a rider said, his frock coat billowing in the wind.

Duncan pivoted around, cupped a hand over his eyes and studied the person. "Hard to believe that that top hat of yours doesn't go the way of the next breeze. Must be lassoed to that fancy ascot of yours. Perhaps God might see fit to hang you by your own device some blustery afternoon. Wouldn't that be grand?"

"The Almighty and I are old friends. That's the truth of it," Tyler Curtis said.

"Interesting choice of words," Alex said. "*Truth* that is. For some it seems to take on the hue of a chameleon, changing its coloring whenever the need arises."

Duncan's vision slid to a second rider who wore chin whiskers and was bald. "Heard you finagled your way into owning the *Sonoma Democrat*."

"No such thing," Thomas Thompson said. "Bought it outright. From the profits made with the sale of the Petaluma *Journal*."

"Word is that a haggle of southern boys bought the *Democrat* for the purpose of using you as their front man," Duncan said. "You know, to spread their views on enslaving the Negro and such."

"I speak for the good citizens of the county who, unlike you, have a sense of what our Constitution stands for," Thompson said.

"Enough with the poor mouth," Duncan said. "Why might you be here?"

"Is it true that you're harboring a colored among your

midst," Thompson said.

"Ah, there's that word again," Alex said. "I'll let you in on a wee bit of what is *true*," and he began the tale of a Scottish lad used by Tory Redcoats for their own end to cut through the ranks of Irish Paddies.

"Told myself then and there that no man should own another," Alex said. "So *tabhair amach*—you're giving out the stink, you are. Best you and your cohort be on your way."

"When Breckinridge is escorted into the White House, the State of Missouri and every other California county will endorse slavery," Thompson said. "Where will you and your darkie be then?"

"Wherever we land, he and I will still be free men…in Sonoma County, not in your flummadiddle State of Missouri," Alex said.

"Your mind is cluttered with the naivety of a newborn," Curtis added. "Progress is at your doorstep. Jump onboard with your brother and embrace it, man."

"Embrace this, you knackers," and Alex drew his hand away from his weapon and dropped his trousers.

Twin cheeks fouled the air as a pair of steeds and their riders steered away and traveled north along the coast.

* * *

Without warning, a lasso caught the corner of a makeshift stand and brought it down. Lemons, apples and copies of periodicals tumbled to the planked porch.

The ruckus caused a Negro, wearing a barber's apron, to rush from the general store. "Weepin' mother of Jesus," and he started to corral wayward fruit and flapping newspapers.

"That fruit is most likely no longer fit to sell," a young rider, with chin-whiskers and prematurely bald, said from his mount. "Don't want to be the cause of citizens going ill, do you?"

"My produce is fit for most."

"You've got some lip on you, boy," Baldy said. "Probably best if you closed up shop and moved elsewhere."

"And if I don't?" the Negro said.

"I'll see to it that your name is vilified throughout the county to the point that not an apple or a newspaper or a strand of hair comes your way," Baldy said.

"And for my part, I will drag your black-ass from this property and put you on the auction block," a dandy added from under his top hat.

"Don't believe this property belongs to either of you gentlemen," the Negro retorted. "Duncans are leasin' the land from Mr. Wright who, accordin' to county records, is the rightful owner of Bodega Corner as well as three miles further down the coast."

"The slavery laws of this state know no boundaries," Dandy added.

"Best leave," Baldy repeated. "You understand my words, nigger?"

"This *Negro* understands quite well. *Igitus sales stulti sunt* (white man is a fool)."

Baldy and Dandy exchanged puzzled glances at the Negro's speech before making their way to the mill.

Chapter Eighteen

With darkness falling, Alex returned to his abode in Bodega Corner. He was played-out, exhausted from his fruitless search for an alternate port as well as his dealings with Thompson and Curtis. The image of his wife on the other side of the entrance caused him to wince. He didn't possess the strength for another bout and turned away. Upon reaching the riverbank he plucked a Philip Morris from a pack and lit it.

The crimson edge on the horizon danced with the ebb and flow of the river as it butted up against sandbars. The unfolding serenity, mixed with several pulls on his cigarette, began to iron out the kinks in his thinking when a familiar figure made his way to him from the mill.

Alex flicked the cig to the ground. "Evening, little brother," and he spied the emptiness in Sam's countenance. "You have the look of a rootless wanderer. What's the problem?"

"Had a visit from Curtis and Thompson," Sam said.

"Lucky you," Alex retorted.

"Not so much," Sam said in a serious tone. "Seems they had a disagreeable meeting of sorts this afternoon. Was that the way of it?"

"Might have been," Alex said as he fumbled for another Philip Morris.

"Frankly, they were none too pleased with the cut of your attitude. Complained about the insolence in your tone not to mention the loosening of your drawers."

Alex put a match to his pleasure and inhaled. "My arse was better than they deserved."

"Perhaps, but the reality is that we either rid the premises of our Negro or they withdraw our easement rights."

"Don't let them put you on the tenterhooks. We've been through worse."

"Without the easement we have no access to Bodega Bay. Without access to Bodega Bay, we have no harbor from which to ship our product. I counsel you to review your stand on the matter. For the sake of Duncansville. For the sake of our families."

No response.

"Your altruism will bury us," Sam continued. "Standing by a secondhand barber instead of our financial good is nothing short of foolhardy. No good ever came from denying the truth of things."

"The *truth* of things, eh?" Alex repeated, heat in his voice. "That word surely has made the rounds lately," and he took another pull, a crown of ash building atop his cigarette. "Mr. Charles Franklin Sloan owns more correctness than those two racist knackers put together."

Sam raised his finger as if to make a point but Alex broke in, saying, "Our *Negro* is going nowhere, little brother. How's that for a fox with no teeth?"

* * *

A four-horse team labored with a loaded railcar as it wound its way up the switchback from the mill at Bodega Corner. A "yaw" and a snap of a whip caused the team to dig in. The climb was arduous even for the Shire breed. Muscular backs tightened in sinewy furrows. Hindquarters tugged in obeyance, as was the nature of the horse's temperament.

Having reached the top of the bluff, the team came to a rest, relieved that the ascent had reached its climax. The remaining two miles proved much less strenuous, winding its way south along a flat trail between the rolling fields and the jagged coastline. Pastures retained their flaxen hue, grasses waving in a synchronized dance along a gentle slope. To the west lay their counterpart, sharp-edged inlets buttressing against agitated seas.

The team railed past Wright's Beach, a spit of sand named after its owner. They soon came upon a cove on the southside of the dunes where the Shires came to a halt. The Duncan brothers had arrived early, anxious to witness the inaugural run.

"For every problem there is a solution," Alex said with a grin.

Sam cringed at the cliché, saying, "Remind me again why we chose this inlet."

Alex took a sip from his flask. "First and foremost, we no longer have to put up with the shenanigans of Tyler Curtis. Secondly, by not making use of the harbor at Bodega Bay we have cut the distance from the mill to a mooring spot by almost four miles," and another smile.

"You're in love with that gob of yours, aren't you?" Sam said.

Once again, Sam had yielded to the desires of his older brother. Nothing had changed. For the younger sibling, it was as if they had never departed from the shores of Ireland. Alex was in charge then. And he was in charge now. Sam's suggestion for the construction of a port at Bodega Bay had gone the way of most of his ideas—into the trash bin. Life would go on, but it was not the one that Sam would have selected.

The brothers suspended the exchange to survey the doings. From a sling-carrier hung a consignment of 2 x 4s, which a brakeman lowered to the deck of a schooner some seventy-five feet below.

The vessel had experienced few obstacles on its voyage north from San Francisco, the greatest challenge being the dodging of the doghole's outsized boulder, which had earned the nickname "Death Rock". Alex Duncan didn't understand why a single crag warranted such distinction. Nor was he sure he wanted to know.

* * *

A brush applied soapy suds into the folds of the customer's face before a straightedge slid down the line of a cheekbone. The patron started to criticize an editorial in the *Sonoma Democrat* when a warning came hard and fast.

"*Tace* (be quiet)!" Charles Sloan said.

"What is that, Latin?" Alex Duncan asked.

"If you don't keep your mouth penned up, you may have more than one hole with which to throw out your complaints," the barber said. "And put down that paper. Like tryin' to shave a jaybird on the wing. Never seen anybody jabber away so much about nothin'."

"Didn't know you spoke Latin."

"*Igitus sales stulti sunt* (white man is a fool)."

"Stop that."

"*Tace.*"

"Maybe Thompson and my brother are right," Duncan said. "Maybe your black arse should be shipped out of the county."

"Then who'd listen to your complaints every Tuesday?" Sloan said before shifting Duncan's head backwards for a better angle.

Duncan flapped open the *Democrat* to the second page and started reading aloud Thomas Thompson's publication of a New York Democratic Party manifesto:

> "'The Creator, Himself, has stamped natural distinctions upon the human family. The unconstitutional demands of leading politicians to bow, for the sake of supposed popularity, to the imperious demands of anti-slavery is cause for serious and profound alarm...'"

"A bona fide knacker, Thompson is," Duncan said in a raised voice, his hands gesturing in rhythm to his heated words.

"Christ on a bike!" and Duncan put a hand to a nick on his jaw. "You attempting to put me to slaughter?"

"Hold still," and Sloan gripped the head of Duncan with one hand while the other leaned forward for another go with the razor.

"There's more," Duncan said as he returned the newspaper to his vision:

> "'And we reject the debase doctrine, as abhorrent to natural instincts and right reason,

that American citizens should place themselves in an unnatural equality with an inferior race.'"

Duncan looked back up at Sloan, saying, "Thompson's talking about you." A smile formed on his face. "Better hightail your arse outta here before it's too late."

And another slip of the razor. "Christ on a bike!"

Sloan patched up his customer's face with wetted wads of tissue before saying, "Ain't my finest work, but it'll do considerin' what I had to work with."

"Hope I have enough face remaining to see me through the week," and Alex rose and felt his cheek. "A mummified Scot is what I am."

A simper leaked from the mouth of the Negro. For a weekday, the event would serve as decent entertainment.

Alex put aside the mockery to take in a new trophy, which had recently found a place upon the wall. "And the mask? What's its tale?"

"Made by the Maasai people. From Kenya. Possesses healin' powers."

"You are, my friend, a wellspring of information. News seems to arrive at your foot faster than lightening to the ground."

"It's my currency. In a way. Customers seem to visit the shop as much for the stories as for the haircut and shave."

"You must have a proper title," Duncan said in a burst. "One that better fits you. *Sloan* is such a pedestrian designation," and he ransacked his mind, his fingers tapping his forehead as if to unlock a thought.

"*Professor*," Duncan said. "That's it. From this day forward you will be known as the *Professor*."

"If it'll bring a coin to these hands, so be it," and the Professor snapped the hair cloth across the lap of his next customer.

Alex headed toward the exit when a request followed from behind. "Where's my tip?"

"Catch you in seven days," Alex said back over his shoulder.

Grumblings from the barbershop faded as Duncan went outside to the stand on the porch. "How's business?" Alex asked Junior.

The eleven-year-old had been hired by the Negro to tend to the sale of fruit and periodicals due to the increase in business. The job seemed to suit the persuasive manner of the lad as well as his pension for finances.

The boy's mouth went slack at the sight of his uncle's condition. "Your face," and the boy placed a hand over his mouth to stop the giggles. "Looks like a pumpkin with the pocks."

"Not your uncle's finest image, I suppose."

They began to share a laugh when Alex's grin flattened at the sight of his brother riding toward them. Sam yanked on the reins and said there was an emergency.

"Got...a...situation," the younger sibling sputtered. "The stableboy...has your...mount ready and..." Sam stopped in midsentence, squinted and leaned closer. "What happened to you?"

"My chin bumped up against a razor one time too many," and Alex shrugged as if to say that was the way of it.

Sorry that he asked, Sam gathered his thoughts and urged his brother to follow him to Death Rock.

The *Bianca* arrived the previous night with Captain Steven Williams successfully directing the anchorage despite strong winds. During the following day, attempts to deal with the unloading of cargo was thwarted by the arrival of 60 m.p.h. gusts and rough seas.

Alex glanced at the seething waters below and thought the task of unpacking goods too risky. "Best option is for the captain to set sail and head back out to sea," he said to Sam.

But before a final decision could be rendered, the schooner broke from its mooring. The *Bianca* began to drag its anchor toward the volcanic monolith.

Every available mill worker hurried from the bluff and waded into the white-capped froth. Shouts could be heard from the broken schooner, men wheeling their arms. The sea lapped over the bridge rails. Sheets of spray passed over the deck. The

Bianca shuddered, tossing and rolling on Death Rock. A sailor attempted to throw the hawser ashore. The lanyard was meant for towing. Perhaps it could be used to release the schooner from the boulder.

William Fraser saw the hopelessness of the effort and dove into the roiling cove. He battled the crashing waves, trying to keep his head high. He coughed up seawater and powered on, reaching the line. With it tied to his waist, Fraser paddled his way back to shore where his limbs dropped with fatigue. Others rushed forward and clutched onto the rope but the endeavor proved difficult as the ship heaved with the rise and fall of the Pacific.

A railcar arrived with more millers who sped to the scene and lent a hand. A team of twenty-plus strong, strung out along the hawser, tugged and swayed with the trundling of the *Bianca*. Words and gestures crisscrossed over each other, mixing with the hammering of the surf. Organized chaos took hold before the men gathered themselves, dug into the shifting sand and synced their movements with that of the vessel. A Negro in a salon apron, owners in three-piece suits, workers in soiled trousers and a sally of settlers threw out with equal sweat. But the vessel wouldn't budge.

With the situation becoming dire, the captain devised an alternative plan for the hawser. Crewmen stepped into harnesses, clipped onto the line and lowered themselves from the foredeck. The sea pitched the figures to and fro, as might a mutt with ragdolls. Heads bobbed up and down, disappearing beneath the water before resurfacing only to repeat the uncertainty of it all. With determination and a prayer, each sailor inched along the line until receiving the beach underfoot.

* * *

Venison stew, pockets of potatoes and hot coffee circulated the table with thanks given on high. Victims and rescuers regurgitated the day's events: the thrashing of the *Bianca* upon Death Rock; the anchoring of the hawser with folk from the mill; the victory over the hungry sea. Jocular and jaunty. Fear and panic on hiatus. It was within this moment of relief that Captain Williams, with drink in hand, staggered to his feet and proposed that the inlet should rid itself of its present moniker and henceforth be known as *Duncan's Landing*. All agreed with raised glasses and hardy voices, saying farewell to Death Rock.

Ann stood behind her husband and placed her hands upon his shoulders. The heat of her touch penetrated his jacket and he swelled with pride. The act reminded him of their walks through Central Park in New York. Innocent and reassuring.

He reached for her hand but the fabric of his coat was all that greeted him. His eyes dropped in disappointment. A counterfeit smile grew as he pretended to savor the entertainment from across the table.

Seafaring tales abounded, which grew in proportion to the amount of drink finding the gullet. The wick of the lantern burned to its nub and the whiskey went dry, sending all to sleep.

The next day, Alex and Captain Williams brought a compliment of men to the wreckage site. With the aid of lighters, the gang salvaged as many items and effects as possible. Twenty hours later the owners' agents and cargo consignees visited the disorder.

After receiving the survey report, the proprietors decided to grab the insurance money and release ownership of the *Bianca* to the underwriters. Beachcombers soon took over, picking at the leftovers. Shorn canvas, forgotten tools, brass couplings and tattered lines found the arms of eager men.

Chapter Nineteen

Bamboo firecrackers flew from hands into the flame. Pops echoed into the ether. The clamor from revolvers joined the celebration along with the howls and jangles of excited men.

The Settlers League—some thirty strong—galloped off into the night, whooping and crowing. They rode with the thrill of Lincoln's victory, arms waving, muzzle fire dotting the blackness.

A two-story mansion came into view, fluttering within the coming and going of a quarter moon. The Settlers crisscrossed each other on horseback. Shouts. Shots.

A dandy in his ascot and three-piece suit appeared from the entrance with a lantern. Next to him stood a bald man with bloated cheeks and chin whiskers.

Words scurried back and forth. Though a mere handful advanced above the din, the rancor clothed within was unmistakable. "Nigger" and "Traitor" and "Fabricator" were exchanged with equal heat.

* * *

He took his seat in the barbershop, scanned the trophy wall and came under the fixed gaze of a large rodent. "What in the name of weeping Mary might that be?" Alex Duncan asked.

"A capybara. From Argentina," the Professor said as he sharpened his razor on the strop.

"Biggest rat these eyes have ever seen," Duncan said.

"Can weigh up to 145 pounds."

"Wouldn't want the likes of it knocking about in my attic."

"Couldn't agree more. 'Sides, you've got enough critters

roamin' around up there already."

"You are one funny man, you know that? Perhaps we should call you Jester instead of Professor. Might be more fitting, eh?"

"*Stultus hominem* (stupid person)."

"Told you before to stop doing that."

"Still owe me a tip from your last visit."

"Don't tip when more flesh is cut than hair," and Duncan started to mine through the *Sonoma Democrat*. On the third page, the newspaper issued a scathing editorial regarding the election results of November 6, 1860. Thomas Thompson said the nomination of Lincoln as the next President was the workings of the "black" Republicans.

Duncan rose with lather on his face. "*Black Republicans?*" and he started pacing. "Thompson's basically calling the Republicans low lives for supporting another race."

"You gettin' back in the chair, or what?" the Professor said.

"Thompson says we should all be pleased with the results. That the Democrats did well in the State of Missouri." Duncan lowered the paper, saying, "that eejit better cease his reference of Sonoma County in that manner or—"

"No time for this. Sit down or leave. Your choice."

"And then he goes on touting how that southern knacker Breckinridge won the popular vote in the county, how the election wasn't over, how things had to be done to save the democracy."

The Professor released a clump of air, snatched the hair cloth from Duncan and gestured to William Fraser to take the chair instead.

Duncan continued to travel across the small confines, rendering a summation of the article. "The gall of the man. Thompson pays a pittance to Lincoln's acceptance speech while printing the entire inaugural address of Confederate president Jefferson Davis. Outrageous."

William Fraser was oblivious to the ranting, rendering a sermon of his own, bragging about the hairs emerging upon his upper lip. A ragged mustache in the making. The Professor feigned an admiration of sorts, saying that in another month or so there might be sufficient follicle to warrant a trim.

The indifference surprised Duncan. He scolded the duo for their lack of interest and tramped outside where Junior tended to his stand.

"Nothing but a land of knackers," Duncan said to no one.

"Got soap on you," the lad said, gesturing to Duncan's cheek.

Duncan wiped away the suds with the sleeve of his coat. "Doesn't anyone give a capybara's arse anymore?"

"A what?"

"It's a rather large rat that…Doesn't matter."

"Maybe you should stop reading the *Democrat*," Junior said, gesturing to the periodical in the hand of Duncan. "Doesn't seem to do much for your nature."

"Why Sonoma was the lone county in the state to vote against Lincoln is beyond me," Duncan said.

"Don't pay much attention to—"

"With Breckinridge and Douglas each claiming to be the rightful nominees of their party, the Democrats couldn't form a unified front."

"Okay."

"Thanks to the Almighty for placing eejits upon this land. Otherwise, this country would've been in a pickle."

"Hallelujah for eejits?" Junior guessed, trying to sound interested.

"Hallelujah."

* * *

A letter opener cut through the casing. The recipient ballooned the envelope open with his breath and tweezered out a letter bearing the official seal of the Democratic Party.

The younger Thompson began mumbling aloud. His head slid across the sentences as might one's teeth working the rows of a corncob.

"Don't just stand there with indecipherable nothings spilling from your mouth. What does it say?" old man Thompson demanded, a cigar dangling from his fingers.

"It's a request for funds," the younger Thompson answered.

"From the Knights of the Golden Circle."

"Funds? For what?"

"For stopping the theft of the election. For putting Breckinridge into the White House," the younger Thompson said before tossing the memo into the wastebasket.

Old man Thompson retrieved the letter, saying that the Knights of the Golden Circle was exactly what the country needed. "The KGC's been operating since '54. Has powerful allies in the South," and he took a pull on his smoke.

"You're not seriously thinking of backing these radicals," the younger Thompson argued.

"KGC possesses an army of 16,000. Might be able to bend the country to its will."

"Sounds farfetched. If you ask me."

"You been breeding with those Yankees down Petaluma way? 'Cause I swear, you've slipped a cog," the old man said. "Grow a pair, for God's sake," and he stamped out his cigar and exited.

* * *

Men hauled drums of fuel across the deck and fastened them to the wire cable. Provisions for the households followed. Wicks, glass chimneys, sacks of flour and chicory, barrels of molasses and whiskey, a cast-iron stove, lace curtains, pocket windows and clothing items. Upon reaching the bluff above, the products were loaded onto flatcars, which the four-horse teams pulled north to Duncansville.

The seven Duncan children rushed to a pile of shoes. A tangle of arms ensued as the kids reached over one another to draw out a boot only to toss it back and search for another. Ann busied herself with the storage of foodstuffs after which she inspected the store-bought curtains with a close eye.

Alex sat in his chair and lit a Philip Morris, waiting. In a matter of seconds his wife would engulf him with her dissatisfactions. He drew on his cigarette. The clock's secondhand ticked, beats measured by the thickness of its nell. Another puff.

Instead of complaints, however, Ann brought a thank-you kiss to his presence. He squirmed and fidgeted. Uncomfortable. Was this some sort of ploy? There was a time during their courting days when such affections were commonplace. Perhaps he was overreacting.

That evening Captain George Morgan of the *Excel* took supper with the Duncans. His presence had become a regular fixture, his good humor and easy-going palette second only to the tales of his travels.

"Parades are becoming so commonplace that even the smallest doghole has taken to harboring a band for a celebration," the captain said.

"Lincoln's victory will change the landscape," Ann said.

"There are some, however, who profess the theory that the election was a fraud, that the result was the work of conniving Republicans," the captain added.

"For one, I'll rest easier when Lincoln is sworn in at his inauguration," Alex said.

"Couldn't agree more, dear," Ann said before adding that rumors were on the wind, that certain groups were raising funds to halt the swearing-in ceremony. "I do hope the actions of a few malcontents do not ruin the day."

Ann steadied her glance upon her husband. "It's as if some know no better...one eejit following another blindly off the cliff like a herd of lemmings." When no response was returned, she filled the space, saying, "You wouldn't do any such thing, would you, dear? There are far too many eejits as it is."

Christ on a bike.

Chapter Twenty

He stepped past masks, a stuffed rodent and a dozen other artifacts and plopped down into the barber's chair. The usual rant began to spill from his lips when an admonishment rained down from behind.

"At least let me get some lather on you before that tongue of yours goes on another rampage," the Professor said.

After several more threats, Duncan settled down, kept his words to himself and let his eyes wander the space. There was always something he noticed for the first time. Below the head of the capybara, a taxidermy posed with its feathers fanned out.

"A rooster?" Duncan said, unable to hold his thoughts.

"Gamecock," the Professor corrected. "Souvenir from some fella who came through here from South Carolina."

Duncan nodded. "So, you know."

"Yes, I do."

"Seems as if the news arrives at your doorstep before it is in print. Quite the accomplishment."

"It would seem."

"And what is your opinion of the events from back East?"

"Don't have one," and he started to glide the straight edge down the cheek of Duncan.

"The Santa Rosa *Democrat* isn't afraid to share its opinions."

"The editor is white. He can afford to speak his mind."

"South Carolina and six other southern states secede from the Union before Lincoln is sworn in, who would've thought?" Alex Duncan said.

"Let the world rest for ten minutes. Please," and the Professor applied an extra layer of lather, hoping that might dam up his customer's hole.

"That knacker of an editor is doing nothing other than pushing his own agenda," Duncan persisted. "A hidebound sot, he is."

The Professor wiped the suds from Duncan's face. Removed the hair cloth. "That'll be two bits."

Duncan rose and examined the work in a standup mirror. "Got more stubble on me than when I came in," and he ran his fingers over his face.

"Next time, leave your mouth at home if you want better service."

"Don't let that rooster peck you in the arse."

"It's a gamecock, you blitherin' idiot."

"See you next week," Duncan said without turning around

He stepped from the general store and went to the stand out front where he observed a bowed expression on his nephew. "Why the long face?"

The boy, without looking up, said, "My mum says your arse is hanging out the window."

"Might be some truth to it," the uncle said with a shrug.

"You going to hell?" the nephew asked.

"Not today."

No response.

"Let's go for a stroll, eh?" the uncle suggested.

Junior hung a CLOSED sign above his stand and walked alongside his uncle toward the Russian River. As they reached the bank of the muddy waters, a foreboding sight appeared before Alex. A wrinkled woman in black clothing bent over the stream with a garment dangling from her grip. She was a stranger to both, which in itself was an oddity. The curiosity piqued Junior's interest and he started for her when his uncle steered him away.

"But I want to talk to her," the lad said.

"No, you don't," the uncle said.

"Who is she?"

"Not from around here. She's from everywhere."

"Don't understand."

"It's best that way. For now. You'll know soon enough."

They meandered upstream along the driftwood-strewn beach, Alex oblivious to the rattling beside him. His mind was cluttered with visions of the washerwoman. Her presence at the river perhaps explained mysterious events of the recent past. At least to his own thinking.

Strange lights and unexpected knocks at the door were omens of a tragedy to come. Scottish folklore told of an old woman known as the Washer-at-the-Ford who would visit homes where death lingered on the horizon. The washerwoman often posed at the side of a stream, cleaning the blood from the clothes of the dead.

* * *

A dandy in his frock coat sat across from a rolltop desk where a balding, bloated-cheeked man had stationed himself. A third paced the room with his cigar, acting important.

Dandy tapped the planked floor with the toe of his button-down shoe. His sentences came out jumbled. His top hat fluttered within his hold. "The squatters mean business," Tyler Curtis said. "Heard they've found backers for their cause."

"Is this concerning the other night?" Thomas Thompson asked in a flippant tone. "I wouldn't worry yourself over a few drunkards."

"They surrounded my house. Shots were fired. Threats thrown at me and the wife."

"Did you really care for her that much?" Serranus Hastings quipped.

"You're missing the point," Curtis said. "The squatters have organized. Go by the name of the Settler League, or some such thing. Have raised funds. Who knows how far this will go."

"If I were a betting man," Thomas Thompson started to say, "I'd guess they don't—"

"If you were a betting man," an older gentleman, with a lean physique and a full head of hair, said from the opened doorway, "you'd be out of purse before the sun set."

"Father, it's good to see you," the younger Thompson said, halfway out of his seat.

"What's this all about?" old man Thompson asked.

Tyler Curtis's nerves didn't have the wherewithal for small talk. "As head of the State Land Commission, can you guarantee that these squatters won't prevail if the issue ends up in the courts?"

Serranus Hastings leaned in. Though he had rid Mendocino County of the troublesome Yuki people, he—like Curtis—needed Robert Thompson's agency to come onboard.

The old man snapped a wooden match on the heel of his riding boot and puffed on a cigar until the tip glowed red. "Nothing is guaranteed in life, gentlemen," and he took another draw before reminding all that his office had sanctioned the dandy's claim to the Mexican land grant in the Ocean Township as well as Hasting's holdings in Mendocino.

"Yes, but will it hold up under the law?" Curtis asked.

"Probably," and another puff.

"*Probably*? I require stronger assurances than *probably*," Curtis said. "Advertisements in your son's newspaper have been running for over a year regarding the sale of my properties. I'd be in a tight hole if everything ventured south."

"Don't be soft, Curtis," the old man said. "As long as my son has your backing, you'll have the full measure of the Land Commission at your disposal. Same goes for you Hastings."

Curtis fingered his top hat. Tapped his foot.

"We do have your backing, correct gentlemen?" Another puff.

Curtis and Hastings both surrendered nods, which was good enough for the old man. "Very well. Shall we get on with the next order of business?"

The old man took a seat at the head of the conference table as if to say that a meeting was underway. "The Knights of the Golden Circle are entreating loyal Democrats to continue the fight against the fraudulent election of Lincoln by those black Republicans."

"Not this again," the younger Thompson grunted.

"You'd be advised to curtail that tone, son." The old man rolled the cigar between his lips, waiting for his only child to settle down. "The KGC has a plan to restore truth to this past election. It will delay Lincoln on his journey to Washington for the March inauguration while a second contingent storms the capital and installs Breckinridge as the rightful president."

"And you expect the military to simply stand down?" Hastings asked.

"Exactly. The Secretary of War, John Floyd, is a member of the KGC in addition to both President Buchanan and Vice President Breckinridge. The secretary will use his position to move munitions and soldiers to the South under the pretense of attacking the Confederacy. That will leave D.C. defenseless and ripe for the taking."

"If our involvement goes public, it'll be the end of any political aspirations you have for me," the younger Thompson said. "You do know this, father, right?"

"Do not dare to lecture me on what I know and do not." And another puff. "You were but a seed in your mother's belly when I was massaging the egos of fellow colleagues in Congress."

"Yes, father."

The old man rose with his cigar. "I shall leave you to the details," and he exited, leaving the door open as if the task of closing it was beneath him.

Curtis leaned into the younger Thompson, whispering. "Don't put the old man into a tizzy. We need him."

"Absolutely," Hastings said in agreement.

"*You* need him. You both do," the younger Thompson corrected. "I've got no use for that rusty old banger."

"Sort yourself out or he'll have us all buried before our time," and Curtis alighted from his chair, dipped into his pocket for his poke and pitched the bag of gold coins onto the table. "See that the KGC gets this. And quit mucking around."

Serranus Hastings contributed as well, leaving both currency and a glare behind as if to warn the younger Thompson that the future was fragile.

* * *

An open casket rested in the sitting room. Vases of poppies, daisies and baby's breath adorned a makeshift altar. A grieving mother busied herself, travelling from the pantry, setting out food and drink for visitors. Mourners came and went for three days to pay their respects.

Junior had never viewed a dead person before. He studied the face of the infant, which was consumed with a peacefulness. Entranced, Junior continued his examination. Miniature hands held a rose. Bare feet, looking as insignificant as a hair's breath, appeared forgotten and forlorn.

"When will my cousin fly with the angels?" he asked his uncle.

"Soon, lad. Soon," and Alex grinned a comforting grin.

"Not soon at all," the mother corrected before gesturing to her husband and nephew to leave.

During the quiet of the night, Ann sat beside the body of her four-year-old son. She avoided prayer, for prayer was for the deceased.

"All will be right soon enough," she said to her son who rested in the coffin. "Your brothers and sisters await your return."

She brought forth a tin cup of small, wooden disks. "When you are well, we can play a game of tiddlywinks. You'd like that, wouldn't you?"

Alex Duncan put on his robe and shuffled from his bedroom toward the prattle. With a delicate touch, he lifted the game pieces from his wife's hold and placed them on the nearby table.

"Come to bed, dear," he said. "The hour is late."

Ann clenched her jaw. Brushed his hand away.

Without another word, he retreated to his quarters, flummoxed as to how to aid his beloved during her time of grief. He lay there motionless. His gaze fixed upon the ceiling. A moistness began to settle in the corner of his eyes. Helpless. The only sound was the brush of oxygen upon his cheeks. A stillness anchored the darkness. The children huddled together in a single bedroom, silent, not able to comprehend the distance that pervaded the home. Ann would remain at her son's coffin, without sleep.

Hugh Duncan was born at Salt Point in 1856. In recent

weeks he had suffered chest pains, fever and night sweats. All was accompanied by pea-green mucus, coughing fits and the occasional expectoration of blood before succumbing to consumption.

Though childhood diseases were commonplace on the frontier, acceptance was always difficult for an aching mother. Alex hoped Ann would come around in a fortnight or two. In the meantime, he would provide as much space as she required.

After the official mourning period, the next three days were meant for dancing and celebration. To honor the boy's Scottish heritage, bagpipers played jaunty tunes.

The whole affair was accented by the recent arrival of a newborn to Sam and Fanny. John James, born December 28th, 1860. Weight, nine pounds, ten ounces. Height, twenty inches. A strappy lad. No matter how hard Ann tried, however, it was difficult to acknowledge the glow on her sister's face.

"May I?" Ann asked her sibling, extending her arms with a desire.

"Be careful to hold his head up," Fanny answered as she placed her baby into the arms of Ann.

Ann drew the infant close, talking baby-talk. The more John James cooed a response, the closer she brought him to her bosom. A bit of fright washed across Fanny's countenance and she motioned for the return of her child. But Ann put her shoulder to the request, shielding John James from his mum.

"Please, dear," Alex said as he stepped to his wife.

"Go away," and she continued to mutter sweet nothings to the baby, calling the boy "Hugh", saying she was so joyful for his return.

* * *

A wooden casket sat on a flatcar near the mill at Duncansville. A four-horse team stood at the ready with their gleaming coats and polished harnesses.

Alex took the arm of his veiled wife, leading a procession on foot. The six Duncan children as well as uncles, aunts and nieces followed, easing from Bodega Corner and up the switchback. Though Sam was present, he carried a somberness, which pushed him into a quiet place during the wake and burial. Alex interpreted this aloofness as rude and unsupportive. Ill feelings festered, adding to the divide between the brothers.

At the insistence of Alex, all employees were permitted to take part, including the Professor. Some one hundred and sixty souls in all. Bagpipes sounded, filling the trek up the windy grade with a haunting melody.

Steel-gray clouds streamed above white caps as the tide rolled in, breaking across steeples of rock. The green grasses of winter frolicked within the breeze, belying the dreariness of the day.

Upon reaching Duncan's Landing, pallbearers hoisted the casket from the railcar onto their shoulders. Hands stiff at the side as all marched eastward to the sound of bagpipes humming.

Hugh Duncan was lowered into his grave at the cemetery next to the one-room schoolhouse. He would have joined his brothers, sisters and cousins to begin his education this coming year. Not to be.

Each member of the immediate family approached the tomb. Some tossed flowers onto the coffin. Others coins. Ann raised an object from her pocket. It was a small, tin box of wooden disks, wrapped with a ribbon and bow. She held it over the chasm. Her hand quivered.

Alex came alongside, steadied her. "It's okay," and he motioned to the tin box, to his son below.

Ann released the keepsake and watched with a tear as her boy received it with his outstretched wings.

Chapter Twenty-one

The weeks went by. The emptiness remained dark and bottomless. The absence of her son wore on her. She laid in bed for days at a time while her husband was left to tend to not only the business but their six children as well. It was not always possible—nor safe—to collect them and bring them to the worksite. Machinery, as well as the manners of employees, could put even the stoutest of souls at risk.

Jeannie, their firstborn and almost sixteen, was of great help especially with Alexander and William who were but three and two years old respectfully. It was no secret that Alex Duncan had paid more attention over the years to the business side of things. Some would even say that Duncansville had evolved into an obsession of sorts for him. This was not lost on his sister-in-law. Whenever Fanny visited, she would chide Alex regarding his ways.

It was easy enough for him to blame his childhood poverty for his attention to financial matters. He recalled his da lecturing him on such at their final farewell in Derry, sermonizing that Alex had better not get himself all twisted up in any slumgullions while in America. This bit of history fell mute upon the ear of Fanny who often blamed Alex for her sister's condition.

The father placed his eldest in charge, mounted his horse and headed south along the coast. Upon completing a brief inspection of the workings at Duncan's Landing, he made his way to the cemetery. Spring had arrived, providing a burst of color. He plucked blood-orange poppies and purple irises and placed them upon the grave. As the father ended a simple prayer with an "amen", his vision lingered upon his son's headstone.

The words *requiescat in pace* came to Alex Duncan. He hoped it was so.

Alex reflected on the date: May 10, 1861. It was the anniversary of another who had perished all too young. He gathered two sticks and fashioned a crude crucifix and pierced the ground nearby. A second prayer. One that Mr. Ogden had vocalized aboard the *Roscoe* on the voyage across the Atlantic. Alexandra was an infant when she passed. So few days on earth. So many unfulfilled quests. The same could be said for the girl's caregiver, Lizzy, who also did not reach the shores of her dreams. Alexandra was as much a child to Lizzy as Hugh was to Ann. Alex prayed that the same despondency, which befell Lizzy, would not visit his wife.

It was during these wanderings that a woman, with coffee-colored skin and midnight-black curls, approached. "*Lo siento mucho por tu pérdida,*" Mrs. Manuela Curtis said, extending her sympathies.

"*Gracias,*" Alex Duncan responded.

The exchange was cordial and Duncan took her statements as sincere and thoughtful. The conversation soon turned toward the tragedies of the time and why the young seemed to be the first to suffer.

"*Mis hijos también sufren,*" Manuela said.

"Your children suffer as well?" Duncan guessed.

Manuela continued, saying that she feared for her remaining three youngsters probably in the same way that Alex Duncan did for his. "*El future es importante.*"

Duncan sensed there was more behind her words than mere sentiments. He bent an ear as she went on to tell of her *niños* and how her husband was stealing their future, how he hoped to sell parcels in Bodega that were willed to them by Captain Smith, their biological father.

"*Qué puedo hacer?*" she asked.

Duncan thought about what she could do, but no plan came to him other than that of the Settlers. "Did you know that the squatters are gathering funds to countersue your husband, to hold onto the land in much the same way as your children desire?"

Manuela seemed frightened by the notion of using the court system. Her husband had threatened that if she brought the law into matters, he would ship her back to Peru.

"*No puedo dejar a mis ninos. No. No. No,*" and she stamped away.

Duncan knew enough to understand that Manuela Curtis was terrified of her husband. *Fecking knacker.*

* * *

A dandy stormed into the office of the *Sonoma Democrat.* His face flush. His movements edgy. Fingers pinched the brim of his top hat, which rose and fell with his agitation.

"I need to know where the Land Commission stands with regards to my claims. And I need to know this very instant," Tyler Curtis said to Robert Thompson.

"My people have—"

"I don't think you realize the situation I am in," Curtis said in a burst. "These squatters will stop at nothing to steal my land."

"Yes, well, that being said, I have—"

"They took over Geyserville in '58. Martial law was declared. The same could happen in Bodega."

"There is no need for —"

"And this Settlers group is taking me to court. You've got to—"

"Will you shut up!" Robert Thompson barked. "You're some kind of handwringer, is what you are. Calm down and take a seat."

"But—"

"Take a seat. Now."

Curtis did as ordered while the younger Thompson and Serranus Hastings showed smirks at the dandy's discomfort.

The senior Thompson placed a quill down beside an inkwell, taking his time. "If you're intending to go about the countryside with your head in a tither, I'm afraid there is no place for you here."

Curtis fumbled with his hat, uttered an apology and

rendered the space back to the old man. "Please forgive my excitement. Very unbecoming. My apologies."

"Probably backed up," the younger Thompson said.

"Excuse me?" Curtis said.

"*Backed up*," the younger Thompson repeated. "I don't have the scientific term at my grasp but it's when a man exhibits an element of extreme disquiet due to blockage of the urethra."

"What?" and an expression of discombobulation began to leak from the face of Curtis.

The younger Thompson exhaled, smacked his lips and said with finality in his voice, "have you had carnal knowledge of your wife lately? Or anybody's wife for that matter? Might loosen the bowels."

The senior Thompson's examination swung between the pair. "I'm washed ashore on a desert island with misfits at my side."

Curtis's angst slid from the twenty-one-year-old to old man Thompson. "My personal affairs are no business of your son's. If he wishes to carry on in this—"

"Hush," and old man Thompson held a finger to his mouth.

Serranus Hastings lifted a couple of cigars from a humidor and surrendered one to the old man.

"If we are done with the theatrics, I would like to share a bit of news," old man Thompson said. "Some good. Some not so much."

The air began to settle and the old man drew in the attention of Curtis. "My friends in the state legislature have procured a sweetheart deal for you."

"*Sweetheart deal?*"

"The regulation is specifically designed to meet your needs. Needs, which I believe you once demanded upon knowing *this very instant*. I believe that is how you phrased it."

"Yes, well, that was most likely a bit hasty of—"

"You will be able to sell, as you wish, your step children's interest in Bodega. With a caveat."

"*Caveat?*"

"All proceeds must remain in their names. As well as any interest, of course."

"But how does that benefit me?"

"You'll have complete access to their accounts," and old man Thompson drew on his smoke, studying Curtis, waiting for a light to shine.

"Ahh, of course," Curtis said.

"And my claims?" Hastings asked the old man.

Old man Thompson scanned both men. "The state is grateful to the two of you for ridding the place of those savages, for cooperating with the authorities to make certain that the land is transferred to those who rightfully deserve it."

Tyler Curtis and Serranus Hastings nodded approvals before glancing at each other with grins and looks of contentment.

"Now for the bad news," old man Thompson said, anxious to move on.

He explained how someone had betrayed the Knights of the Golden Circle. News leaked as to the circle's intention of waylaying Lincoln at Baltimore. Thousands of KGC members were either arrested or chased into the hills. There would be no storming of the Capitol Building, no swearing in Breckinridge as president.

"But the movement continues," old man Thompson said. "The KGC will gather the Confederacy of the South and couple it with other like-minded governments."

The younger Thompson bided his time in hopes of a further explanation from his father. It was a game often played between the two. Lessons learned, never to be forgotten. Or else.

"Mexico, Cuba and most of Central America will join the cause," old man Thompson continued. "A better Union will rise up. One that touts self-government and the superiority of the ruling class. One that could overwhelm any challenger."

"And what is our part in all of this?" the younger Thompson asked.

"Bring the Civil War to Sonoma County."

"But how?"

"Remember, son, where there is strength in numbers, the will of the people can be bent."

* * *

A man with square-shoulders and a receding hairline approached the newsstand. He paid his usual respects to his nephew, collected the *Sonoma Democrat* and entered the general store. Canned goods, flour sacks, drums of kerosene, linens, cookware, hardware and various other items caught his perusal before wandering to the one-chair barbershop in the rear.

Alex Duncan fingered the latest piece of memorabilia—a red cloak with bronze buttons and gold-thread trimming. "Made of silk. Very nice," and he surrendered an approving glance toward the Professor.

"Don't touch," and the barber slapped at the hand of Duncan. "Sit down and behave yourself."

"Some sort of ceremonial robe?" Duncan asked.

"A priestly wrap for a minister of the International Order of Odd Fellows."

The mention of the fraternity caused Duncan to swivel his head back around. "Odd Fellows?"

"Negroes were first admitted in '43," the Professor said. "Back in Philadelphia. Lodge No. 646, I believe."

"Did I ever tell of the time when I was crossing the Atlantic and—"

"Be still," the Professor admonished. "Anyways, the movement of allowin' blacks into the IOOF was started by an Ogden fella."

"Yes, that's him. I'll be damned. Never thought he'd—"

"Stop talkin'", and the Professor clamped his hand upon the head of Duncan. "Like I was sayin', 'cause of this Ogden fella's efforts, IOOF lodges have started up in Petaluma and Santa Rosa and other such places."

They concluded their business and Duncan rose. "Mind if I say something now that you don't have a razor at my throat?"

The Professor smirked and raised his hand as if to say go ahead. Duncan went on to tell the story of his meeting Mr. Ogden who was the chief steward aboard the *Roscoe*, of how close the two became during their many troubled episodes while voyaging to New York City.

"No need to exaggerate," the Professor said. "You wanna

steal my thunder, be my guest, you big-mouth cracker."

"No. It's all true. He and I were like brothers."

"You sure you ain't Irish? 'Cause that's a heap of blarney that be spillin' from that gob of yours."

Duncan bypassed the mirror in the Professor's hand and stepped to the robe. His vision slid upwards above the collar where a white wire-mesh mask, with red lips and rosy cheeks, was perched.

"The mask part of the ensemble?" Duncan asked.

"Think so. Don't know its meanin'. Just like its looks."

Duncan was about to say his goodbyes when he spotted a pin attached to the lapel of the barber's jacket. Alex leaned forward for a better looksee but the Professor covered the medallion with his hand.

"Is that—"

"Thank you for your patronage, sir," and the barber whisked Duncan from the other patrons, guiding the babbling man outside where they looped around to the side of the general store. "You want to get this Negro attached to the end of a Confederate rope, is that it?"

"Is that some sort of Odd Fellow's regalia?" Duncan asked, gesturing to the pin.

The medallion displayed three links of chain with three letters attached—F L T (Friendship, Love, Truth).

"Been a member of Petaluma Lodge No. 30 for a month."

"Why?"

"The three founding members were a boat builder, comedian and a vocalist. Figured I might fit in with such a group of odd balls," and the barber shrugged as if that was the whole of it.

But Duncan grew suspicious. "Can't argue with the logic. In fact, you might be overqualified. But why put yourself at risk like that?"

"We never speak of this again. There's people who don't wanna see a black man in a society made for whites. Understand?"

"No. I don't."

The Professor returned to the general store while Alex

Duncan proceeded toward the mill. His mind was in an uproar. Not only did he carry this disbelief that the Professor belonged to a secret society, but he also had to deal with an altogether different concern related to a second employee.

He motioned for William Fraser who was laboring over a conveyor belt, and the pair walked to the office. Duncan closed the door behind them while Fraser worked a rag through the grime of his hands.

"Afraid I've got a bit of bad news," Duncan said.

Fraser cocked his head in anticipation.

"Seems as if the courts have sided with Tyler Curtis."

Fraser's brow furrowed with the statement.

"You're homeless," Duncan said to clarify.

"How's that possible?"

"Curtis has been granted the right to sell off the Bodega lots. Arranged some sort of deal with the state legislature. Most likely with the help of Thomas Thompson's da. Nothing but a knacker, those two. Don't know what else to tell you."

There was a pause as William Fraser thought about his options. "Can my family board with you and yours?"

No response.

"Just til we get back on our feet."

It was almost the same phrasing Alex Duncan profited from when he made a similar request of Fraser upon first arriving at Bodega Corner. No use in denying such, and Duncan nodded without a word and exited.

Chapter Twenty-two

The Civil War was in full bloom with the falling of Fort Sumpter to the Confederates. In his editorials Thomas Thompson was declaring that the conflict would be over in a fortnight, that the South would rise up in all its glory and deliver the Promised Land. States' rights would be restored. Slavery would be legalized forever, written into the Constitution as Breckinridge and others foretold.

The bickering between the citizens of Santa Rosa and Petaluma continued to heat up. Until a third party put a damper on things. Mother Nature had a mind of her own and would let all know who was in charge.

Her terror rained down upon California for sixty-five days. Seventy-two inches fell between November 9, 1861 and January 14, 1862. The deluge melted the Sierra snowpack. The American and Sacramento Rivers overran their banks, collapsing levees. The newly elected governor, Leland Stanford, was forced to flee the capital and reconvene the legislature in San Francisco. The city's *Call* reported: "Sacramento has been drowned out of existence."

Matters in Sonoma County were no better.

* * *

It set out ninety-five miles from the northeast, gathering strength along the way. A hundred yards wide and full of piss and vinegar, the mass grew, gathering up everything in its path. Two-story clapboards, water towers, carriages, bovines and human carcasses lay within its roiling waters, destined for the unknown.

The Russian River fed upon the storm, swelling beyond anything previously seen. With no thought of deportment or civility, the muddy current bullied its way through canyons and towns, over crops and fields. By the time it hit Big Bottom, it possessed a force all its own. Some forty residents fled to higher ground. Boarding house—gone. General store—gone. Sawmill—gone. Blacksmith shop—gone as well as some twelve family homes, shanties and little snuggeries. Many were carried off their foundations, heading downstream.

Austin Creek joined the rampage as its emerald green waters slid under the muddy torrent. The surging debris flow bulged during the next few miles, swallowing uprooted trees and brush as it took aim on Duncansville.

* * *

The thunderheads stalled over the coastal range. Sheets of precipitation poured down, sluicing off hillsides, off the switchback trail. The ground swelled up into a gooey mess, drenching the flat of Bodega Corner.

Junior rushed into his oilskin slicker, ignored the pleas of his mum and went to the aid of the animals. He slugged from one foothold to the next, trudging toward the paddocks where he opened the gate while his uncle harried cattle and sheep and hogs from certain death. The duo then sped to the stables and freed the mules and horses. Blinded by the rain, neither could see which direction the animals went.

"Return to your mum," Alex howled over the downpour. "Get her and the others to the hotel on the bluff."

With the knowledge that the women and children of the village were heading along the rail line to higher ground, Alex turned his attention to the mill.

"Can we load the saws onto the railcars?" Alex shouted to William Fraser.

"Horses and mules have scattered to God knows where," Fraser said.

Christ on a bike. Alex clenched his teeth, upset at his decision to release the animals before thinking things through.

"Use the men."

Fraser nodded and sloshed away toward a clutch of timber tramps. Communication grew difficult as the wind picked up. The northerner whipped the area into a frenzy. Employees bent their backs to it. Hands shielded faces. Eyes squinted to read the lips of their supervisor.

Fraser split his men into three different units, each one commandeering a specific area of the battered mill. No time to rescue the donkey engine or the giant circular saws. Chains, rigging, belts and tools of every device were gathered up and loaded onto railcars.

A crew of eight, including the Duncan brothers, slipped into harnesses and pulled the railcar up the grade. Alex and Sam, covered in muck and sludge, put aside their differences and crowed words of encouragement to the men. Upon reaching the top of the bluff, the collection sank to their knees. Spent and beaten, the storm could do with them what it wanted.

Without warning, a remembrance came to Alex. He wiggled out of the rigging and retraced his steps to Bodega Corner. Sam yelled for him to stop but the phrasing evaporated amidst the storm's bluster.

The door to the general store flapped open with his touch. Alex entered, stepped to the barbershop area and collected masks, robes and other trophies from the wall.

He bumped his way back through the aisles and reached the porch where the whoosh of the gale partnered with an ominous sound. Alex glanced sideways. A mountain of wreckage sped toward him. He held tight to his bundle and tried for the tracks along the switchback.

* * *

The squall withdrew beyond the ocean's horizon as a weak sun eased up from behind the clouds, putting a bit of light upon the chaos. An outhouse sat atop the smithy shop while a wagon wheel's spokes spun in a lazy circle. The space once reserved for the bunkhouse was littered with window sashes, a kitchen counter, cots and a boat's transom. The cookhouse, pens and stables had also washed away, replaced by slime and gunk. Cut logs—some ten feet in circumference—lay scattered about the river bank and meadow.

A gang of Irish and Chinese recovered a team of horses and salvaged what timber had not found its way to the Pacific. The usual rift of curses filled the ether. Tempers flared as fatigue set in. The condition was not relegated solely to occidentals and celestials. A Scot and a Negro were affected by the state of things as well.

"Had a notion you'd be a bit more appreciative of the effort," Alex Duncan said as he went on to mention the retrieval of a ceremonial robe, a white wire-mesh mask and other collectables.

"Pass the mop," the Professor said, extending his hand in a presumptive manner.

"Perhaps your tongue lacks the ability for gestures of gratitude," and he handed over the item requested.

No response.

"Let me be of assistance and suggest that the price of my next haircut and shave should be free of charge. What say?"

The mop was tossed into a bucket of water as the barber gazed up from his task, saying, "You gonna stand there and do nothin'?"

"I could, if that pleases you, but wouldn't you rather have me entertain you with my Scottish charm?"

The barber shook his head and went back to work with Duncan matching the steps of the Negro, regurgitating the printed word from the *Democrat*:

> "'The death toll statewide from the tempest has exceeded 4,000 while 25% of all buildings are believed ruined. The Mojave Desert and the Los Angeles basin are lakes while California hovers on the edge of bankruptcy.'"

And a sip from his flask.

The barber padded to the next aisle, hoisting goods to various display racks while Duncan leaned against the shelving.

"Ah, here's an interesting piece: 'O.H. Lovett offers a full line of coffins and grave clothes for local consumption.'" Duncan flipped the page and cited an article that told of some five hundred souls lost in the Bay Area alone, many being Chinese laborers killed during the cleanup.

More mopping. More brushing.

"I suppose recent events will fill the purses of an undertaker or two in the months to come," Duncan said. "But that's the way of it, isn't it?"

The front door squeaked open to announce another. "Can you give me a hand?" Sam called out to his brother.

"Afraid not. Lots to do here," and Alex took another pull from his flask.

"Take him," the Professor said. "In all that is holy and just, I beg of you, take him," and he jammed his mop into the bucket, water splashing over the rim.

"As you wish," Alex replied. "I know when not to overstay my welcome."

"Doubt it," and the barber retreated to another task.

The Duncans exited and went to examine what remained of the mill. Grime occupied every cleft and fissure.

"Circular saw as well as the donkey engine have gone the way of most things," Sam said, pausing, gathering his thoughts. "We have a situation here. You know that, right?"

"Relax your crack, little brother," Alex said. "All will be fine."

"By my count we've lost nearly seven million board feet."

No response.

"Don't you have something to say?" Sam asked.

"Think I'll retire for the day," and Alex raised his whiskey to his lips as he headed home.

The door and windows were open to air out the place. While the structure managed to hold fast to its foundation, two or three inches of the river had crept inside, wreaking enough disarray to put everyone out of sorts.

Alex tucked away his flask as he approached the entrance when, without warning, a pile of fabrics flew to his feet. "Burn 'em," a woman ordered from the shadows.

Pieces of his wife dipped in and out of a ban of light. Her face appeared drawn, showcasing wasted cheekbones and sagging eyes, punctuating the tiredness that engulfed her.

While a frazzle was evident, there was also present a bit of fortitude. Tragedies often do that to a person. And so was the case with Ann.

She lifted a corner of her pinafore and wiped the sweat from her brow before pushing back tendrils of hair, which had loosened from her French braid. Her pose accentuated the curves and subtleties she had always possessed. Memories of their early courtship looped through his mind and a grin began to form on his face

Perhaps a comforting prospect from the flood was that it provided the woman with an escape from her mourning. Son Hugh had met his end the previous year, but now Mother Nature demanded her full attention. The time for tears had passed.

A communal pyre received the bundle from Alex. Curtains, linens, pillows and bedcovers soaked up the flames as splotches of green and black mold dissipated within the blaze.

He returned to his home where Jeannie and Sammy Alexander were busy removing furniture to the outside. The four younger ones were nowhere to be seen. Probably over at Aunt Fanny's, Alex guessed.

Without being asked, he put away his yearning for a cigarette and dug in. Words were not exchanged as there was no space for such luxury. He latched onto one end of a bed while his wife lifted the opposite side. The pair stamped through the exit with their load and rested it alongside a dresser and a rocking chair under the afternoon sun. The chore was repeated until the floors appeared as a whole, showcasing a fine layer of silt.

The flood waters went where it wanted. Not even the sanctity of several outhouses fell within its respect. Scat and urine were carried and dumped to the four corners of Duncansville, leaving an unwelcomed toxicity behind.

Galoshes, slickers and gloves covered the body parts of the Duncan clan as they squeezed the filth from their home. It was a rare occasion when the family operated as one and Alex celebrated the moment, as feces floated past.

Chapter Twenty-three

The younger brother revisited an old itching, stating that the mill should have been constructed on higher ground to begin with, that any rebuilds should transpire at a safe distance from the unpredictable Russian River. The oldest persisted with his belief that the flood of '62 was a rarity, that such an event wouldn't recur within their lifetime.

As usual the argument was won by Alex. During the following year, the bunkhouse, cookhouse, pens and smithy shop were restored as well as repairs made to the general store and the residences of the two Duncan homes. As far as the mill itself, a double circular saw was installed, plus an edger and planer.

In addition, a post office was acquired, officially putting the place on the map. A curiosity of sorts, however, soon reached Bodega Corner. Mail started arriving with the address DUNCANS MILLS. Rather than deal with the labyrinth of government, the brothers decided to leave well enough alone and accepted the fresh moniker. *Duncansville* was no more. Didn't matter what you called the place, a financial turnaround was needed to diminish the losses from last year's flood.

* * *

A man with square-shoulders and a receding hairline stood alongside another who bore the resemblance of a matchstick. Below was Duncan's Landing where the two-masted *Far West* had been moored for two days.

"You sure about this?" Alex asked.

"Do we have a choice?" Sam retorted.

The weight of the truth caused Alex to go quiet. The loss of so much product to Mother Nature had put Duncans Mills on the brink of bankruptcy. While aiding the cause of the Union remained risky business within a rebel county, it was make or break time. Besides, the North needed lumber to build their warships.

"The swells are picking up," Alex said, switching his attention to the *Far West*. "Perhaps she should head out."

"Her deck is but half-full," Sam argued.

"Better to cash-in on a partial load than squander it all, wouldn't you say?"

"We can little afford to—"

And a thwack rang out with the crashing of a load of cut timber. The brothers hurried to the brakeman in the tower who confessed to losing control of the sling-carrier's descent. But that didn't top the list of misfortunes.

Alex surveyed the situation below. "She's pitching badly."

Sailors stumbled about the deck of the *Far West* in their attempts to restore order as the weather picked up. A rogue gust from the south roared in. The vessel threatened to turn turtle. Stacks of lumber shifted. Crewman lost their footing.

Without reason, the uninvited disturbance slackened as quickly as it had appeared. Men took advantage of the lull to redistribute much of the cargo.

Commands spilled from the captain's miniature microphone: "Cast off lines…Weigh anchor…Unfurl the sails," and the *Far West* heeled to starboard as it headed toward the open sea.

"It'll give my head peace knowing she made it to Frisco," Sam said.

"Frisco?" Alex said in burst. "The words you carry with you baffles all sensibilities."

"That's your concern, big brother, my use of a pseudonym for your beloved city?"

"Some would say such uttering is nothing short of slander. Might go so far as to say an epithet of the worse kind."

"If a Confederate warship confiscates that shipment," Sam said, "Duncans Mills will be reduced to a curse. How's that for becoming *of the worse kind*?"

* * *

The Santa Rosa *Democrat* printed the details around the capture of the rebel schooner *Chapman* in San Francisco Bay. Loaded with weapons, it was headed for New Orleans to boost the Confederate cause. The crew was tried, fined and imprisoned while the munitions were stored on Alcatraz Island along with a cache of Union gold. The paper called the incident a dark day for justice.

A second article featured the waylay of another vessel. This one, however, was a schooner with a shipment belonging to northern sympathizers: "The *Far West* off the Sonoma Coast has disappeared with its cargo reputably taken by a Confederate warship."

* * *

"Can't believe the words of that Thompson. His rag is nothing more than a Copperhead sheet," Alex said to his brother. "The *Far West* was lost to bad weather. Not to eejits from the South. That'd be the truth of the matter."

"And you're a blathering shite in a bucket," Sam retorted. "A Confederate warship. A storm. Doesn't matter. Either case, there's a goose egg on the bottom line of our ledger."

But Alex wouldn't let go, insisting that such talk by that knacker of an editor was nothing short of sedition. "Printing such falsehoods will embroil the citizens of the area to commit unfounded acts of violence, sure of it I am."

"Only sure thing is that your thinking has gone to muck."

* * *

"Forces are gathering on the horizon against me," the younger Thompson said, tramping across the small confines of his office. "Those Union sympathizers from Petaluma and the squatters and millers along the coast…It's…It's a conspiracy, I tell you," and he gnawed on his lip. "Not sure if I have the will to deal with it."

"Of course, you don't," old man Thompson said in a chiding tone. "That's why I'm here."

The younger Thompson paused at the remark, threw a look at his father and continued his pacing. It wasn't enough that halfwits like Alex Duncan and others rose to oppose him, but now his own kin was applying irritations as well?

"We shall meet force with force," old man Thompson said before gesturing for his son to calm down, to take a seat. "I have discovered a legal loophole that may serve our purpose."

The younger Thompson lifted his eyes from his depression. The noise in his head continued but respect demanded that he at least feign an interest in his father's words.

"Did you know that fire service exempts one from jury duty and poll tax?" old man Thompson said.

"Of course, but why is that—"

"It frees one from military service as well," and the old man picked a cigar from the humidor and lit it.

* * *

With the false declaration by the *Democrat* that the Confederate army had won the Battle of Atlanta, a score of Santa Rosans went to the town square to celebrate. Most all wore the uniform of one of the town's two fire companies, which exempted them from the Union draft. If you were a supporter of the South, you possessed little desire to fight on behalf of its enemy. Thomas Thompson made himself captain while using his newspaper to enlist additional recruits who would do his bidding, fighting any and all fires no matter what form they should take.

"We gather today to commemorate the licking of that Union blowhard, William Sherman," the younger Thompson said, his hand held high in a victory pose.

He nodded while pushing his voice over the whoops and hollers that rose from the throng. "The Union forces scattered from the heart of Georgia like cockroaches from a firepit."

Confederate flags waved amidst the bluster of firemen. Shots rang out. Howls and hoots spilled over one another in concert with the sharing of whiskey.

"We will not be deterred by those in our county who hold with the sentiment that the colored man deserves a seat at our table," Thompson said in an agitated tone.

More gunfire. More swigs.

"Slavery shall one day be part and parcel of the Confederate Constitution, forever etched into our proud history."

The hoopla attracted business owners, customers and pedestrians from nearby. The town square bulged with radicals, curiosity seekers and the idle. Thompson enjoyed the attention, his voice brimming with confidence. Until.

A detachment of thirty-something outsiders, donning scarlet-colored robes and white wire-mesh masks, began to chant a haunting refrain:

"Why do the heathens rage behind the firehouse
Where the scoundrel sits upon the wall to preach?
The boys gather pearls of wisdom
Falling from his mouth.
Wash off the blood.
Wash off the whiskey."

The phrases pierced the armor of Thomas Thompson. Darkness seeped inside. He balked as his gaze floated toward the rear of the square.

His faithful spied his uneasiness and several swung their attention toward the distraction. Upon spotting the source of the disturbance, the Johnny Rebs filled the space with curses and the showing of weapons. The costumed outsiders started to march across the edge of the town square toward the offices of the *Democrat*.

A fireman lowered his pointy Confederate flagpole and charged as might a knight with his lance. An outsider fell with his wound. Fearing all sorts of wild happenings, the young Thompson ordered his men to stand down, that this was not the time or place, that their services would be required soon enough.

The crowd dispersed as well as the outsiders with their ceremonial robes and puzzling chants. The area grew quiet with the exception of a low hum, which often followed such events.

On his trek home that evening, Thompson's head replayed the chorus of the outsiders. His men were the heathens. He was the scoundrel who preached.

His eyes remained fixed upon the cobblestones. Could he be the man that his father wanted? Did he own the ruthlessness required to deal with "outsiders" and such? These doubts occupied his thinking until the sound of footfalls from behind brought him out of his wanderings.

A shadow stretched from under a lamppost. Pieces of someone dipped in and out of the light—a scarlet robe; a white mask.

Thompson slipped into an alley, looked back. Nothing. With the heel of his hand, he rubbed the fuzziness from his eyes. Took another gander. No one. Must be the stress of the day, he thought and continued on his way.

* * *

"Leave a bit on top, if you will," Alex Duncan said to the barber.

"Can't say there's more than a bit to work with," the Professor said.

"Do what you can."

"I'm a barber, not a miracle worker."

"See you've returned your Odd Fellows' robe to the wall. And the mask as well."

No response.

"Was missing for a fortnight, eh?"

No response.

"Heard some of your brethren from the Petaluma lodge were at that ruckus in Santa Rosa last week."

No response.

"Didn't know you boys were acquiring a thirst for politics. Thought you were all about fraternal brotherhood and that sort of hogwash."

The Professor leaned forward. "And I thought we had an agreement to never speak of this."

"Thought wrong."

The noise from atop sounded more like the flapping of a card against the spokes of a bicycle wheel than the gentle clip of a barber's scissors.

"You thrashing through a hayfield up there?" Duncan said. "Appreciate a tad more restraint."

"Don't think I can," and the Professor ramped up his attack until a collective neighing of horses arrived at the newsstand out front.

Duncan steered his vision to the entryway while the Professor held his scissors in abeyance. A clutch of men cut down the aisle toward the rear of the store.

"Thought I might catch you here," a bald-headed young man with chin whiskers said.

"Here for a shave?" Alex Duncan said with an impish grin.

"Need a word with the nigger," and Thompson gestured to the barber.

"His name is Charles Franklin Sloan," Duncan said, "but we refer to him as the Professor, seeing as how he can recite history by the yard."

"A nigger is still a nigger. Can't dress it up any other way," Thompson said. "Now, if you don't mind, we'll be having a private moment with the man."

"*We?*" Duncan asked.

Thompson nodded toward his men. "These fine citizens wish nothing more than to enforce the laws of this land."

Duncan eyed the badges on the chest pockets of a few. He pushed aside the hair cloth, stood up and stepped forward for a closer inspection.

He fingered the badge of one, saying, "It would seem this is the insignia of the Santa Rosa Fire Department. Not the coat of arms of the sheriff's office."

Thompson was about to render a retort when he spotted a robe and a white mask hanging from a wall. Within the space of his mental lapse, he didn't hear the onslaught of words from another.

"The use of taxpayer money to reinvent the purpose of your fire department would be a breach of civic responsibility," Duncan said. "Not to mention the misuse of tax dollars."

Thompson's concentration waned as the vision of Odd Fellow's memorabilia continued to puncture his sensibilities. Images of men in scarlet wraps and white shrouds flashed across his mindscape. He didn't know why such ceremonial nothings should haunt him so, but there it was.

"…and the use of these men for no greater purpose than that of a vigilante committee is beyond—"

"Is this the outfit of the IOOF?" Thompson asked, motioning to the robe and mask.

The Professor was about to answer when Duncan stepped in to assist with concealing any presumed association of the barber with the fraternity. "It is. Petaluma Lodge No. 30."

"A curious item to decorate a barbershop with," Thompson said.

"No more so than a rodent and other souvenirs from around the globe," Duncan said.

Thompson stepped to the Negro. "These yours?"

"Yes, sir," the Negro said.

"You a member of Odd Fellows?"

"Things fall into his lap from passing travelers," Duncan interjected, being evasive.

"Let the nigger speak for himself," Thompson said to Duncan before returning his attention to the barber. "Show me your papers."

"*Igitus sales stulti sunt*," the Professor said in Latin.

"What'd you say, boy?" Thompson said in a biting tone.

"I said I don't need to."

"You got some lip on you."

A half-dozen firemen drew closer.

"I'll ask one last time. Show me your papers."

"Don't believe I will."

Duncan spied a few of the vigilantes put a hand on their firearms. "Perhaps the Professor is being a bit hasty," and Duncan glared at the barber. "Why don't you produce your papers for the gentleman so that he and his thugs can be on their way?"

"And you," Thompson said to Duncan. "I could have you arrested for abetting a runaway. Fine of one thousand dollars and six months jail time."

"Well, we wouldn't want that, would we?" Duncan said.

"Enough," Thompson said before signaling to a couple of his fellow Confederates to step forward.

"The Fugitive Slave Acts of 1793 and 1850 been repealed. By Congress," the Professor said as he struggled within the hold of two men. "No longer legal to return runaway slaves to their owners, or to imprison or fine those abettin' such persons."

Thompson glanced around the small space. All eyes upon him, waiting.

"A new order will soon rise up under the leadership of Jefferson Davis," Thompson said. "Whereupon the State of Missouri will go the way of the South," and he started to lead his men back down the aisle when he turned around with his frustration and said to Duncan, "Be careful with the nature of your dealings or you might incur the same fate as the *Far West*."

"There's one item your empty head continues to dismiss," Alex Duncan said.

"And what might that be?"

"We're Scots. Ornery to a fault. Difficult to put us down."

Duncan stared at the backsides of the gang as they withdrew from the general store. *Fecking knackers.*

Chapter Twenty-four

The election of 1864 once again witnessed Sonoma County as the only district in California that failed to vote in the majority for Abraham Lincoln. The area was living up to its title as "the State of Missouri". The local results produced outrage from the *Petaluma Argus-Courier*, printing that "Judas is among the brethren, the black spot and only spot on the coast where treason has polled a large majority…Every home has its cesspool and California has its Sonoma County."

* * *

The Confederate cavalry of the Bloomfield Guards rode out of the oak forest and onto the grassy glen. The heads of a hundred steeds lathered at the bit, ready for action. Muskets loaded. Bayonets fixed. With banners flying, Captain Arthur raised his saber and gave the order to charge. The snorts of horses and the bloodthirsty cries of soldiers in gray rose up.

The thunder galloped toward the infantry units of the Emmett Rifles of Petaluma. The Union soldiers planted themselves four ranks deep. Major James Armstrong ordered the first line of defense to hold their fire. Though outnumbered, the men in blue would defend their town to the last man.

The Confederate cavalry stormed across the narrow valley: 300 yards; 200 yards; 100 yards. Shrills and shouts spilled forward.

"Hold…your…fire. Hold…your…fire," Major Armstrong yelled in a deliberate voice to the blue coats of the Emmett Rifles.

"Fire!" and the first line of defense unleashed holy hell.

Major Armstrong repeated the order each time a new rank of men stepped to the front. Weapons at the ready.

The gray coats of the Bloomfield Guards kept coming...and coming. The icy breath of their mounts now visible to the enemy.

"Fire at will!" Major Armstrong shouted.

Volley after volley rang out. The discharge of smoke and sulfur filled the air. The bristle of bayonets and the rattle of musketry told all that a battle of some making was underway.

With the skirmish far from decided, the cavalry unit of the Bloomfield Guard and the infantry brigade of the Emmett Rifles withdrew a short distance and formed a line opposite each other. Enemy facing enemy.

Without warning, soldiers doffed blue and gray hats to acknowledge the cheers from the spectators.

Following the reenactment, a procession was formed on Main Street, headed by the participating squads. Captain Arthur's Bloomfield Guards rode ahead of Major Armstrong's Emmett Rifles, who endured the pungent aroma of Confederate horse dung. Cornets and saxhorns of the Bloomfield Brass Band trailed behind, belting out the notes to "Florello Quick Step". Horse-drawn floats weaved their way through downtown Petaluma with the grand entry being a fourteen-foot-high representation of the Goddess of Liberty. Fifty members of the local I.O.O.F. joined the celebration, marching in their scarlet robes and white masks.

Cheer upon cheer occupied the space. Handkerchiefs waved a victory salute. Bunting adorned the lampposts while flags fluttered from porches. The parade ended in front of the American Hotel where several dignitaries spoke to the assembly.

From the mayor to Captain Arthur to Major Armstrong to the Noble Grand of the local I.O.O.F., each recited the same theme: that all had gathered to honor not only the termination of the Civil War, but the salvation of the Union. Petaluma would remain indomitable in the face of local Confederate hoodwinks and fabrications. Thomas Thompson of Santa Rosa's *Democrat* was mentioned as one who promoted the lie that the South had not been defeated, that the fight still raged on. Major Armstrong made it a point to hold the man and his allies as accessories, aiders and abettors.

Roars of exaltation rose. The sharp repeat of gunfire rang out, followed by the Petaluma Glee Club, which surrendered a rousing rendition of "The Battle Hymn of the Republic".

* * *

Four days later, a different type of parade made its way through the avenues of Petaluma. Lincoln had been assassinated. Shops were closed. Black armbands adorned coat sleeves. Flags were at half-mast. Units of the Odd Fellows and City Guard led a funeral march accompanied by an empty hearse, a riderless horse and pallbearers. Church bells tolled. On the half-hour, from sunrise to sunset, a cannon sounded a tribute.

The *Argus-Courier* wrote: "Petaluma is in mourning… Never before have we witnessed so widespread and unutterable sorrow."

But the tone was much different at the epee center of the State of Missouri. Santa Rosans, led by their two fire departments, crowded the town square with their jubilation. Meanwhile, in the back office of the *Democrat,* a quartet of men questioned what the next step should be.

"Lincoln deserved nothing better," old man Robert Thompson said.

"I agree," the younger Thomas Thompson said. "But we can't let those Petaluma Yankees make a martyr of him. After all, look what they did with that parade falsely celebrating the Union victory at Appomattox. Not only did they erroneously proclaim it was the end of the Civil War, but they used the event to elevate the status of Sambo and the Black race. Shameful."

"Your paper can't just ignore the death of a president, can it?" Tyler Curtis asked.

"Sure, it can," old man Thompson said. "No need to make a fuss over the man.

"Curtis has a point," Serranus Hastings said. "Though Lincoln was a waste of American tax dollars, his office should be recognized with some sort of obituary."

"Nonsense," and the old man gathered his things and departed.

* * *

They rode north along Stony Point Road. Major James Armstrong and his Emmett Rifles rumbled with the anger of fifty souls. This raid, however, would not be some parade for the citizens of Petaluma. This raid would not see weapons firing blanks. Blood ran hot amongst the troops with the *Democrat's* assertion that perhaps the murder of Lincoln was a "good event".

Armstrong fed his troops promises of ransacking the Copperhead newspaper. As a bonus, they might attack the Santa Rosa courthouse and carry the county seat in their saddlebags back home to Petaluma.

The militia came up fast and hard to the headwaters of Washoe Creek. With the ride chaffing at parched throats, the major relented to requests for some refreshments at the local stagecoach stop and saloon. Entranceways, barback mirrors, chandeliers and a framed photo of Abraham Lincoln were draped in black crepe. Servants of the Washoe House tried to keep up with the demand for whiskey, but the effort proved futile.

In the meantime, one of the few remaining Johnny Rebs in Petaluma rode ahead to Santa Rosa. He stormed past the secretary and into the back office of the *Democrat* and delivered a warning. Old man Thompson thanked the operative for his service before dismissing him.

"If those Yankees set foot within the city limits, we'll be ready enough," the old man said to the others sitting around the table.

"They wouldn't dare do such a thing," Curtis said.

"Wouldn't be so sure," the younger Thompson argued. "Mobs in Frisco laid siege upon the offices of the *Alta* and

Bulletin," the younger Thompson argued. "Types and presses were cast out of windows. Papers were distributed on the wings of the wind. Door frames were torn out of their fastenings and thrown into the streets where the debris was gathered and set afire."

"Falsehoods," Serranus Hastings said. "Lies promoted by Republican publications. No truth to the matter."

"Two companies of armed police were called out to put down the violence," the younger Thompson added. "Nothing says it couldn't happen here."

"Better assemble your firemen," the old man said to his son.

"What, and restart the Civil War?" the younger Thompson argued.

"Sounds like a splendid notion," Curtis said while Hastings concurred with a nod.

"No," the younger Thompson said. "No, it doesn't."

"You've inherited the backbone of your mother. Gather a bit of manhood about you and stand your ground," and old man Thompson slipped into his overcoat and gloves, saying that he rued the day his seed brought such a weakling into the world.

Firehouse Stations No. 1 and No. 2 emptied as the men marched to the Santa Rosa town square. Sixty strong danced and whooped and fired their weapons. The killing of Lincoln would act as a salve for the unfounded rumors that the South's Lee had surrendered to Grant's Union Army at Appomattox. Hope filtered through the pack.

Thomas Thompson heard the gunshots from his office and feared the worse. With a bit of urgency nipping at his nerves, he sent his staff home and bolted shut the doors and shutters.

"I believe I'll be on my way as well," Tyler Curtis said.

Serranus Hastings joined him saying, "No need to concern ourselves with such handwringing."

"Thought you two were all giddy about the prospect of battle," the young Thompson said.

"Seems as if you have things handled on this end," Curtis said. "No need for us to tarry about," and he included Hastings with his look.

"Wouldn't want my affairs to upset you," the younger

Thompson said in a barbed tone.

"Awfully decent of you," Curtis said before he and Hastings exited.

* * *

The whiskey caught up with the militia group as they continued to drown the dust from their throats. The hotness of the day subsided and the Emmett Rifle brigade laid down their angst in favor of more trivial pursuits. Talk of storming the Santa Rosa *Democrat* waxed and waned until diminishing to a spate of broken sentences.

Night's curtain fell with nary a single soul wanting to vacate their barstool with the exception of a disagreement or two regarding who was sleeping with who's wife or other such matters. Fisticuffs erupted in sporadic fashion from different corners of the saloon. The brawl would have to do as it was all the men could muster under the conditions. Some would later expand on the event, christening it "The Battle of the Washoe House".

With the relief that the boys from Petaluma were stuck at the public inn, Thomas Thompson secured his office and began the trek home. He passed the town square where a trickle of men still held out hope that a skirmish was in the offing.

One man spilled away from the group and headed toward his captain. "And where might you be headed?" he said with a slur in his voice.

No response.

"Firemen from both stations…gathered at the bidding of…of your old man, but you…you were nowhere to be seen," the man said with a stumble in his phrasing.

No response.

"A captain's supposed to lead…to…to be an example for his men. But you're nothin' but an arse who's runnin' home to hide behind locked doors."

Thomas Thompson pinched up his collar and livened his pace. Harsh words fell to the wayside as the editor rounded the corner. The stress of the day was taking its toll. He had faltered in the eyes of many. His inactions were those of a coward and a milquetoast. Perhaps his father was right. Perhaps he did own the spine of an old woman.

A city employee stepped along the dirt avenue on a pair of stilts putting a flame to the gaslights. Shadows sprung every which way from a fence or a garbage bin or a carriage. Besides the lamplighter, the bark of a caged dog was Thompson's only company.

At 301 2nd Street, he turned the key, opened the door and entered. After lifting a glass chimney and putting a match to the lamp's wick, he set about fixing a meal for himself.

Most nights harbored the same loneliness. Silence grew to become his worst enemy. It was within the stillness that sinister images used his mind as a playground. He tried to keep himself occupied with the tasks at hand, slicing a tomato or brewing a cup of tea, but the torment was never far away.

A scratching sounded against the window. He carried the lamp and knife to the parlor and leaned the light toward the commotion. The naked branch of his apple tree brushed across the pane.

Oxygen fell from his lips in silent relief. Thompson started to return to the kitchen when a similar sound came to him from behind. But this one possessed the grating shrill of slashing fingernails. Not the sound of some silly branch.

The unknown drew him in and he turned around with his fright. A second slash along the glass. His breath thickened. Thompson eased forwards.

The image of a scarlet robe and a white mask flitted across the window. The lamp fell from his grip.

* * *

Alex Duncan walked to the sixteen-year-old at the newsstand. "Seems you're long overdue to accept a more substantial job."

"Sounds about right," Junior answered.

"Report to William Fraser tomorrow. He'll have something for you."

The lad nodded before handing over the latest edition of the *Petaluma Argus*. The uncle started to slip away when the lad uttered the usual theatrical cough, palm extended. "Did you forget something?"

Alex Duncan grinned and tossed a coin to the boy. "Becoming more like your da every day…By the way, where is that knacker? Haven't seen him in a while."

"Been busy," the boy said. "You should try it sometime."

"Like I said, definitely growing into the cloth of your da," and the uncle folded the periodical under his arm and stepped toward the rear of the general store for his weekly haircut and shave.

The Professor slapped open a cloth and unfurled it over the lap of his customer. "You're gonna put the piss to me if you read from that paper," and he reached for a neck strip.

"See your Odd Fellow's regalia is missing," Duncan said as he examined a blank space upon the shelves. "Has your robe and mask been busy again?"

The Professor responded with a tighter than usual application of the neck strip.

"Trying to choke the life out of me, eh?"

Barber and customer went back and forth—as they often did—regarding the proper etiquette in the shop. The following quiet was welcomed by the Professor until the routine of chitchat resurfaced not long afterwards.

"Heard that Thompson was burned out of his place," Duncan said. "Some say it was an accident. Others that it was the work of those Yankees from Petaluma. Still others insist that the Odd Fellows had a hand in it."

No response other than the snip of scissors.

"Know anything about that, eh?"

Snip. Snip.

"If your lodge brothers had a part to play, I'd be rooting them on, don't you know."

Snip. Snip.

Duncan snapped open the *Petaluma Argus* and read aloud an editorial:

"The plot to assassinate the President was doubtless well known in the wigwams of the Knights of the Golden Circle, and no sensible person will attempt to deny that leaders of the Democratic Party of Sonoma County were members of that organization."

Snip. Snip

"Would you hold an opinion on the matter?" Duncan said as he started to glance backwards when a stiff hand told him to do otherwise.

Exacerbated and tired, the Professor took the bait and said, "This Thompson fellow has acquired hate on the cheap. But now it's gotten a hold of him and he can't set himself free."

"He speaks. Praise be."

"Be still."

"You may be correct in your thinking," Duncan said. "Perhaps hate does own men like Thompson. Perhaps it will be with him to the grave."

"We can only hope that it digs the hole as well."

Chapter Twenty-five

While the displacement of so many things told of a tragedy, the day could have been worse. The mill was spared as well as the homes of the Duncans and the post office. The bunkhouse, cooking shed, storage facility and outhouses were nowhere to be found, most likely fodder for the Pacific.

As had become custom, all took refuge at the hotel on the bluff, above the mill. The tight quarters brought everyone closer, both physically and emotionally. In the case of the Duncans, this did not playout as a welcoming.

* * *

A man with the carcass of a matchstick peered out the lobby window and gazed at the line of thunderheads romping over Goat Rock. More rain to come, he thought.

Though the torrent of that year bore little resemblance to its kin of four years previous in '62, it was still a meritorious effort in the eyes of Mother Nature.

"You're a peck of trouble, aren't ya?" Sam Duncan said through the glass pane to the skies above.

"She does seem to hold onto a bit of an attitude from time to time," a person said from behind.

While keeping his gaze upon the growing storm, Sam said, "She does indeed."

Alex noted a skein of brown pelicans gliding along the crest of a wave. "We are nothing more than guests on this spec of dirt. Most critters recognize that. We should too."

Sam swung around. "This is the fourth washout since we've arrived. That is what I recognize."

"Can't put the moral lash on me for what Mother Nature decides to do."

"Oh, but I can."

"Is that so?"

"Look around you," Sam said. "What do you see?"

"Afraid I don't take your meaning."

"We are standing on dry floors, which happen to be attached to dry walls, which are holding up a dry ceiling."

"Don't be chewing on my tail, little brother. You were the one with the notion to move south of the Russian River. Not me."

"The mill should've been constructed on this site. Standing next to the hotel. High and dry."

"You're beating a dead horse. We've wagged our chins over this from day one."

"And you got it wrong, didn't you, *big brother*?" Sam said in a snarky tone before brushing past Alex and stepping to the reception counter.

Alex took Sam's spot and gawked at the parade of gray clouds. *Fecking Mother Nature*, and he picked his flask from his coat pocket.

* * *

A few days later, after the Russian River had receded, all returned to Duncans Mills to address the cleanup. Ann Duncan was growing weary of the onslaught, but she never expressed such. Truth be told, it was her idea to abandon a comfortable life in New Orleans in favor of northern California's rugged frontier, all in the name of "family". And as of late, it seemed as if that concept had enlarged. With William Fraser and his family taking up temporary quarters in the house, the walls were closing in.

She had but one release and she would avail herself of it at every opportunity. "That Scottish charm of yours isn't going to clean this mess by itself," Ann said to her husband as she gestured with a mop to the silt and sludge.

Alex waved off the request, saying that he had business

elsewhere. "Sorry, dear, but duty calls," and he started for the exit when an irritant chased after him.

"Your duty belongs here, ya lousy Irishman," Ann said in a raised voice.

Alex paused before reclaiming his pace, knowing that any further hesitation would result in a sermon of some duration. His actions, however, did not serve the intended results as reminders followed him past the entranceway and onto the meadow.

The general store withstood the ravages of the Russian River only to act as a collection bin for muck and grime and all manner of foul things. With the cleanup still in progress, the Professor established shop outside.

Alex stepped to a nearby flat where a deserted crate served as a barber chair. Other items littered the area as well. A cash registrar sat upon a barrel of nails. Shelving rested on its side. Wares and goods of various shapes and kinds lent an aura of a forgotten outdoor market.

The deluge, however, would not waylay certain rituals. Alex Duncan's weekly haircut and shave took its proper place atop a backlog of urgencies.

"You've acquired a new memento since our last visit, I see," Alex Duncan said, gesturing to a placard with the words HEALD & GUERNE etched across its length.

The barber placed a cloth and neck strip on his customer, saying, "Souvenir of the flood. From the new mill upstream in Big Bottom. Some fella by the name of George Guerne has made an impression upon the folks there."

"Well, he's certainly made an impression upon me," Duncan said. "Want to thank him for his donation."

"I wouldn't say the sendin' of lumber downriver should be labeled a *donation*," the Professor said, reaching for a pair of scissors.

"No matter. Donation or not, the timber will sell just the same."

No response.

"The boys back in D.C. just ratified the 13th and 14th Amendments. Seems as if your black arse is free for all time."

"Nothin's free."

"Does away with the California Indian Act as well. I'm guessing those Kashaya folks will be liberated from Fort Ross."

"*Liberated?*" the Professor repeated. "No such thing for coloreds, no matter what shade their skin takes on."

"Well, go ahead then," Duncan said, noticing the irritation in the barber's voice. "Let's hear the rest of it."

The Professor suspended his scissors in midair, pondering if it was worth the effort before taking a chance. "People like the Yuki and Kashaya have been stolen from their land, not unlike my ancestors. Religion and language and every strand of culture were stripped from them, replaced by those of their captors. Home reduced to a distant memory."

"But the Amendments?" Duncan said with optimism in his voice. "Days ahead will be different. You'll see."

"Words on a paper do not a solution make."

But Duncan remained hopeful, saying, "Negroes and Indians will be able to roam the streets as naked as a jay bird…I'd toss a gold piece in the ring to witness that, I surely would."

"You're an idiot," the Professor said as he began trimming Duncan's sideburns.

"Appears to be the general consensus."

"*Naked as a jay bird* comes from the penal colonies Down Under, depictin' a convict's introduction to prison when he went to the showers, after which he walked the length of the cellblock naked. That how you see me, barebone in my birthday suit with my red brother walkin' beside?"

"Relax your crack," Duncan said. "Didn't mean much by it."

"Hatred's a malignancy," the Professor said. "Always searchin' for a new host to infest."

"There you go again. Be nice if you took some of that riddle out of your speech."

A gleam filled the eyes of the barber as he sharpened the edge of his razor on a strop.

* * *

In a barn on the outskirts of Santa Rosa, a gathering of men took place after nightfall. It was by invitation only. Exact location revealed only hours earlier. No uniforms permitted. Keep it nondescript. Pedestrian. More important than ever to maintain a low profile.

Buggies and wagons crowded the entrance. A lean-physique of a man, with a full head of hair and a cigar pinched between his fingers, greeted each arrival in turn. His self-assured demeanor oozed confidence. If the man called, you came.

Robert Thomas never lost the swagger that had become his trademark. Glad-handing was second nature, noting another's past accomplishment or his superb selection in a wife.

Old man Thompson said hello to a dandy, admiring the person's attire. "Only you could carry such grace into the shed of bovine and other uncouth critters."

"As always, your compliment humbles me," Tyler Curtis said.

"I understand that you'll soon be departing from our midst," old man Thompson said.

"Manuela and I are opening a leather goods enterprise in Frisco."

"And those contestable children of hers? Will they be accompanying you as well?"

"Of course, they hold the strings to the purse."

"Comforting to know you have obliged yourself of my counsel."

"Indeed. Those brats of Manuela's may have title to Bodega, but I have retained control of their bank accounts."

"Well done," Thompson said between pulls on his cigar. "I've written a particularly enthralling speech for my son, which should entertain you to no end," and a nod told Curtis that it was time for him to move along.

A hundred men filed into the barn, milling from one cluster to the next, a hum drifting along for the ride.

A bald person, with sideburns running down a bloated face to chin whiskers, stepped atop a hay bale and brought a paper to his eyes. "Welcome, my fellow brothers. The night grows long…as does the arm of those black Republicans," he said in a stilted voice as he read from his father's notes.

Men turned every which way until all squared up to the person whose words cut through the chatter. It had been a while since Thomas Thompson had stood in front of them with a meaningful phrase on his tongue. Fresh on everyone's mind was his recent absence at the Santa Rosa town square where the hopes of a skirmish once rose high.

Glances were exchanged.

"Illegal amendments to the Constitution have upended states' rights. What will those Yankees do next? Will it be the legislation of universal suffrage? The legalization of mixed-blood unions?"

The yammer swelled.

"A new enemy has joined the fray. The yellow infidel wishes to join Sambo, to seek equality with the white man."

Agitation salted the air.

"Foreigners and..." He paused, wetting the tips of his fingers, turning to the second page. "...and darkies threaten to steal gainful employment from you and yours."

Curses rose.

"Will you join me...and...and restore decency to our county, to our state, to...to America?" and he hoisted his arm in an awkward plea for unity.

While the request may have fumbled from the lips of an unseasoned orator, shots rang loud with a definitive answer.

Chapter Twenty-six

In 1867 a Chinatown of sorts began to emerge along the banks of Santa Rosa Creek near the town square. Lean-tos and shacks spiraled off from a washhouse, noodle shop, an opium den and a makeshift temple. Most of its occupants were men who had jobs at nearby farms or as house servants. Some had drifted to the site from the recent completion of the county's first railway, the Petaluma & Haystack, which was two miles long and powered by mules. The smell of progress was in the air. Many clung to the hope that a railroad cyclone of some description would soon be unleashed.

Sunday lazed forward as men in their queues and pajama-like clothing sat cross-legged, smoking bamboo pipes. The few women in attendance were washing laundry in the stream or hanging clothes on lines. Calm proclaimed the area.

Until it didn't.

Packs of whites marched toward the area, a muted cacophony drawing closer and closer. Some carried a complaint. Others an armament.

A Chinaman rose from the ground and approached the apparent leader who was bald with sideburns running down to chin whiskers. "My name Guy Ah. It mean handsome. What yours?"

"Don't give out my name to chinks."

"Guy Ah like your whiskers," the Oriental said in the third person. "You like mine?" and he jutted his chin outward to display three strands of hair.

"Not allowed to smoke in public," Baldy said.

"This not public. This home," and Guy Ah gestured with his hand to include all that surrounded him.

"Your kind's taking work that belongs to Americans."

"You fella from paper?"

No response.

With the realization that his effort to diffuse the situation would not reach fruition, the Chinaman decided to have a little fun and said, "Your paper excellent for catching turds," and he showed a grin.

The backhand of Baldy sent the Celestial to the ground. He rose, swiped the dirt from his pants and wiggled his jaw.

"Sausages make for puny weapons," and Guy Ah pointed to the lard-like fingers of Baldy as if to say the man punched like an old woman.

Baldy spat into the face of the Chinaman and a riot broke out with the exchange of shrieks and flying objects. The tin of a washbasin found the arse of an occidental. A billy club sucker-punched an oriental. Frying pans and cooking pots took flight. The toe of a boot made its mark.

* * *

A square-shouldered man with a receding hairline travelled to the mill where he met up with two workers who were busy navigating the extraction of a mulesaw from the clutches of a log.

Alex Duncan asked what the issue was.

"Broken saw," William Fraser said.

"Whole line's shut down," Junior added.

Duncan surveyed the scene. With the ripsaw unable to reduce the behemoth to half its girth, the parade along the conveyor belt lay idle.

"Junior," the uncle said, "go round up the smithy."

At the entrance to the blacksmith shop, the lad met up with a muscled man steeped in black dust, feeding charcoal into the furnace. Junior talked over the whoosh of the bellows as it expelled its breath, and in the short of things he was off with the required tools.

The team wrestled with the snagged saw for the next hour until its teeth were freed. No nods or handshakes were exchanged as this was emblematic of another typical workday. But for Junior, the task furthered his education with the family business. Without being told, he stepped to the far end of the conveyor belt where circular saws sliced through the log. A whine rose to a steely pitch. Junior turned around, garnered the attention of his uncle and gave a thumbs up, grinning as if his opinion mattered.

Duncan escorted Fraser to the outer edge of the din. "I see where some of your fellow Missourians conspired with a mob of Micks to take on Santa Rosa's Chinatown."

"Told ya, they ain't mine no more."

Though the topic of Fraser's allegiance had been perused years previous, Duncan thought the issue should be revisited. "It would disappoint me greatly if you harbored any sentiment toward Thomas Thompson and his gang of thugs."

"Got no energy for such foolishness. Me and the wife have enough troubles. No reason to take on more."

Not completely convinced, Duncan put forth a test, saying, "You attending that Democratic barbeque in August? All the ribs you can eat in exchange for providing a hearty welcome for the governor."

"Doesn't temp me in the least," Fraser said.

"Good to know."

"Ribs that is. Pork fella myself," and Fraser hoisted an eyebrow as if to say he was more than up for a game of wits.

* * *

Politicians had built the city's first fairgrounds a half-mile west of Courthouse Square. It was to mark the advancement in Santa Rosa's march toward legitimacy. The effort, however, did not go well. Marred by violence, gambling and heavy drinking, the fair was abandoned and the space plowed under. The area's reputation continued to plummet with the infestation of celestials who soiled the place with their uncivilized ways, so said some. The situation often called for constant policing by Thomas Thompson's band of vigilantes as well as other patriotic groups.

To avoid future disturbances, a rancher was kind enough to donate his private racetrack several miles south for an upcoming event that deserved as much civility as the town leaders could muster.

The orchestra of the Free Masons sat on folding chairs at the foot of the platform, which was draped in banners reading WHITE MEN SHALL RULE. Miniature flags fought for space with balloons and crepe paper and wreaths. Red, white and blue smothered the place.

A gaunt fellow wearing a three-piece suit, gray hair and half a beard stepped to the podium to the tune of "Hail to the Chief". Little Caucasian girls held hands with little Caucasian boys while adults surrendered a rousing tribute.

"Ladies and gentlemen, it is my great privilege to be here today to celebrate the official incorporation of Santa Rosa," Governor Henry Huntly Haight said in a raised voice.

Scattered clapping erupted from different corners.

"I want you to know that I stand with you in your fight to save your beloved town from ruination. For I come from the same place where you have been. I married my lovely Anna on January 24th, 1855 in St. Louis, Missouri, forever the proud gateway to the west."

With the annunciation of the word "Missouri", the throng went berserk. Arms windmilled. Mouths yelled hallelujahs.

"While we are many miles from the plains of our childhood memories, we bring the treasures of our upbringing with us. God and family shall show us the path to the promised place, unfettered by the foreign infidel."

Thomas Thompson rose with other dignitaries to cheer. He scanned the crowd, his vision sliding from one end of the grounds to the other, from front to back until coming upon the last row where a string of white masks returned his gaze with a stare.

He blinked and they were gone.

* * *

"Junior thanks you for assigning him to the mill," Ann said

in a polite tone.

"And his auntie?" Alex asked with a twinkle. "Does she thank me as well?"

"She does. She does, indeed."

"The boy was ready for an advancement," Alex added. "I believe he's up to the task."

"Wants to be like his uncle. A timberman."

For Alex, his wife's fresh demeanor was a welcomed change. Perhaps she had gotten past the demise of their son Hugh. Perhaps she had grown accustomed to the meager doings of frontier life. Whatever the reason, the moment did not go unnoticed. And then he opened his mouth.

"Wanna give the boudoir a spin?"

"Alexander Duncan, quit acting the Irish Paddy and clear off."

"Is that a *no*?"

A missile of some making hissed past his head with the answer.

Outside, he built a cigarette before rummaging through his pocket for a match. With a flame rising from the sulphury tip, he suspended his intent to study the approach of a man on horseback.

"Tell me it isn't so," the man said as he reeled in the reins.

"And what are you cracking on about now?" Alex asked his brother.

"Secure a mount. We ride across the river," Sam said.

"Not until you tell me why we're—" and the match burned down to its nub. "Christ on a bike." Alex flicked his fingers to ease the pain, knowing that more discomfort was most likely on the way.

* * *

An Irish bullwhacker by the name of Harrington oversaw the worksite. His chest puffed out his soiled shirt while his stained teeth notched an unlit cigar. His gruff manner and attitude of entitlement reminded Alex Duncan of his landlord back in Strabane who never gave a quarter but expected one in return.

Curious how events had come full-circle. At one time the Duncans were under the whip of the Irish. And now, Scottish brothers ruled over this Mick and all his countrymen.

Dew rose to join the mist until all retreated to the Pacific as the sun sat on its afternoon perch. Gonna be a hot one, Alex thought, unbuttoning his coat.

Choppers—one left-handed, the other right-handed—stood on either end of a springboard, which was supported by two stout staves and iron wedges. The men faced each other some twelve feet above the ground, the springboard quivering under the blows of their axes. They had begun the undercut the day before, nearing a goal of slicing two thirds into the giant's girth.

The bullwhacker hollered at a lone Chinaman who was assisting with the building of a crib. "Christmas be only four months from this day," he said with an Irish accent. "Fixin' to spend it with a bottle and not some shiftless heathen."

The Oriental, wearing a queue, black clothing and a bamboo hat, took the bull's meaning and started to gather more branches, duff and such. The litter would form a pad some three hundred feet in length, which would absorb the shock of the fallen tree. The construction of the crib was in its third day and behind schedule.

"Don't be carin' much for chinks," the bull said to the Duncans as they drew upon the scene. "Don't be speakin' American and they be worshippin' the wrong god."

No response

"Got kin and such down in Frisco," the bull added. "They might do."

"The thugs of Dogpatch, from the south slot of Market Street?" Alex said with a smirk.

No response other than a challenging glare.

Sam sensed the heaviness occupying the space and changed the topic, saying, "How much timber can we claim til the forest runs its course?"

"Be enough for six months, I suppose," the bull said to Sam Duncan.

"We'll let you get back to it," Sam said.

At a safe distance from the prying ears of employees, Sam said to his brother, "This is your idea, I'm thinking."

"Only a matter of time before Guerne and other millers start hiring Chinese," Alex argued. "Might want to get ahead of the practice. The Chinaman I hired is named Guy Ah. Has connections. Can bring in as many laborers as needed."

"Can't afford it."

"He's grateful to have the work. Pay him what you will."

No response.

Alex spied the hesitation in his brother and added, "The Chinese will take the jobs that Micks don't want any part of—digging and grading skids, water slinging and such. Filthiest tasks in the forest."

No response.

"And all done for less wages and without a complaint. I dare you to say that about these Irish wankers."

"The practice is frowned upon by most," Sam argued. "Even the governor said as much in Santa Rosa last month. If Sacramento is backing the scourge against these foreigners, it'll be the Indian and Negro situation all over again. We can't risk it."

No response.

"You came to the aid of those Yuki up at Salt Point, which brought us within a hair's tip of a bout with the Eel River boys," Sam said. "Then you hired on the only Negro in the Russian River Valley, which was followed by more brushes with trouble. Now you want to introduce an Oriental to the area? Are you on a mission of self-destruction, big brother?"

No response.

"You can't correct all the evils in the world," Sam said.

"No, but I can correct all that I can," Alex said before adding, "Look, if you want to compete with the likes of Guerne, this'll be the way of things. No doubt about it."

"And who's to say the Chinaman won't bounce from one mill to the next in search of better compensation?"

"Pay them in coin rather than scrip. Never knew a man who didn't prefer a gold piece over paper," Alex suggested before removing his coat and packing it away in his saddlebag.

The issue sat unsettled as the brothers returned to the logging endeavors of the crew. The springboard was transferred to the opposite side of the redwood and the second cut began. Alex marveled at the balancing act of the choppers as the platform teetered and the tree trembled.

The work progressed into the afternoon until the bull whistled that it was time for a break. Tired men slumped to the ground. Conversation was not forthcoming as they saved their energy to sip water from a passing container. Though the sun had started its downward descent, the air grew thick with the heat.

In need of a bit of fun to brighten spirits, the bull collared the Chinaman and placed him further down the crib bed, along the projected fall-path of the redwood. The others began to realize the intent of the bull and started to return to their feet.

"Don't ya be movin', ya yella chink," the bull said, straightening the foreigner's frame as might a marksman with his target.

A puzzled look occupied Guy Ah's expression. His head swiveled to a clutch of workers in search of an answer, but the goad of the bull thrashed the dust with a warning.

"Move again," the bull said, "and I'll be havin' your gonads for me supper."

Guy Ah restored his head to its original position. Pupils went wide with fright.

Money from various hands reached the hold of the bull as a rapid exchange of words ensued, which Alex couldn't make out at first. His best guess was that several of the men were placing bets on where the tip of the giant redwood would land: thirty feet in front of the Chinaman? Twenty feet? A foot?

"Shouldn't you be doing something about this?" Alex asked his sibling.

"Big brother, you are absolutely correct in what you speak," and Sam nudged his steed forward to the bull and placed a wager.

The sequoia began to topple. The two choppers stepped from their perch and sped a few feet to either side. A single, sharp crack echoed off the forest wall as the tree continued its descent. The giant sheared the branches of other redwoods, flinging them hither and thither. The rain of needles and limbs continued until a thump as loud as a thunder peal shook the woodland and all in it, coming to rest four-feet in front of the Chinaman.

"And that, as they say, is driving a stake with a tree," Sam said as he collected his wages, steering a smug look in the direction of his brother.

"*And that, as they say, is driving a stake with a tree,*" Alex repeated to no one, the corner of his mouth turned up in sarcasm.

Several of the timber tramps, as well as the bullwacker, showed a tightness with their glares, upset that their employer had drained the betting pool dry. Bad enough to lose a wager, but to line the pocket of some daft Scotsman was almost too much to bear. With this disappointment, the crew went back to work.

The buckers arrived with their long saw, standing on opposite sides of the felled redwood, cutting at fourteen-foot lengths. The men slid the tool back and forth, working in rhythm as a single unit. The iron bars of barkers came next, prying off the outer skin of the tree, carpeting the forest floor with its waste.

Could use the bark for shingles and siding, Alex thought. Might process it into flour for the making of bread, or ship it to textile factories to be shredded and woven into clothing. If he was to have absolute control, things would go a different way.

Snipers, with their double-bitted axes, went into action, making 45° cuts into the nose of the logs for smoother traction during hauling. Suglers strung bridle chains from the front end of a log to the backend of another.

The bull paced across the earthen floor, shouting orders, fingering his whip, appearing agitated. The shift in the man's deportment might have been due to wages surrendered during the "felling game". Or to the simple fact that he was Irish. Unpredictable.

"Best be linin' up the beasts," he growled at an employee.

Seven yokes of oxen reacted to pulls and yanks,

maneuvering over broken branches and bark and skids. The bull exchanged his whip for a goad—a pole with a nail protruding from its end. The bull stood on the leading log, gripping a chain for balance with one hand while the other put the goad to the backside of the last oxen, the prick prodding the animal forward.

"Haw, ya mangy critters," the bull shouted.

The queue of Guy Ah flew in the breeze as he sped along the makeshift roadbed with buckets attached to the ends of a shoulder pole. He ladled water upon the skids, trying to keep them slick for easier hauling of the logs.

Sweat trickled down the arms of the bull who hurried the Oriental along with curses and such. "Quit your driftin', ya miserable chink."

Additional men trotted to the area, guiding pack mules loaded down with canvas water bags, filling tubs along the way. But no matter how much water or how fast it was applied to the skids, the oxen continued to bog down.

Frustrated that profanity didn't resolve the issue, the bullwhacker released his grip on the chain, marched forward along the log and leaped onto an ox. He walked the entire length of the team, stamping hard with his caulked boots, yelling like a demon from hell.

"Ya feckin' maggots. Get your legs into it," the bull shouted.

The felled timber, however, continued to catch onto the skids. The bull pricked the Chinaman with the goad.

"Don't believe corporal punishment will bring a solution to the day," Alex said to Sam.

"Hiring this foreigner was your idea," Sam said. "We should let this run its course."

Alex bit down hard on his brother's statement, unwilling to admit that there was some legitimacy in it. Couldn't play wetnurse every moment of the day.

Another prick and the Chinaman fell under the goad's strike. Alex started his horse forward, but the hand of his brother intervened.

Guy Ah nodded and started to collect his hat from the

ground when another prick caught his backside.

"Ya be gettin' your yella carcass back on the line," the bull ordered.

The bull attempted another strike but Alex Duncan caught the goad on its downward flight and ordered the man to stand down.

The bull started to dispute the interference but Duncan hushed him. "It's too hot for water. Skids are soaking it up in the quick of things," Alex said. "Tallow will grease the path good enough."

"Ya be spillin' your mouth, ya are," the bull challenged.

"What we have here, gentlemen, is a lack of respect for the chain of command," Alex said in a raised voice for all to hear.

"Only thing the Scottish be good for is givin' out the stink," the bull said.

Duncan nudged his horse closer to the Irishman, telling him to collect his things. "And don't let me see you in these parts again, understand?"

The bullwhacker showed his back, tossed his goad to the side and stomped off.

Alex Duncan summoned the Chinaman. "Let me have a look at you," and he turned the employee's head one way and then the other. "Not a pretty sight."

"Boss man wrong," the Chinaman said. "My name Guy Ah. It mean handsome."

"Not today it doesn't."

Chapter Twenty-seven

"**EXCURSION**. To the people residing in the neighborhood of Heald & Guerne's Mill on the bank of the Russian River: the steamboat *Enterprise* will make her inaugural trip to Duncans Mills at the mouth of the river tomorrow."

The notice in the *Democrat* was not news to the one hundred and thirty inhabitants of Big Bottom, as most were employed at the mill where the first stern wheeler in these parts was constructed. George Guerne and his brother-in-law, Tom Heald, closed their lumber company for the doings as did the keepers of the town's other businesses—the general store, boarding house and the blacksmith shop. With the shuttering of the saloon, it was official—June 4th, 1869 was a day to be recorded in history.

A parade commenced down Main Street toward the wharf. A quadrille band lifted its horns in a jaunty tune as citizens followed in ragged formation, out of step but with a grin on their faces. Thomas Thompson and the Board of Supervisors were on hand as well, eager to take whatever credit might come their way.

Half pints were raised from the hands of well-wishers who cheered and hooted along with tykes and old alike. The planked walkways creaked under the weight of the festivities. No stomp was too harsh. No hurrah too loud.

The fuss continued for two blocks to the dock where musicians and politicians and day-trippers boarded two barges, which were attached to the steamboat. Brassy sounds continued nonstop, adding to the merriment that showed on the faces of all present.

Captain John King tipped his hat to the crowd from the opened window of the pilot's cabin. With that rejoinder, he gave the order to throw out the bow and stern lines. The engine thumped. The paddle wheel turned. Water churned and spat alongside steam, which rose with a blow from the ship's whistle.

The thunder from onlookers peaked as the *Enterprise* separated itself from the wharf. Though the vessel eased downstream, the townspeople had reason to linger. One hundred yards ahead was a lock. Nothing of this nature had been conceived before, at least not on this waterway. There were no certainties, and this alone drew excitement, if not downright trepidation. Whether the process worked or not, entertainment would fill the day. All one could ask for.

The sternwheeler approached and the lock opened. Three feet of water rushed forth, carrying the *Enterprise* westward. Another round of howls could be heard from the riverbank before the citizens of Big Bottom retreated to their everyday lives.

From one barge came the giddy chitchat of patrons who had paid $2.50 for the roundtrip excursion. From the second barge came the melodies of "Little Brown Jug" and "Shoo Fly, Don't Bother Me" with Brahms and Mozart making a brief showing.

Thomas Thompson turned to one of the supervisors, who owned a prodigious nose, saying, "Such classical melodies are proof that even in this godless frontier, there is still room for civilization."

"Must preserve our culture," Supervisor Big Nose answered as his hand did slow figure eights as might that of a symphony conductor.

Under the lively notes of the band and the chatter of toadying men, a sailor stood on the prow and lowered a line, with knots at one-foot intervals, into the stream. It was hoisted and the crewmember noted the depth: "Mark four." The process was repeated: "Mark three." The third attempt was completed with some urgency, the sailor yelling toward the pilot's cabin:

"Mark two!"

Captain King spun the wheel starboard, reversed paddles and prayed. He peered out the window to spy a sandbar passing by.

"Mark three."

"Mark four."

"Mark twain."

The captain swallowed hard, relieved his ship had reentered safe waters. Though the *Enterprise* possessed a draft of a mere twelve inches, there was no guarantee that it would survive the shallows of the Russian River. Nautical charts were nonexistent. Wouldn't matter as not even the Lord Almighty could tract the shifting sandbars and snags of this stream.

And what if the *Enterprise* was bursting with coal and timber, what then? The future of the steamboat as a means of connecting inland towns with the coast was tenuous. This run was far more than a mere outing. It was a test of what was to come.

The next six miles lived up to the *Democrat's* billing. Redwoods jutted upwards from ridgetops, resembling the teeth of a timber tramp's long saw. Behind the curtain of evergreens, no doubt hid untold accounts of adventure. The minds of children and adults whirled, curious as to what tales of the wild such forests might keep?

They didn't have to wait long as the sun glinted off the pupils of some beast secreting away in the darkness. One passenger guessed a bobcat, another a mountain lion. Some moaned a discontent as the spectacle passed their detection.

The flotilla corkscrewed its way along the edge of a sixty-foot granite wall. The river turned dark. Its bottom indiscernible.

Patrons bent over the railing to capture a look of an ugliness, which only folktales had spoken of. The snout of a prehistoric-looking creature rose from the depths. All went awestruck. The nine-foot-long beast's eye steadied its examination upon the fleshy inhabitants of the boat. A second later, it showed the bony plates of its tale before vanishing into the deep.

Thompson identified the specimen, saying, "The sturgeon may present itself in a hideous manner, but its roe makes for a caviar beyond luxury," and he grinned, pleased with the sound of his own voice.

The *Enterprise* eased its way through the redwoods and entered a brief expanse of open land. The skies opened and the sun surrendered its warmth. Nearby, men toiled with the framing of a structure, the embryo of a future village.

A bend in the river showcased foam-lipped eddies near the bank. The captain cranked the 15-horsepower engine to its max and steered the ship past the whirlpool.

The stream corrected itself and straightened for a few miles as the forested hills pinched inward once again before hitting another crook where Austin Creek joined the party. From here, the woodland began to melt away in a more serious nature as golden pastures rolled forward toward the coast.

Captain King announced the arrival of the flotilla with a blast on the whistle. The Duncan clan as well as millworkers stood on the shoreline, welcoming all with waves and cheers.

The *Enterprise* moored at Bodega Corner while passengers and crew stretched the stiffness from weary muscles after the four-hour journey. Musical instruments and sore bottoms were put aside as all stepped down gangplanks to a meadow teeming with wild peonies and poppies. Tables and benches, decorated with linen cloths and vases of flowers, sat in an uneven line below a bunkhouse.

The eleven children from the two Duncan families, which ranged in age from seven to twenty-five, served pitchers of buttermilk, a mélange of vegetables and an unknown beef dish, which had most folks furrowing their brows in question. The recipe combined veal, ham and bread crumbs with a lemon egg wash for a French flavor. The meatloaf was well received to the relief of Ann and Fanny.

Captain King rose with a toast. "My appreciation is extended to the Duncans for hosting this affair."

Polite applause leaked from different sections with the exception of a contingent at the far end. The supervisors followed Thomas Thompson's cue, providing nothing more than nonplus looks.

"This day defines tomorrow for the Russian River Valley," the captain continued. "No longer will inland provinces suffer from want of goods. Nor shall their products of timber and the like sit idle in yards and warehouses," and he paused before unloading a surprise. "With the addition of two locks upstream, I believe the *Enterprise* could sail from Healdsburg to Duncans Mills."

A man choked on his meal. Another spat ale from his mug. Singular applauses from Guerne and Heald rose as an exception, telling of how preposterous the project seemed to most everyone's ear. Adventure enough accompanied the journey south from Big Bottom. Adding another eighteen miles would be a daunting task, indeed.

After everyone's palette was met with satisfaction, William Fraser and Junior led all on a tour. Clusters of men joined the narrated trek while the women and children remained behind, satisfied with a game of cribbage or croquet or a walk along the riverbank.

Alex seemed excited regarding the possibility of new business arriving at Bodega Corner, going as far as postulating the prospect of obtaining a schooner to handle the influx. "I envision hulls of silver exchanging hands," he said to Captain King as they walked side by side.

"And what are your expectations?" the captain asked Sam who was trailing behind.

"Your goals for the *Enterprise* are ill thought out."

"Don't mind him," Alex said. "He puts on the sour side of things most often."

Nervous laughter followed from the captain who sensed something amiss. Without knowing how to respond, he returned his attention to the older sibling, talking about the marketplace in the tomorrow of things.

Sam faded away as the duo accompanied the tour into the plant where Junior started to give a detailed description of the milling process. The twenty-year-old savored the opportunity to show off his acumen with the offering of a demonstration. Saws buzzed. Conveyer belts hummed and dust flew.

The clatter prompted Alex and the captain to visit the quiet of outside where financial aspects could be furthered. The discussion was truncated, however, when a clutch of suits approached.

"Do you remain the lone employer of a nigger in the Russian River Valley, Mr. Duncan?" a bald person with bloated cheeks said.

"I'll leave that bit of accounting to you and your racist rag," Alex Duncan answered.

"I do not stand alone when I say that the county is fast evolving into the society we all envisioned," Thomas Thompson said before gesturing to his colleagues to include them in the prediction.

"You mean a society filled to the brim with white fanatics? Would that be your vision?" Duncan said.

"Your tongue, sir, knows no bounds," Supervisor Big Nose said from the rear of the pack.

"Aye, that could be the truth of it," Duncan said. "And would *your* tongue, sir, be owned by the likes of Mr. Thompson here and his deep-pocketed da?"

"My father has taken leave for Frisco," Thompson interjected. "To serve on the justices' court."

"Please render him my heartiest congratulations," Duncan said in a cheeky tone. "Still, I have no doubt that his wallet will find its way north to continue the purchase of politicians on your behalf," Duncan said to the young Thompson.

Supervisor Big Nose took exception and started to step forward when Thompson seized the moment and said, "You should not upset the powers to be, Mr. Duncan. They can be an awful nuisance. If they've a mind to."

A standoff ensued with both sides measuring the others resolve. Captain King felt displaced and took his awkwardness to the tour group, which was heading toward the general store.

Thompson eyed the captain and the passing throng when a curious sight crossed his vision. A man of small stature, wearing a queue and pajama-like clothing, exited the store and vanished behind the crush of visitors.

"Is that…" and Thompson left his words in the wake of his

outrage and stamped forward. The others in his entourage stood flatfooted, exchanging glances with one another, unable to guess their leader's purpose.

Thompson shouldered his way through the crowd, peering over heads. Some objected to the man's intrusion and voiced as much. A burly sort straight-armed Thompson with an admonition.

But Thompson's obsession pushed him forward. Beyond the line of tourists, the clearing showed his prey entering the smithy shop. Determination showed in Thompson's expression and he marched ahead.

Without warning, a horn's blare roared. Scores of millworkers left their meatloaf and ale and dashed toward the railcars. Tourists, politicians and newspapermen stood aside.

Thompson strained to squeeze through the stampede, muscling timber tramps aside. He made his way to the smithy shop, but it was empty. His gaze shifted to the railcars and a team of horses making their way up the switchback. He squinted for a tighter inspection and detected a black queue flickering in the wind.

At the top of the bluff, the Duncan brothers and the troop of workers unloaded from railcars and rushed toward Goat Rock where a frightfulness of sorts loomed before them. A two-masted schooner lay on its side.

When they reached the narrows south of Goat Rock, Alex Duncan spied the vessel's name on its transom. "It's the *May Ann Sophia*. She was scheduled to arrive last night."

"Must have bypassed the cove in the fog," Sam added.

"Probably mistook this inlet for Duncan's Landing."

"Think there are any survivors?"

"Best we split the men into two teams."

Alex and a dozen others combed the dunes north of Goat Rock while Sam led the second party south. The Pacific rolled up crags and heads, causing Sam's contingent to time their dash to the next spit of sand with care as the tied rolled in. Thirty minutes more was all they had. After that, their retreat would be awash, their party stranded with the cliffs on one side and the ocean on the other

Alex and his men continued north along the rolling beach. The search provided little except for the occasional seaweed root, which from a distance was confused for a body. After another mile, they arrived at the mouth of the Russian River, which had hit the incoming tide and started to back up. The stream too deep to cross. Even if that were possible, the coastline further north was near to impossible to navigate on foot with sky-high cliffs rising from the sea.

By the time both parties returned to the mill, Captain King's paddle wheeler had departed. Picnic-goers, tourists, curiosity seekers and politicians had seen fit to leave the tragedy behind. And why not? There was more than likely an ample supply of such misery waiting upstream. It may not arrive that day, but it would arrive soon enough.

The silence stifled the air as timber tramps and others collapsed to the benches where a celebration had not long excelled. No need to discuss the negative outcome of their efforts. It had happened all too often before. During the previous year alone, two vessels had come to their end along these same shores. The schooner *C.P. Heustis* sank ten miles offshore below Fort Ross. Its crew of five were able to scramble into a lifeboat and row to land. The *J.A. Burr* was not as fortunate, sinking off Bodega Point with all lost.

Sam Duncan feared that the fate of the *May Ann Sophia* would imitate the later. "This is no country for a Scottish farmer from Ireland," he said to his brother.

"If this isn't," Alex said in a quiet voice, "it'll have to do till the right one gets here."

Chapter Twenty-eight

The Chinaman examined his image in a handheld mirror. Satisfied, he vacated the chair and exited the general store where he encountered his employer.

"Guy Ah have shave," the Chinaman said in the third person.

"Let's have a looksee," and Alex Duncan peered forward as if sincere in his study. "The Professor has performed an honorable job. Yes, indeed."

"Guy Ah now more handsome than boss man," and off he went with a strut in his step toward the smithy shop.

Duncan laughed a quiet laugh before entering the general store and stepping to the barbershop in the rear. "Are you charging Ah by the follicle?" He asked the Professor. "Can't imagine a profit made any other way."

"We're exchanging services," the Professor said as a way of an explanation.

"What services?" Duncan asked as he took a seat to wait his turn.

"None of your concern," and the Professor stifled a grin.

Duncan caught the gesture and a suspicion grew. "What business does Ah have with the smithy?"

"None of your concern," the Professor repeated. Another grin.

"Having fun, eh?" Duncan said. "Keep your little secret. Most likely nothing but folly and fudge," and he mined through the Santa Rosa *Democrat* to busy himself.

He turned to the back page when, without warning, the title to an editorial appeared: "Boycott Companies that Employ Chinamen."

Thomas Thompson went on to chastise Latham Cal Pacific for hiring Chinese crews. The railroad company had recently entered a heated competition with the San Francisco and North Pacific line to see which could lay down track fastest from Santa Rosa to Healdsburg. Two roadbeds ran parallel to each other over the sixteen-mile route, which was lined with the local citizenry who treated the race as a sporting event.

Thompson went on to write that the Chinese of Latham Cal Pacific and the Irish of the SF&NP worked side by side, heaving curses and dirt at each other. At the height of the battle, the Micks struck for better pay. The Chinese crew went on to win the race to the dismay of many who had placed a hefty wager on the Irish to win.

Duncan gazed sideways into the blank wall with his thoughts before dropping the *Democrat* to the floor and rushing out the exit. The Professor crunched up his face, wondering what was so important to cause Duncan to forfeit his weekly pleasure.

Duncan crossed the open field to the smithy shop. "Was Ah here?" he asked a weary sort with charcoal dust running down his face and arms.

"Can't say," the blacksmith answered, the ringing strike of his mallet filling the air.

Duncan, bored with the mystery around Guy Ah's visit to the smithy, started to leave when he spotted a peculiar sight. White, wire-mesh masks lay piled atop one another in the recesses of the shop. Duncan formed a question in his mind but the words never left his mouth and he withdrew to continue his search.

At the bunkhouse, the Chinaman slid from one cot to the next, hands extended. Guy Ah received a coin, bowed, said a chirpy thank you and side-stepped to the next Mick and repeated the routine.

With the task completed, the Chinaman swung around to the row of disgruntled faces. "Guy Ah thank you. Today I most happy," and he presented a toothy smile and retraced his steps to the exit as "chink" and "slant-eye" accompanied him.

The smirk never left Ah until he butted up against his

employer at the doorway. "Ah need to go," and he attempted to pass when a hand collared him.

"Not so quick with the giddy up," Duncan said. "We need to talk."

"Talk about Guy Ah's money? Ah win bet on railroad race. Fair and square."

"You knew," Duncan declared with surprise in his voice. "You knew the Irish were going to strike, didn't you?"

"Guy Ah know many thing."

It was at that moment that Duncan realized he had hired the right foreigner. "You enjoy working here?"

"Guy Ah enjoy very much."

"Then I must ask for a favor."

"You boss man," and he smiled and deposited the coins into the pockets of his pants.

* * *

The Spring of '70 loomed promising. California Assembly Bill No. 217 advocated for improvements to the Russian River. Captain John King hoped passage of the bill would furnish the money required to build additional locks, turning the voyage from Healdsburg to the coast a reality.

Alex Duncan was ecstatic. His brother, not so much. Sam contended that Thomas Thompson's father still owned powerful connections in Sacramento, that the bill was doomed to fail.

"Nothing would please the Thompsons more than the failing of an establishment which harbored the only Negro and Chinaman in the Russian River Valley," Sam asserted.

"There you go again, little brother, putting on the sad face," Alex said. "The legislatures won't vote against the measure. Not with George Guerne and the citizens of Big Bottom in the mix."

No response.

"Besides, it's too late," Alex added.

"Too late?" Sam asked.

"I may have hired on fifty more Chinamen."

"May have?"

"Well, there's a good probability."

His brother's words struck like a bell clapper. "You fecking eejit. You're willing to pay the salary of fifty extra men on a vote in Sacramento that hasn't even taken place yet?" and Sam turned away.

"One more thing," Alex said in a low voice to his brother's back.

Sam halted, pivoted and stood with a wary expression.

"We've invested in King's venture."

"*We*?" Sam repeated in an aggressive tone. "*We've* invested?"

Alex thought of covering the awkwardness with a charming repartee, but nothing came to him.

* * *

Bill No. 217 did not pass and the Russian River was officially deemed "unnavigable". The setback, unfortunately, did not deter Captain King.

On February 26, 1870 the *Enterprise* took advantage of the winter runoff and set sail from Big Bottom for Healdsburg. The entire affair was chronicled by Santa Rosa's *Democrat*.

With a load of cut lumber and shingles, the vessel backed upon a snag and sunk a mere quarter mile upstream from the Guerne and Heald Mill. But the indomitable Captain King got her afloat with the help of new arrivals. After another three miles, her engine went kaput. But once again, the captain refused to surrender and babysat the ship until a new sixty-horsepower engine could be installed. Just above the mouth of Mark West Creek bad fortune revisited. The *Enterprise* ran aground, requiring the use of an ox-team to haul her over a series of sediment mounds.

* * *

The lad scampered through the lazy mist with the newspaper tucked under his arm. Clumps of oxygen leaked from his nostrils as he hurried down an aisle of the general store to the barbershop.

His uncle received the *Democrat,* saying that the delivery reminded him of old times when the boy worked at the newsstand out front. "This is an unexpected pleasure."

"Not today," the Professor said before throwing out a tsk-tsk, snatching the paper and placing it in the magazine rack. "Sit still," and he went back to the scalp of Alex Duncan.

But Junior retrieved the *Democrat* and thrust it back into the hands of his uncle. "Better read the editorial...Before my father does," Junior said in spurts, his words trying to catch up with his thoughts.

The Professor witnessed the urgency on Junior's face, withdrew from his work and told his customer to go ahead. "Never could stop ya before. Don't know why I'd be able to now."

Duncan fingered through the periodical until arriving upon Thompson's article. His lips twitched with the silent uttering of each word, his countenance growing tighter and tighter:

> "...The *Enterprise* moved slower and slower each day, until she became firmly grounded five miles south of Healdsburg. Captain King dismantled his ship and left her hull as the ghost of a wreck on the gravel bar."

"Christ on a bike!"

"Should read the rest," a voice sounded from the end of an aisle.

Alex gazed up at his brother, saying, "I'm guessing you've seen the edition. Why don't you render a summarization for all?"

"Be glad to," Sam said as he went on to tell of the *Enterprise's* demise, of how its creditors were enraged. "It seems as if several held doubts as to the efficacy of such a venture, seeing as how it took Captain King four weeks to travel twelve miles."

"Does seem a tad pokey when you put it like that," Alex said.

"Guerne and Heald own first rights on any salvage attempts.

Of what might remain at least," and Sam drew closer to the barber chair. "Please tell me, big brother, that Captain King possesses collateral other than his demolished vessel."

"As a matter of fact, he does. Or rather he did as I have procured the asset and sold it for a handsome profit."

"So, we are in purse once again?"

"On our way."

"What are you saying?"

No response.

"Alex, look at me," Sam said in a stern voice. "How far *on our way* are we, exactly?"

"*Exactly?*" Alex repeated, stalling.

And Sam gestured with his hand as if requesting the surrender of the particulars.

"I was able, with much cunning and business acumen, to legally take possession of Captain King's Gypsy."

"*Gypsy?*"

"A purebred lab. Which fetched $200, I might add."

"A dog?" Sam said with an incredulous look. "You're saying that the company's sole reclamation from this fiasco is…a dog?"

"A *purebred*," Alex corrected, raising a finger to emphasize the point.

Chapter Twenty-nine

*T*rumpets, French horns, tubas and trombones protruded from the wired lips of white masks. Scarlet-colored robes hung on the frames of musicians as they slow-marched to the beat of a dirge. A Grand Marshall came next, wearing an ill-fitting smile and carrying a baton draped in black crape. A banner arrived with its rendition of three interlinked circles. Embroidered in gold stitch below the symbol was the club's motto—"Amicitia Amor et Veritas" (Friendship, Love and Truth). The Outer Guardian followed but without his sword. There would be no protection for the deceased as he was not worthy.

Pallbearers carried an open coffin as they exited from the charred remains of a home. The deceased, a bald man with bloated cheeks, lifted his eyelids and scanned the walls of the pine box. With all the energy that remained, he rose to a sitting position and peered over the edge at the doings.

The procession passed through the town square, which lay empty. Not a single relation bothered to attend his burial. Not Serranus Hastings, not Tyler Curtis, not a member of the Board of Supervisors, not even his own father.

Mournful notes continued to rise from the brass band as the cortege entered the reek of Chinatown. The scent of rotten fish mingled with the sharpness of ginger and garlic, producing an unpleasant bouquet.

The coffin was lowered into a cesspool. People, each in turn, approached and surrendered an aversion for the man to take with him to Hades. The deceased gazed upward from his filth to witness the thrust of a ceremonial spear into his heart. A Kashaya nodded and retreated. The Grand Marshall came next *and removed his white mask to reveal an ebony face. The Negro smiled an uneven smile and tossed his disguise into the pit. A Chinaman, wearing a black queue, went to his knees, leaned forward and released a wad of spittle.*

The newspaper publisher sat up ramrod, wiping his hand over his damp face. Breathed fast and hard, blinking the sleep from his eyes. He pushed his legs over the side of the bed and slipped into a pair of moccasins. The effort to rise proved fruitless and he sat there, staring at the carpet.

The stillness assailed him. A growing concern ate at his soul. The men whom he had trusted had abandoned him. Or so it seemed. Serranus Hastings busied himself in Mendocino with the spoils of victory over the Yuki people. Tyler Curtis had vacated the county for the potential of San Francisco. As had Thomas Thompson's old man. Was the son to become a rootless wanderer or would he shed his taciturn ways and emerge from the shadow of his father?

These thoughts and others swirled around him. Doubts began to crease his face and he tried to shrug himself free, but the weight of his thinking returned him to his pillow.

* * *

He sat in the barber chair and rifled through the *Democrat*. Nothing other than the banal tidings of commerce, boasting of products and services made *by* whites, *for* whites.

"Don't think he's thought it thru," the Professor said.

"How's that?" Alex Duncan asked.

"With the disappearin' of us coloreds, who's gonna do the white man's bidding?"

"I'm tired of hearing the same old story. Tired of my own voice," Duncan said before submitting a request to the barber. "Give me something to cheer the day with, eh?"

"Doubtful," the Professor said.

Duncan braced himself for more bad news. "All right, give me what you got," and he expelled a wad of air.

The Professor obliged and spilled the latest stories from

passing travelers. "*Emma Adelia* capsized near Russian Gulch. Two men drowned."

"Christ on a bike."

"There's more."

"Always is."

"The schooner *Liberty* is lost. Up near Timber Cove."

"Does your mouth possess anything that might give my head some peace?"

"Not today," and the Professor brushed the cuttings from his customer's torso.

* * *

The crisp edge of fall needled his face as he exited the general store. He took a pull on his flask and headed toward the mill, which appeared weak and forlorn through the milky haze of the rising dew.

Alex Duncan entered the plant, noticed a small gathering inside the office and steered that way. Upon reaching the entrance, he was greeted by an employee with a steel scraper in his hand.

"Congratulations, sir," the employee said from his knees, in the middle of his task.

"Excuse me?"

The employee pointed with his tool to the frosted glass of the office door. The words AND SAM DUNCAN were partially effaced.

Alex nodded a thank you, not wanting to spend time in search of further explanation and stepped inside. Brother Sam, nephew Junior and William Fraser stood in a huddle, talking in muffled voices.

Alex stepped forward and inquired as to the reason for the assembly. "What I'd miss?"

"Just finalizing a few things with everyone," Sam said.

"*Finalizing?*" Alex repeated.

"Fanny and I are leaving for San Francisco."

"Excuse me?"

"I'm retiring from the family business," Sam said in a

matter-of-fact voice. "Junior wishes to remain behind. To work at the mill."

The agitation of his brother's announcement caused Alex to hiccup into silence. He felt whipsawed. Blindsided. Didn't see that coming.

Sam spied the befuddlement aboard his brother's countenance and added, "The business has caught up with me. Not the man I once was."

"Well, that's a soddy notion, isn't it?"

"You'll be fine," Sam said.

"No, I won't."

* * *

The *Alex Duncan* had been recently built to handle the extra commerce that would be forthcoming to the family via Captain King's plan to sail his *Enterprise* up and down the Russian River. Not only were both his vessel and the promise of trade literally dead in the water, so did it appear the Duncan clan was as well. Furthest from the imaginations of the eldest was the idea that the *Alex Duncan's* first job would be the exportation of kin.

Nieces and nephews exchanged kindnesses. Ann approached sister Fanny with a warning, telling her not to let her life be reduced to a crutch for the wounded psyche of her husband. Fanny met the statement with a rejection, saying that Sam was not ill in the head, that it was his body that was the concern.

Sam stood by the wooden tower and gazed beyond the railcars to the tracks, to the coastline north. Nothing. With the realization that his brother would not be arriving with a farewell, Sam turned to his family and announced that it was time.

He went to his son, gripped him by the shoulders and said, "Tell your uncle goodbye for me. Tell him that he need not take on every fight that knocks on his door."

Samuel Montgomery Duncan Junior nodded with a promise before telling his father to take care. Sam senior returned a gesture in kind and then turned away to guide his wife and four younger children to the travelling sling-carrier, which carried all to the *Alex Duncan* below.

* * *

Ann entered the house, witnessed the condition of her husband and told the children to busy themselves outside. She closed the door behind the kids and went to open the curtains when Alex ordered her to keep them drawn.

But she paid him no mind and continued with her intent, talking along the way. "You'll not be putting a shroud upon these premises with your self-pity."

His face grew tense. A pane of light unfurled across the floor to further stir the frenzy in his head. To smooth out the edges, he started to take a pull on his whiskey, but Ann snatched the flask from his grasp.

His gaze remained fixed upon the grooves of the wooden planks. "We shared no point of sympathy, save the name we held in common."

"Don't give way to that," Ann said, kneeling beside him, placing a hand upon his. "Your brother is dispirited. Needs to clear off for a bit is all. He'll be back before the long of it, rest assured."

"I appreciate the varnish you brush your sentiment with, dear, but I fear you are wrong."

She stretched her touch along his arm in silence.

He continued with his laments, laying out the blueprint of how things had turned sour with his brother. Controversy broiled inside his head. Anger became the goad that pricked his brain. The feel of his wife did little to assuage his guilt and he picked a pouch of tobacco from his coat pocket. He began to build a cigarette when Ann latched onto his pleasure.

"Drinking and smoking won't help with your thinking, dear," Ann said.

"Well, if that's the case, I surely am bait for the rat's tooth," and he rose and bounded through the exit.

Ann's eyes followed his path. *Men. Whose idea was that?*

Chapter Thirty

With the initiation of a stagecoach line connecting points along the coast, news of various calamities came into the hands of the Professor post-haste. He relayed to Alex Duncan and others regarding the wreck of the schooner *Osceola* near Fort Ross, of how the apron chutes at the Russian Gulch Mill were washed away, and of the most recent tragedy with the grounding of the *Sovereign* nearby.

The two-masted schooner, with Captain Ross at the helm, left San Francisco on June 30, 1873 and stopped at Fort Ross for the night. On the morning tide, it made for Fisk's Mill, nine miles north. However, a storm set in with different intentions. It pushed the *Sovereign* twenty-three miles in the opposite direction where it struck a volcanic boulder near the opening to Duncan's Landing.

Heavy seas swept over the decks. Captain Ross ordered the spars to be cut away. Crew swung their axes. Rain rushed in sideways, stinging faces. The gale increased.

Passengers sought refuge in the hatchway until water and foam spilled over them. A ginger woman seized an opportunity to escape and stepped from the bowsprit onto the nearby boulder. She clung to its edge while Captain Ross, his wife and child skuttled along the same route.

Alex Duncan, William Fraser, Junior and other millers sped down the bluff, using clumps of ice plant and ferns as footholds. The boulder was but seventy-feet away and Junior started for the water when his uncle shouted above the wind for him to stand down. Junior and Fraser argued, saying that the lady appeared weak, that she wouldn't be able to hold on much longer.

It was then that Alex Duncan noticed the mainmast, which had separated from the schooner and was rolling in the froth. His men inched into the cove until chest-high, snatched onto the mast and redirected it toward the rock. The woman released her grip, slid back into the water and swam the short distance to the mast. Junior, Fraser and a half-dozen other men reeled in the pole until the woman was brought to shore.

She collapsed to the sand and with a frail wave motioned back toward the rock. Duncan returned his examination to the boulder where he spotted three additional people hanging on for dear life. Men repositioned the mainmast and yelled encouragement, but they were too late. All stood gaping at the scene, feeling helpless, as the sea swept the bodies from view.

* * *

"Any survivors?" the Professor asked as he clipped his customer's sideburns.

"A woman. Has a ginger complexion," Alex Duncan said. "Everyone else is listed as missing including the captain and his family."

"Shame," the Professor said. "Life's a precious commodity, but when an entire clan disappears in the blink of an eye, that…that…" and he stumbled over his words before saying, "Well, it just ain't right."

"You saying family is all important?" Duncan asked.

"What else is there?"

"You should've told my brother that."

"Your brother's a good man," the Professor said. "Just didn't deserve you is all."

"I'd choose your next words carefully if I was you," Duncan said in a cheeky tone.

The silence ballooned until the Professor asked, "Heard you made a tidy profit from the salvage of the *Sovereign*."

No response.

"Usin' the reclaimed parts to make improvements to the *Alex Duncan*, is what I heard," the Professor said.

"And how has that become your concern?"

"Folks say you've shut yourself off, spendin' all the day's time held up in that boat of yours. Even sleepin' there. Surprised you remembered your way back here to the shop," and the Professor swapped out the scissors for a straightedge.

"Maybe next time I'll have better luck and forget the path. Might save me from the clatter that comes with this place."

"Big groundbreakin' ceremony down in Sausalito the other day," the Professor said as he slapped the razor along the length of the strop. "Hear about it?"

"Got your gob working overtime, eh?" Alex Duncan said in a flat tone.

"Gonna start layin' tracks over a 4,200-foot trestle across Richardson's Bay. Continue to San Rafael and points west."

No response.

"Might even reach the Russian River."

No response.

The Professor withdrew his straightedge and peered into the eyes of Duncan. "You could get into the game and put in your two cents. That is if you came out of that boat of yours long enough to see matters clearly."

No response.

"Someday you're gonna have a voice so you better have somethin' to say," the Professor added. "Best you throw away that hangdog expression of yours. Ain't nobody gonna give a sow's tit what you got to say with that on your face."

"Only face I've got."

"You borin' as *a fecking knacker*—think that what you used to say. Rather have that old blatherin' eejit who came in here every week than the one sittin' in front of me."

"I paid for a trim and a shave," Duncan said. "And that's what I intend to receive."

"For starters, you ain't paid for nothin'. Not in two years. Secondly," and the Professor's mind stalled out before saying, "Hell, I reckon that's reason enough. Now git," and he pulled the cloth from Duncan's lap.

* * *

A world-wide recession began in 1873, the same point in time when Sam Duncan abandoned the mill. Alex often wondered if his little brother had anything to do with the economic downturn. *Would be just like him.*

Alex—for all practical purposes—had taken up permanent residence aboard his schooner, bringing it up to a standard beyond perfection. The project grew to an obsession of sorts. Not even Alex understood why. Perhaps it was to prove something. Perhaps it was meant as a distraction from the troubles of the world, from the reflections of his lost hours with his brother. He didn't know. Truth be told, most things of late had escaped his understanding. Except for the value of a good smoke and a generous pour of whiskey.

On July 26, 1875 there was a bang on the hatch of the *Alex Duncan*. "Uncle, I need to talk with you."

"Go away."

"There's news from my family," Junior said in a loud voice.

"Not interested. Now leave me be."

Junior swallowed hard and blurted, "My dad has passed on."

No response.

"Uncle?"

With silence the only reply from the other side of the hatch, Junior walked to the foredeck and climbed aboard the sling-carrier. He started to make his way back up the bluff when a racket sped to him from below. Shrills and curses filled the cove alongside the thumps and whacks of untold disarray.

It didn't take Junior long to reach out to the only person whom his uncle would pay any mind to. Ann travelled to Duncan's Landing and peered downward to the rocky shore. She eyed Junior. Then the sling-carrier. Back to Junior. Doubt filled her mind. Nothing tormented her more than that contraption. Other than men.

With a lump in her throat, she descended along the cable, wondering why she was jeopardizing her existence for the sake of his. She stepped onto the deck, marched to the hatch and knocked.

"Alex Duncan, let me in this instant."

Another knock but with more gusto. "Alex?"

Ann balled her hand into a fist and raised it for a third try when she recoiled at the sound of the latch coming free. She pushed aside the portal and stepped down into the galley. The area had turned upside down. Pans lay strewn about. A cooking pot's handle had pierced a cabinet as if flung there like a dart. An axe lay imbedded in the sink. Cushion fragments were strewn across the area alongside splinters from the dining table.

Her husband sat on the floor; his head buried in the palms of his hands. "I've pushed him away. Forever and more. Couldn't let go of the notion that he was my *little brother*, that he required my presence to walk him through life."

Ann remained quiet, attentive. Not the time to bring up his shortcomings.

"Never brought his counsel into the seriousness of the day. He went deft to my ears. I countermanded his every action, not trusting in its value."

Memories of yesteryear sifted in and out: the day Alex insisted on establishing Duncansville near the bank of the Russian River; on the selection of Duncan's Landing for the mooring of vessels; on the hiring of a Negro barber and a Chinese timber tramp. All of which Sam opposed. All of which brought trouble. As predicted.

With the awareness that words would not be enough, Ann knelt, wrapped her arms around his frame and drew him close.

Little fight remained and he went limp within her touch. His body quivered, unable to hold back the tears.

* * *

Sam and Fanny moved to the East Bay from San Francisco on the recommendation of doctors. The biting fog of the city had played havoc with Sam's system. He had been laboring with his breathing. He struggled with his speech, and his craving for food was almost nil.

Samuel Montgomery Duncan passed away of consumption on July 26, 1875 and was buried at Mt. View Cemetery in Oakland. It was a quiet affair. Immediate family only. Junior provided a heart-felt eulogy, extolling the virtues of his father:

his unrelenting work ethic; his pious nature; his devotion to the well-being of family.

Junior returned to his seat, comforted along the way by the nods and grateful eyes of the assemblage. A lengthy pause ensued. Heads glanced one way, then the other. Ann nudged her husband who appeared stuck with the meaning of the moment. Another nudge. He blinked aside his wanderings and began to rise, but the weight of all that was present began to test him. He hesitated. Looked sideways to his wife. She surrendered a soft smile as if to say it would be all right. He sidestepped his way out of the pew, past his children, past Fanny and her family. Upon reaching the aisle, he glared at the pulpit. At the coffin near the altar. And he turned away and retreated down the aisle.

* * *

In many respects—as odd as it may seem—Alex Duncan and Thomas Thompson experienced many of the same emotions during that period. Alex suffered from the weight of unresolved issues with his brother while Thompson endured a similar fate with his father, who died shortly thereafter from cardiac arrest.

Over the years both had distanced themselves from blood. Neither possessed the wherewithal to mend family differences, which had swelled to the point of no return. They felt abandoned while the compass moving forward lacked direction. Then, without forewarning, destiny intervened to provide new impetus for each, albeit ones that landed on opposite ends of a moral compass.

For Alex Duncan, the stimulus arrived on a nondescript spring day while bringing his schooner back to life. As he was replumbing the sink, a trio arrived and began to lend a hand. Not a word was exchanged. The reassuring presence of William Fraser, Junior and Ann was all that was required.

A kind of harmony began to ease into the space. A purification of sorts, slow and steady. Cushions were mended. The dining table was put whole. Cabinets were renewed. In addition, the gang replaced the bowsprit as well as topsails, gaff rigging and anchor.

Upon completion, not only did the *Alex Duncan* appear fit for most any job, the time together matured the pack into an inseparable unit. A week later they carried this bond with them as they departed the schooner and boarded the sling-carrier to the top of the bluff, ready to confront whatever might come their way.

Thomas Thompson's reason for advancing his agenda also came in the form of allies. Hate and bitterness were his constant companions. They would enable Thompson to dig himself out from under his father's lingering spirit. Not only had old man Thompson departed, so had Tyler Curtis and Serranus Hastings. Good riddance. Feck 'em all. The younger Thompson's passion to return civilization to the area would be enough.

The Board of Supervisors remained in the pocket of Thompson. He would use the group to control local politics, to shape Sonoma County into a land born out of Manifest Destiny, free from the stain of native heathens and darkies and foreign infidels. The State of Missouri would become a model for all to follow.

Thomas Thompson's pen would coerce the supervisors to bring regulations more in line with his thinking. For instance, the poll tax laws would be amended to include non-property owners, following the recommendation of the *Democrat*:

> "In the city of Santa Rosa there are found to be at least 500 Chinamen, transients and residents, who can't escape paying street taxes."

If you couldn't physically drive them off, perhaps you could tax them into oblivion. It would be a new beginning, and Thomas Thompson felt invigorated.

Chapter Thirty-one

A thirty-seven-year-old lifted a cigar from a humidor, which once belonged to his father. Thomas Thompson snipped off the end of the corona and lit it. Along with the curls of smoke, a sense of satisfaction rose to fill the confines. Besides passing on this symbol of propriety to his son, the old man—through his death—also gifted freedom to the lad. Freedom to prove his worth. On his own terms. He—and he alone—would sit at the head of the table, orchestrating the future.

Cigars were handed to members of the Board of Supervisors who had gathered in the back office of the Santa Rosa *Democrat* to absorb Thompson's scheme for the State of Missouri. The body had evolved into a powerful entity with individuals holding different reasons for moving forward. Some desired to implement the ideals of the South into the county. Others saw the cabal as a means to personal gain, whether it be political or monetary. Preferably both.

A supervisor sniffed the Cabaña with his prodigious nose. "Full and rich." Another whiff. "Perfecto."

"So glad you decided to remain part of our little circle," Thompson said between pulls.

"Yes, well, about that," Big Nose said as he rummaged through his pocket for a match. "I understand that there might be a grand jury investigation into your actions as of late. Any truth to the matter?"

"Not a concern," Thompson said before putting a flame to the supervisor's cigar.

Big Nose nodded a thank you and said, "Some of these tail-wagging Republicans are spouting rumors that you're running a corrupt ring to control the politics of the area."

"Corruption has received such an ill-gotten reputation over the years. A bit of degradation is needed now and then to put seed into the groundwork of civilization," and Thompson released a grin, pleased with his phrasing.

"Can't do much tilling if you're peering down on the cement floor of a cell," Big Nose said.

"Your fellow supervisors are with me. If they waiver, it is understood that my paper would put a rather sizeable dent into their careers. Not to mention their marriages." Thompson rolled the cigar between his lips, saw the uncertainty in Big Nose's expression and added, "You'd be amazed at the volume of photos memorializing the many jaunts to our local whorehouse. Quite the collection."

Big Nose cocked his head to better determine Thompson's meaning.

"If all else fails, there is the loyal following of my fire departments," Thompson said. "As their captain and founder, they served the Democratic cause well during the Civil War. They will continue to do so. Guaranteed."

"Can't afford to have my name associated with a criminal investigation. You understand, right?"

"I understand that these are uncertain times, that certain people go to great lengths to present falsehoods, conducting old fashion witch hunts and such. It is time for people to decide which side of the line they wish to place their legacy upon."

No response.

The discussion drifted to the world-wide recession and the recent national strike of railroad workers. The entire transportation system had been shut down.

"The citizens of Frisco are blaming the Chinaman, saying that the infidel is benefitting from the situation at the expense of whites," Big Nose said, trying to find his footing.

"The *Chronicle* told of race riots," Thompson added. "Of how vigilantes raided Chinatown. Burned businesses. Maimed chinks. Calling it the Sandlot Incident. We could use some of that here."

Big Nose took a pull on his smoke, nodded, letting it be known that he would not be a problem.

The meeting came to an end with the bunch exiting and going in different directions. Thompson meandered toward the town square where he spotted a peculiar sight at the corner of Mendocino Avenue and Fourth Street. Kitty-corner from the Santa Rosa courthouse, a file of Chinamen stood outside a two-story brick structure with the initials IOOF emblazoned above the entrance.

"What the...," Thompson said to no one before strolling to the scene.

He slid around the line and brushed clean his coat as if a contagion might have passed his way. Inside, he followed the human column to a kitchen where soup and bread were being served.

Thompson approved of the lodge's "whites only" status regarding membership. Much sounder point of view than the Petaluma lodge, which was rumored to have at least one colored amongst its ranks. But this...this disgusting display of kowtowing to the needs of foreigners baffled him.

He turned to leave with his angst when he crashed into another. A white wire-mesh mask met him face to face. Thompson stumbled backwards, knocked over a pile of trays. He regained his balance and straightened his tie as an assemblage of eyes followed him to the exit.

* * *

"*Carolita* went aground up at Stewart's Point," the barber said to his customer. "Total loss."

"How many is that?" Duncan said as his head tilted sideways with a nudge from the Professor. "Over a hundred just this past decade?"

"Pacific knows no mercy. Not somethin' you wanna trifle with," the Professor said.

"And let's not forget this damn river. Fourteen floods since the mill's been here. Almost one every year."

"Maybe your brother was right," the Professor said. "Maybe this ain't no country for Scottish farmers from Ireland. Maybe it ain't no country for no kinda farmer from nowhere."

"Might be the truth of it," Duncan said. "Should have listened to him."

"Oh, you was most likely listenin'. Just not payin' attention."

"Probably time to move."

"Pro'bly," and the snip of scissors.

* * *

The North Pacific Coast R.R. pushed their line from Sausalito to Tomales Bay, past Freestone and through the forests and over the Brown Trestle to Howards (Occidental). With the digging of a fifth tunnel, the tracks reached Russian River Station (Monte Rio) and further, continuing west along the river bank to Moscow Mill.

With a little charm and a little loosening of the purse strings, Alex Duncan convinced the railroad to extend the line across the stream to a meadow big enough to accommodate a town and a rising enterprise. While the construction of the rail bridge was underway, the settlement at Bodega Corner was heavy with activity.

Barges sat in tidy rows, waiting. With the absence of the usual breeze off the coast, the work turned uncomfortable.

Guy Ah and his Chinese crew struggled with the transfer of the post office to one of the barges. Duncan supervised the event, much to the dismay of Guy Ah while Mandarin and English fouled the air with dos and don'ts.

"Leave Guy Ah," Guy Ah said in the third person.

"Get the logs secured beneath the platform," Duncan said.

"Guy Ah know what he do. Boss man go have shave," and the Chinaman motioned toward the general store.

But Duncan didn't budge. The project was too important. If you owned a post office, you were more than a "place". You were a "town". The Duncans had not journeyed this far only to slide backwards. No, sir. Not today.

The afternoon progressed as did the building of a skid upon which a team of horses pulled the post office down to the riverbank where a donkey engine brought the structure up a gangplank to a barge.

The Chinaman turned to Duncan and said, "Told you Guy Ah know what he do," and a simper stretched across his face.

Duncan returned a half grin but without humor. Need a drink, he thought and slipped his fingers to the inside pocket of his coat. Nothing but air and a few strands of forgotten fuzz.

Christ on a bike. Hell of a time to go sober.

He had made a promise—not so much to his wife but more so to himself—to forego the taste of whiskey as well as cigarettes. The surrender of one vice would be a noble sacrifice indeed. But two? Not even Saint Andrew could accomplish such a feat.

Another concern crept into his thinking and he stepped to the plant, weaving between millers who busied themselves with the dismantling of machines. "Can we talk?" Alex said to William Fraser.

The pair went to the privacy of the office, where boxes pinched the air out of the place. They stood in a rare open space next to the filing cabinets. A pensive look on Duncan's face. A curious one on Fraser's.

"Bad news," Duncan said. "Manuela Curtis passed away."

"Sorry to hear," Fraser said in a matter-of-fact tone, wiping the grime from his hands.

Duncan spotted the nonchalance in the man's speech. "Don't think you understand."

"Sorry?"

"With Manuela's passing, her knacker husband was able to sell her interest in Bodega Bay."

No response.

"Your property belongs to another."

Fraser's head drooped, searching the floorboards for answers. As a squatter, there was always the chance that his home could be sold from under him. He just couldn't believe that the day had arrived.

"You can relocate with us upstream," Duncan said. "Plenty of room for you and the family."

"Can little afford to do otherwise."

"Good. It's settled then."

Fraser nodded and shuffled back to the only existence he had known since reaching adulthood.

* * *

Sweat continued to drip from tired bodies during the following weeks as yoked oxen hauled one barge after another three miles upstream. Upon arriving at the flat of an inviting meadow, men unloaded cargo and began the process of rendering a new home for Duncans Mills.

"Could make another trip before day's end," Duncan said to a trio of men. Guy Ah, William Fraser and Junior looked at each other with the eyes of spent souls.

Silence hung between them until Junior said, "Might be best to wait til tomorrow."

Guy Ah confirmed, saying, "Boss man should drink. Boss man better when he drinks," and he widened his eyes as if that was the truth of it.

"Harness your talk, Chinaman, or you'll find yourself without a job," Duncan barked.

"Guy Ah always find job," the Chinaman said. "Guy Ah handsome," and he ran his hand over his chin in a theatrical manner to showcase the results of yesterday's shave.

Duncan showed a disbelieving expression before resigning to the wishes of his crew. Ann, her daughters and the other women set about unpacking foodstuffs and preparing a meal over a ten-foot-long firepit. With quiet speech, the workers stepped along a line, holding plates, nodding a thank you to the ladies who ladled up portions of creamy beans and corn pone. One by one, the men retreated to a tree or a chest of drawers or a wooden box and sat, mopping their dishes clean with the heel of the bread.

Ann went to her husband who peered out onto the meadow, shadows growing with the passing of the day. "A gold piece for your thoughts," she said as she handed him a bowl.

He blinked from his wanderings, accepted the food and said, "Sam. Wish he was here," and he turned his gaze to her's. "I'd like to think that he'd be proud of...," and emotions caught him by surprise. Words stuck in his throat.

Ann leaned in and completed his thought, saying, "I'm sure he would," and she hooked her hand under his arm as they returned their vision to the meadow where a town would soon be.

The night dawdled on with crickets and bullfrogs providing a background melody. An untethered cloud drifted free to the east, passing in front of a full moon, which appeared to slide along the distant ridge.

The morning dew mingled with smoldering fires as the long finger of dawn showed itself. The sounds of dogs and roosters replaced the soft music of the previous night and the camp came to life.

Duncan stretched from his bedroll, exited his tent and took in the morning with a yawn. Scents of the new day made their way to him when he realized that something was wrong. Not the smell of bacon from a skillet. Not the aroma of wild poppies. This was distinct and unwelcomed.

He rubbed away the rheum from his eyes and studied the sky. Trails of smoke travelled toward him from the coast. He saddled a horse and rode. The blue of the day melded into a sinister black, maturing with each mile. The steed nosed around a bend and reared up, nostrils flushing. Duncan dismounted and stepped toward the inferno.

The bunkhouse. The general store. The smithy shop. His house. Gone. All gone.

Fecking hell.

He walked closer, the fire's heat reduced to a scorching of sorts. His examination worked from one edifice to the next.

While the buildings were replaceable, they stood as proof of nearly two decades of sacrifice. His angst grew with the onslaught of such reflections.

And then, without warning, a different reasoning began to creep into his thinking. His fury started to abate much like the dying embers from a hearth as the blueprint for this new rational unfolded.

A quiet laugh curled his mouth and he shook his head as an image appeared before him. He stole a peek toward the heavens and said, "You're a sly bugger. I'll give you that," and he chuckled again. "Well done, brother. Well done."

He started to step through the rubble when a peculiar sight came into his periphery. A Negro was picking through the remains of the smithy shop. Cradled in his arms was what appeared to be a stack of masks. Couldn't be sure. Duncan didn't think it worth his time to investigate and rambled forward when another notion bore down. But this time a curse echoed in his head, not the playful horselaugh of a moment ago. With dread in his thoughts, he remounted his horse and headed up the switchback toward the coast.

At Duncan's Landing he hitched his ride to the wooden tower and marched to the edge of the bluff where he took a peek. The *Alex Duncan* slept in the cove, at peace with the world.

He grinned and looked skyward. *Didn't get her, did you, little brother? Guess that makes us even.*

Chapter Thirty-two

On July 13, 1877 a funnel of smoke rose from the balloon stack while one long whistle signaled its approach. The iron horse clickety-clacked across the bridge and eased into Duncans Mills. Cheers went up from onlookers waving miniature stars-and-stripes. Horns trumpeted a welcome.

Steam hissed from the boiler dome as the train came to a stop alongside the depot. The 0-4-0 train type (four wheels at midpoint) was dressed in black while cut logs peaked from a tender with the name BULLY BOY painted in gold leaf lettering on its sides. Coupled behind were two first-class smoking coaches with clerestory roofs, three second class coaches, hunting coach, baggage and mail car, and a caboose.

Passengers debarked and exchanged greetings with the locals. It was not your everyday event as all were aware of its significance. This was the first hour of many more in Duncans Mills, which was now the terminus of the narrow-gauge North Pacific Coast Railroad.

Workers unloaded provisions, valises, hat boxes, fishing gear and rifle socks along with the town's first mail delivery.

Alex brought his Scottish charm to the tracks and gladhanded the arrivals, looking more like a politician seeking reelection than a lumberman. He escorted travelers, passing warehouses and the post office while enroute to the hotel. The Julien contained a commodious dining room, smoking parlor, reading room and accommodations for one hundred guests, not including tent cabins for any overflow.

"Mr. Julien is the owner and proprietor of this fine establishment," Alex said as he introduced a rail-of-a-man with flattened hair and waxed mustache.

The Frenchman bowed to the acknowledgement with his hands folded in a polite pose. "Welcome. It is my privilege to be your host for the duration of your visit with us. In honor of the occasion, I invite you for a sip of our finest champagne," and he showed a paper-thin smile before summoning a porter who guided the guests to the dining room.

Duncan tagged along in case there were any questions, acting the consummate town squire. With the completion of beverages and a bit of caviar de salmon, the porter began describing that evening's fare.

"The entrée will consist of andouille with wild boar, marinated and braised in a blend of turmeric, cumin and ginger, topped with hog curry. A medley of—"

"Perhaps the folks are a bit weary from their journey," Duncan interrupted in a soft voice.

The porter returned the group to the lobby where the check-in process was completed in short order. To everyone's relief. They had ferried across the bay from San Francisco to Sausalito and trained some seventy-seven miles, crossing untold number of trestles, passing through five tunnels and enduring seventy different stops along the way. The entire affair—from door to door--could have taken seven hours from one's day. But that was part of the allure. A journey to remember.

Alex left the bunch and made a beeline for the saloon where most of the remaining visitors had clustered to enjoy the company of one of the valley's wealthiest saloon keepers as well as bartender par extraordinaire. John Orr wore a barrel-chest, a braided beard and a no-nonsense approach. He owned much of the land in the area before selling off lots and some 4200 acres to the Duncans Mills Land and Lumber Company. In addition to retaining his cattle ranch, Orr kept a sliver of the town for himself, turning it into the largest tavern in the state.

"Got a special treat for ya," Orr said to Duncan. "They're bringing it over now."

"What're you up to?" Duncan asked in an anxious tone.

"Don't get your crack in a twist," and Orr left to meet a couple of employees at the entrance where they were unloading goods from a handcart.

Along the side of his saloon, Orr spotted a malfeasance he was not willing to ignore. Not now. Not ever.

He marched to the sin and ordered a quartet of gambling Chinamen to leave. "Gotta put up with your existence 'cause that's how Mr. Duncan sees it. But I won't tolerate your ways near my saloon. Now git."

"You no like Guy Ah," the Chinaman said in the third person as he gathered a pair of dice from the ground. "You no fun."

"And you be gone," Orr said, pointing to a path to nowhere.

Alex drummed his fingers upon the redwood slab, waiting, biding his time with a survey of the crowd. Every stool along the forty-foot bar was occupied while others sat at tables drinking ales and whiskies, chatting it up. The scene reminded him of the action at the waterholes along the wharf in San Francisco. Rowdy and loud. Full of piss and vinegar. Just the way he liked it.

Threads of conversations hung in the air. Duncan could feel the exhilaration. It was contagious, spreading from one corner of the room to the next.

Orr returned with a bottle and filled the patron's glass. "Came in with the train."

Duncan's curiosity slid from Orr's sappy grin to the glass and took a sip. He smacked his lips to get a second accounting and said, "Tastes a bit like root beer."

"Sarsaparilla," Orr said to clarify and held the bottle in abeyance over the glass, waiting for a refill request.

"Aye," and Duncan pushed his glass forward.

"Knew ya were off the sauce," Orr said.

"What a man does for love, eh?"

"No gettin' around it."

The conversation turned to the opening day festivities and the first batch of arrivals. Orr was of the opinion—and a sound one at that—that the anglers were a bit tardy, that the salmon and steelhead were seven months gone.

"Smallmouth bass and bluegill are all they'll find," Orr said. "Hunters might have a better go at it. Especially if boar is to their liking."

Duncan finished his drink, tapped the brim of his hat in a thank you and left Orr to relish the good fortunes of the day. Alex stepped across a dirt road to the livery stable and bid a good morning to the owner.

Christopher de Quien was a former Pony Express rider from Louisiana and supposedly of French royalty. The lad had style with his frock coat, starched winged collar and ascot. Too much of a dandy for these parts. Reminded Alex of that shite Tyler Curtis from Bodega, leastwise in appearance. Duncan wasn't sure how long a person would last with a moniker like *Quien* (pronounced Queen). In any case, the lad appeared enterprising enough. For one who shoveled dung for a living.

Duncan made his way past the blacksmith shop and the bootmakers to the company store, a two-story white clapboard. He entered, strolled down an aisle of well-stocked merchandise and went to the back office, which had been converted to accommodate another business.

"Quite the day," Duncan said as he sat in the barber chair.

"Quite the day," the Professor repeated in a nonplus tone before flapping a cloth over the customer's torso.

Duncan caught the lack of interest and said, "Why the long face? Thought you'd be happy with all the new customers."

"Thought I was gettin' my own place, is what I thought," and the Professor secured a paper strip around Duncan's neck.

"Have the necessary rent money, do you?" Duncan asked.

"Ya know I don't. Lost whatever I had in that fire down at Bodega Corner," and he snipped away.

Duncan motioned with his head to a shelf where souvenirs were stacked one atop the other. "See you recovered those creepy masks of yours. Though I doubt they would add much to your purse."

"Keep still," the Professor hissed.

Snip. Snip.

"Why you holding onto them?"

"Plan on usin' 'em for a ceremony to honor the establishment of a new lodge."

"The IOOF?"

Snip. Snip.

"Figured I'd follow in the footsteps of that Peter Ogden fella. If he could establish the first black lodge on the East Coast, why couldn't I do the same on this end?"

"Afraid to break the news to you, but you're the lone Negro in the entire Russian River Valley. A count of one does not make a lodge."

"Suppose that could be an issue," the Professor said.

Finished with his business at the barbershop, Duncan exited and walked toward the finest ornament in the town. He had built the place for Ann. It was always a dream of hers to live in a large Victorian, but like so many dreams, it was deferred by the rigors of everyday being.

The home rested on the slope of a hill, with a grand porch where the couple could sit and take in the beginnings of their new life together. The remaining six children had attained adulthood with Sammy becoming clerk of the mill and Jeanie taking on the position of postmistress. Though a few of the children had relocated to San Francisco to seek out their future, the family structure was stronger than ever. Perhaps it was because both had witnessed death up close. With the passing of son Hugh and Alex's brother Sam, the couple had a renewed appreciation not just for life but for each other.

The boudoir, however, remained tepid. In the eyes of Alex anyway. He would have to rein in his loins, temper his enthusiasm.

Chapter Thirty-three

Anti-Chinese sentiment had been building in the late 1870s and early '80s. With his political base at an all-time high, Thomas Thompson took his campaign of white supremacy to Sacramento and was elected secretary of state. But the bosses of the Democratic Party soon realized he would never own the charisma of his old man, and they sent him packing without supporting his bid for a second term. The setback demoralized Thomas. It was confirmation that, even in death, his father's shadow would always be there. Thomas hid his scars and returned to the only place where he might revive some dignity.

* * *

Several county supervisors sat around in the back office of the Santa Rosa *Democrat*, pulling on cigars, chewing on the news of the day.

"Good to have you back," one supervisor said who owned a big nose. "Sacramento's loss is our gain."

Thomas Thompson feigned a thank you at the hackneyed phrase. He required a fresh start and the Board of Supervisors would play a key role in that. Had to keep them in his pocket. For now.

Though his radical views were too much for the California Democratic Party, Thompson still had his eye on the national political scene. Such a run would begin where it always had—in the State of Missouri.

"Many of our leading citizens are disturbed by the proximity of Chinatown to the town square and the new courthouse," Thomas Thompson said, the heel of his boot resting upon the conference table.

"Time to crank up the rhetoric. The people are with you," Big Nose said as he rolled his cigar within his lips.

"Those damn chinks won't take the hint," Thompson said. "We arrest them for smoking on public property. Jail others for vagrancy. Throw street taxes at 'em. But they're still here...What's a fella gotta do?"

"For what its worth, Congress has officially taken your side," another supervisor said. "Passed the Chinese Exclusion Act. Bans immigration of Chinese laborers for ten years. Requires those already here to carry I.D. on them at all times."

"Not enough," and Thompson removed his boot from the table, stood and paced the room.

"Patience, my friend," Big Nose said. "Patience."

"Been patient," Thompson said, his vision travelling along the floorboards. "All it's gotten me are nightmares of men in white masks, lurking about, stalking me, waiting for another chance to burn my house. To burn *me*."

A few supervisors glanced at each other, perplexed by the man's words. What the hell did white masks have to do with the Chinese problem? Not the articulation expected from someone with renewed purpose.

Thompson continued his pacing, thinking. "You mentioned something earlier regarding *cranking up the rhetoric*. Perhaps I can do that," and he paused, looked at Big Nose. "After all, I do own a newspaper. Two in fact."

Besides the weekly *Sonoma Democrat*, Thompson started publishing the *Daily Democrat*. More ink was now available to attack his enemies with.

"That's the spirit," Big Nose said, happy his comrade had returned to his senses. "Not to worry. Something will come along."

And then an idea came to Big Nose and he added, "There are always stories available regarding those prostitution rings down in Chinatown. Or of the opium dens. Could use something of that making to kick those infidels out of the county."

Thompson stared into the frosted glass separating his office from the lobby, giving weight to the supervisor's suggestions.

"And let's not forget the unsanitary conditions sweeping through that slum," another said. "Have to protect the health of the good citizens of the city. It'd be irresponsible not to."

But the elation aboard Thompson's countenance waned. "Nope. Won't do. The moment requires something more immediate. Something with finality to it."

No response.

And Thompson's eyes went wide with the answer. "Could follow the example set down in Frisco. Those vigilante boys got their message across in no uncertain terms."

"Just need an excuse to set things in motion," Big Nose said in agreement.

There was a lengthy pause within which minds strained to arrive at an angle. Something to light the fire with.

* * *

> "His head drooped. His chin rested on his breast...The dinner plate was upset in his lap. The plate of his wife, which was opposite, had potatoes on it and was undisturbed. There was a piece of pie at each place. The chair which had been occupied by Mrs. Wickersham was overturned."

The above account was rendered by Marshall Blume at the site of the Wickersham ranch in Skaggs' Springs and printed by the *Daily Democrat* in its January 26, 1886 issue. The article described in some detail the murder of Jesse Wickersham, shot in the back of the head while sharing a meal with wife Sarah who was then dragged to the bedroom, tied to the bedposts and raped.

The column went on to say:

> "People gathered at every settlement along the roadside to get a sight of the sad procession. The crowd that awaited the arrival of the bodies

was a large one, and when the crude coffins were placed upon two express wagons, the citizens forming about escorted the remains to the undertakers."

Though there was no evidence to support Marshall Blume's contention that the Wickershams' Chinese cook committed the murders, the editor of the *Daily Democrat* continued to sensationalize the account to serve his own ends. It gifted Thomas Thompson a new, powerful weapon to demonize Chinese people as crazy, unpredictable, and—for the first time—extremely dangerous.

A few days after the publication, 1,500 men crowded into Santa Rosa's Armory. Thomas Thompson lurked in the shadows at the rear of the congregation with a grin on his face. Speaker after speaker came to the podium to condemn the Chinese presence in Santa Rosa as a "source of great evil" and a "detriment to the white race".

After a sufficient amount of frenzy had occupied the hall, Thompson stepped to the speakers' platform, saying that the City of Roses should follow the example of Cloverdale, Healdsburg and other neighboring towns. "We should all do our very best to show these infidels the road out of town, to avoid another Wickersham incident from happening again, to protect our women and children!"

Affirmations echoed off the rafters as the first meeting of the Santa Rosa Anti-Chinese League drew to an end.

In the weeks that followed, gangs of fifty or so League members visited wholesalers and retailers, "encouraging" them to expel any foreign employees by March 1st. Or else.

* * *

A pair of power brokers enjoyed cigars and bragged about the progress of the Anti-Chinese League.

"Had business down at the courthouse the other day," Big Nose said. "Walked under a banner stretched across Mendocino Avenue, which read: THE CHINESE MUST GO. WE MEAN STRICTLY

BUSINESS."

"The League has made its presence known," Thompson said. "Thanks in no small part to your endorsement and that of your fellow supervisors."

"You are most welcome, my friend. But don't sell yourself short. Your pen has been prolific recently," Big Nose said.

"Ink seems to have an indelible imprint upon the minds of the people," Thompson said.

"Indeed," and Big Nose took a draw on his corona. "I've noticed several citizens advertising the startup of white laundries. No Chinese employed."

"The raids on Chinatown have had their effect as well," Thompson said. "Must give credit to my men from the fire houses for that. They have acted nobly on behalf of the League to return civilization to Santa Rosa."

"The washhouses and opium dens are damaged beyond recognition. So too are most of the Chinese shanties around the town square." Big Nose paused with a thought before adding, "The Board of Supervisors will render the necessary paperwork to register the structures unfit for public use moving forward."

The actions by city and county officials as well as those of Thomas Thompson caused many of the Chinese to vacate. During the next three months, their population dwindled from six hundred to a mere hundred or so. Of those that remained, they were deemed "unemployable" and reduced to foraging and boiling greens along the banks of Santa Rosa Creek.

The biggest employer of foreigners outside the city limits was the Duncans Mills Land and Lumber Company, located along the lower reaches of the Russian River Valley. Alexander Duncan had to be made an example of. For the sake of all that was righteous. For the good of the race.

* * *

Alex Duncan kissed Ann goodbye and made his way from his Victorian toward the village center. With a sense of satisfaction, he passed the El Bonito Hotel (formerly Julien Hotel), a meat market, the post office and warehouses. During the past nine years, the town had swelled to over two hundred and fifty strong with some fifty employed at the mill and an equal number working in the forests and logging camps.

He made his way to the plant, which was another source of pride for the Scot. It had a cutting capacity of 35,000 board feet per day, larger than any other mill in the area including the mill in Guerneville (formerly referred to as Big Bottom or Stumptown and named after George Guerne).

With a tune in his head, Duncan entered and strolled amidst the whirring of saws and the scent of freshly cut logs. He passed the new planning—, picket—, and shingle machines, sliding a hand across the contrivances as might a father with a newborn.

He patted his nephew on the shoulder, leaned into his ear and said they were going on an adventure. "How'd you like to take a ride up to Ingram's (Cazadero)?" the uncle said.

The thirty-seven-year-old nodded with a glint in his eye for he had not as yet journeyed along the recent rail extension by the North Pacific Coast R.R. They boarded Engine No. 9, sharing the cab with the engineer and water tender.

The train rumbled seven miles along the northern edge of the Russian River to Austin Creek where it crisscrossed the stream before reaching Ingram's. Uncle and nephew debarked and borrowed a couple of steeds to survey the landscape that had come under the company's purview. They road up Kidd Creek and greeted William Fraser, recently promoted to "puncher" for the freshly acquired donkey engine.

There was little time for discussion as bucked logs were on the line. Even Guy Ah, who was busy with the building of a skid, had no thought of a chat. A rarity for him.

Fraser signaled with two short whistles and the haulback line was reeled in. Chokermen, yarding crew and puncher worked in a synchronized dance within the hissing of the steam engine.

"It'll expedite matters tenfold," the uncle said to Junior. "Through a system of cables, we can now haul logs to a collection point."

"Are you saying the day of yoked oxen is nearing its end?" Junior guessed.

"Perhaps, lad. Perhaps."

With an adieu to William Fraser and a promise to meet up later at the saloon, the pair continued their inspection. They backtracked along the railbed and arrived at the confluence of Austin Creek and the Russian River where a millpond had been built to store felled logs.

"Would you look at that fella?" Alex said. "It's as if watching Robert Burns in motion. Poetry it is."

Junior followed his uncle's study to a boom man. A fine mix of raw bone and grace, the fellow toe-tapped from one log to another with his pike pole. It was during this flash of admiration when a rider galloped toward them.

Dirt flew from the hooves of the horse, neighing in protest with a yank on the reins. Sweat wandered down the rider's taut expression. His breath came in clumps as he told of trouble in the village. Without another word, Alex Duncan and Junior sped toward the calamity.

Chapter Thirty-four

"You got some nerve closing shop with the light of day still upon us," Alex Duncan said.

He had been looking forward to his weekly visit to the barber's. This wouldn't do. Though most wouldn't classify the event as an "emergency", it did in the thinking of Alex. All that mattered.

"Your damn Masons are clutterin' up the second floor of the company store at night with their card games and such," the Professor said. "Got to use the space when available. Even if it means closin' my shop during business hours to do so."

"Remind me again why you need to use the upstairs."

"For rehearsal."

"Rehearsal? What?" and Duncan crunched up his face.

"Since there aren't enough of my kind to start an all-Negro Odd Fellows, I decided to invite my lodge brothers from Petaluma to put on a play for the folks here," the Professor said. "We talked 'bout this."

"The hell we did," Duncan said.

"See. There you go again. Pretendin' to listen when all you're doin' is hearin' who's talkin' in your own head."

"And there *you* go again. Banging on about this and that."

"Tell you what. You order those Masons to place their arses elsewhere at night for a week so I can work out the kinks in the play and I'll open the shop," and he raised his palms as might a broker with a deal.

"And I get my haircut and shave?"

"That'd be the size of it."

"Now?"

"*Now?*" the Professor repeated in a surprised voice. "As in this very moment?"

"Only kind of now I know."

The Professor placed his mind on the proposal, trying to wring the most from the moment. "It's a deal," he said before adding, "If..."

"There's an *if?*"

"If you promise to build me a proper barbershop."

"You trying to stitch me up or something of the like?" Duncan said. "Sort yourself out on the matter or I'll—"

"Or you'll what? Throw me into a smaller corner of the company store?"

* * *

The conversation settled into the tidbits of the week, as it often did. News from travelers and such. No event off limits.

"Heard Serranus Hastings built himself a law school down in San Francisco," the Professor offered. "Least ways it has his name on it. Hastings Law School, or some such thing."

"Most likely built from the money off his ranching," Duncan guessed. "Up in Mendocino County."

"Blood money is what it is," the Professor said. "Killed or drove those Yuki people to the reservation. Took the land for himself."

"All with the government's blessing," Duncan said.

"Who says hate doesn't pay," the Professor said.

Snip. Snip.

Duncan's ruminations drifted to the Yuki father and his two daughters who were on the run from that Jarboe fella and his Eel River Rangers. The Yuki's name was Elsu, or so Duncan thought. He and Ann hid the family before sending them on their way south to join up with the Kashaya people at Fort Ross.

"Any word on those natives at Fort Ross?" Duncan asked.

"William Benitz sold the place. New owners kicked the Kashaya and others off the land."

Duncan recalled that the Kashaya would not, under any circumstances, move to the Round Valley Reservation. Too many unsettled tribal grievances awaited there. Probably left to the whims of fate, Duncan thought.

And he hadn't done a damn thing about it. *Christ on a bike!*

Snip. Snip.

"Fella came through here the other day," the Professor said, on to the next topic. "Claimed the *Lammermore* ran up on Bodega Rock."

No response.

The Professor caught Duncan's faraway look and said, "You payin' attention here? 'Cause I'd take disfavor if you wasn't."

"Sorry," and Duncan blinked away his wanderings, sat up and said, "Yes, the *Lammermore*. Please," and he gestured for the Professor to continue.

The barber cleared his throat, eyed the level of mindfulness from his customer and started up again. "Captain misjudged the entrance to the Golden Gate by forty-five miles…No accounting for stupidity."

Snip. Snip.

"Funny thing about stupidity," the Professor persisted, on a roll. "Seems to have a ripple effect. Only people it pains are those on the outer circles, not the fool at the center," and he hoisted his scissors with another point. "And you can throw in that incident last year at Fort Point regardin' your precious schooner. Same foolishness, if ya ask me."

The *Alex Duncan* had begun servicing other mills, bringing products to and from San Francisco. In '85 she lost her mooring below the apron chute at Fort Point, crashing into the rocks. Most feared the schooner had seen its last days.

"Didn't come here so you could chew on my tail," Duncan said. "Besides, we salvaged every last bit of her. The *Alex Duncan* is up and running as good as ever."

"And after all that money and so forth makin' her into the first steam schooner to sail these parts. And for what?"

No response.

"Seems as if you white folk love to swing your dicks around. Make a big show of things."

Snip. Snip.

* * *

Night began to fall within the gathering dusk. Raptors, hooded like hangmen, shifted along the telegraph lines. A warm breeze entered from the east, hissing. Splotches of light flickered from different structures. Inky figures came and went from the windows on the second floor of the company store where the Professor and other members of the Petaluma Odd Fellows rehearsed for an upcoming play. Behind the store, smoke curled from woks at the Chinese shotgun shacks. It was dinnertime throughout the village.

Venison stew simmered in the crock while Ann busied herself with a bit of needlework. She looked up and gifted a smile in that shy, slow way that made Alex feel tingly all over.

He attempted to display a gesture in kind but struggled. Not wanting to betray his true feelings, he hid his expression behind the front page of the *Daily Democrat*. Had to take things slow. Let the matrimonial bed come to him. Worked before.

The latest headlines regarding the apparent murder of a white rancher by his Chinese cook was disturbing. The Anti-Chinese League had been formed. Raids upon Santa Rosa's Chinatown had increased. Everyone was running scared. And now Thompson was taking his hate to the countryside.

Not far from where his brother started his first mill, vigilantes flexed their muscle, killing a Chinaman near Bloomfield. Thompson used his political pull with the Coroner's Jury to cover up the mishap. His *Daily Democrat* went so far as to print a nonsensical version of the incident, saying that the Chinaman in question had buried an axe into his own head, after which he managed to stumble a quarter mile to a potato field where he was eventually found.

Hogswill. The narrative of editor Thomas Thompson was untethered to anything Alex Duncan recognized as true. Racist bile. But one thing was certain. Evil was on its way.

A blankness rose from Alex and he gazed over the periodical with his concerns when, without warning, he caught sight of Ann twisting her cotton pinafore. He accepted the distraction as a current of affection shot through him.

Alex rose halfway out of his chair to profit from the scene, but a banging on the door stole him from his intentions.

Before he could reach the knob, Junior exploded inside. "Got a situation," and he slid his awareness from his uncle to his aunt, back to his uncle.

"We were about to have supper," Ann said. "Care to join us?"

Junior steeled his attention on his purpose. "Can't," and he motioned with stealth for his uncle to come along, not wanting to put the fright into his aunt.

Alex spotted Junior's desperation, saying, "If it's that no-account barber again, you can tell him to—"

"We've got visitors," and Junior's eyes widened with an alarm.

* * *

Alex faltered to heave the door open against a sudden gust before they hurried outside and down the slope and across the tracks. At the meadow behind the company store, a cluster of riders had gathered in front of a string of shotgun shacks.

Must have been fifty strong, carrying lit torches and a sour disposition. Facial stubble and unkempt hair spoke of their disdain for respectability. Clothes to match—haggard uniforms of yesteryear with a mishmash of Confederate and firemen outfits.

The scene pulled on the curiosity of townsfolk. Timber tramps emptied the saloon with their whiskies. A few employees, working the late shift, stepped from the sawmill and warehouses. Hoteliers arrived along with city slickers and hunters and fishermen.

Duncan gazed upon the intruders and recognized the man out-front. He was dressed in a three-piece suit, wearing a bald head and bloated cheeks.

"What's your business here?" Duncan asked Thomas Thompson.

"We meet again, sir."

"An unfortunate event, I'm of the thinking."

"I come with the full force of the Anti-Chinese League."

"How nice for you."

"The federal Chinese Exclusion Act requires all infidels to carry I.D. on their person at all times."

"By *infidel*, I assume you are referring to one of low moral character with little religious foundation to their being," Duncan said. "Perhaps we should start with your troupe of soul-sucking eejits," and Duncan gestured with his chin to the riders alongside Thompson.

"Have your celestials come forward," and Thompson unholstered his .45 and pointed the barrel to the row of shotgun shacks.

"Well, you see that might be a bit of an issue as its supper time and—"

Thompson fired a round from his revolver. One by one, men with their black queues slipped from behind closed doors.

Thompson, his gun resting in his hand upon the saddle's horn, nudged his bay forward. A muted neigh the lone sound of the meadow. Onlookers fidgeted with the unknown. Tension hung in the ether, unsuppressed.

"You not work here no more," Thompson said in his best pigeon-English. He continued, trying to convey to the celestials that they were to leave, to pack their things and depart the country. Immediately.

The message caused a murmuring to speed from one Oriental to the next. Heads bobbed up and down. Smiles began to show themselves.

One came forward to translate for his people. "We are most happy to return to our homeland," Guy Ah said. "Most kind of white man to pay for our travel to China. We happy now," and he looked back over his shoulder with a grin to his compatriots, proud of his rendering.

"What?" Thompson said with an incredulous look. "No, we're not paying for a damn thing. Chinaman pay for his own ticket."

"White man not pay?" Guy Ah asked.

"No. White man not pay."

Guy Ah turned back around, said something in his native tongue to his comrades and then returned his vision to the white man. "Then Chinaman not go. Stay here."

"The hell you will," and Thompson raised his .45 with a warning.

Rifles slid from scabbards. Pistols jumped from holsters. Pics and axes showed themselves as well. Both sides at the ready.

Duncan put up his arms, calling for calm. "No need for this to go sideways," and he took in the wooden stares of horsemen, of millers and tourists, of John Orr and his saloon patrons.

"Then tell this chink and his fellow Chinamen that they either bring forth their I.D.s or they come with us," Thompson said.

"Guy Ah remember white man," Guy Ah said in the third person, pointing a finger at Thompson. "You still bald. Guy Ah not bald. Guy Ah handsome."

"Son-of-a-whore!" and Thompson dismounted, stomped forward and started to lower the butt of his .45 into the Oriental's skull when another's hand intervened.

Duncan knocked the weapon from Thompson's grip and drove his knee into the man's groin. Thompson bellowed like a castrated calf and folded up on himself, retching, collapsing to the ground. When he looked back up, the barrel of a .32 caliber Slocum was planted between his eyes.

Guy Ah leaned past Duncan to Thompson for a better look and said, "You still have sausage-fingers. No can fight with sausage-fingers. You stay on ground. Best advice Guy Ah can give," and he picked up the .45 and handed it to Duncan who now held a revolver in each hand.

Duncan ordered Thompson and his men out of town. The newspaper editor rose, hand-brushed the dust from his suit and started to put a foot in the stirrup when figures entered his peripherals from the second floor of the company store. He glanced up and spied a line of people peering down at him from the opened windows. Each wore a scarlet robe and a white, wire-mesh mask.

He faltered, unable to remount. Glanced away from the haunting sight. With the awareness that several of his men were studying him, he regained some composure and climbed back into his saddle. Words came to him, urging him to press onward, to burn down the Chinese shanties. Torches held high.

Thompson couldn't hear the pleas of his fellow League members. The clutter in his mind started to have its way with him as eerie images from the second floor pulled on his sensibilities.

An unseen force entered and pressed him to take another gander. He executed a slow pivot back toward the company store. White masks at the windows. White masks on the balcony. White masks everywhere.

He tore himself away from the witchery. His heart pushed out his chest. The ebb and flow of his breathing quickened.

Within the next minute, his surroundings began to reintroduce themselves. He started to recognize the voices of the horsemen on either side. The meadow came into focus bit by bit. Buildings. Chinamen. Alex Duncan.

"Did you hear me?" Duncan said. "I want you out of my town. Now."

Thompson narrowed his vision. Focused. "You'll be hearing from us soon enough."

Without answering the objections of his fellow League members, Thompson led his pack back across the tracks and eastward toward Santa Rosa.

Chapter Thirty-five

While Duncans Mills never saw the likes of Thomas Thompson again after that fateful Saturday of April 17, 1886, both sides battled each other through the order of law and the power of the printed word. Duncan brought in a U.S. Marshall to protect the Chinese workers while Thompson squawked over the involvement of a federal officer instead of using local police, which he controlled. Furthermore, he used his *Daily Democrat* to urge all citizens to boycott timber products.

But Alex Duncan helped to mobilize lumbermen and farmers against the evils of Thompson and the Anti-Chinese League. In the face of a potential economic crisis, a subcommittee of the League wrote to Thompson, saying that a boycott of tillers and timbermen would cause "strife and bitterness" in the county.

* * *

"That'll be a dollar," the barber said as he removed the cloth from his customer's lap.

"Dollar?" the customer said. "Was a quarter last visit."

"Owe me for a month's worth."

"How about I charge you for the construction of your new shop? Ought to make us square for the next twenty years."

"Had no intention of stayin' that long. Wouldn't be inclined to put up with that Irish gob of yours for such a length."

Duncan took the jab with a quiet laugh—as friends often did—and the pair took advantage of a lull in the day to stroll outside and enjoy a smoke. Alex Duncan rummaged through his coat pocket for a sack of tobacco, built a cigarette and lit it. It was a vice that Duncan had revisited. Calmed him. Needed it after that raid upon the village's Chinatown last year.

"No accountin' for the grandeur of hate," the Professor said before gesturing to Duncan to pass his cig. "Got that Thompson fella elected as California's Secretary of State. Probably send him off to Congress one day," and a puff.

"Where he can expand the federal restrictions of the Chinese Exclusion Act, no doubt," Duncan added.

"No shortage of fools in this county. No, sir," and the Professor returned the cigarette to his friend.

"Hate can weigh on you," Duncan said. "I grew up hating the Irish. Hating the Brits. Had to get out before it ate me alive."

"Doesn't stand to reason how a soft fella like Thompson could make it in the world of politics."

"Not with all that shite brewing inside," Duncan said before taking a pull. "Not a man standing who could carry that much repugnancy around with him. Might as well be living in a glass house next to a quarry."

The pair continued to share a smoke while catching up on the news. The Professor extended his condolences on the death of the *Excel*.

"Went on the rocks by Black Island. Down in Georgia," the Professor said.

Duncan nodded. The schooner held found memories for the clan. The *Excel* had transported the family north to Salt Point where Alex and his brother Sam started a new beginning. He recalled Junior's awe at watching seals play on the sandbar by the mouth of the Russian River. Ann's unpleasant experience at losing her expensive bonnet. A lifetime had passed. At least it felt that way.

It was during this moment of unhurried nothingness when Junior rushed toward them. "It came across the wire a few minutes ago," and he handed the message to his uncle.

Alex Duncan studied the trepidation in his nephew's expression before lifting the correspondence to view. Alex read it with a heavy breath and looked skyward, wondering if this was just another flummadiddle or if his deceased brother was up to his old tricks. He ripped the alert into shreds and headed toward the livery stable.

The pieces of paper drifted to the ground like confetti under the curiosity of the Professor who gathered up the bits and reassembled them for an examination. Railroad irons had been dropped overboard from a salvage vessel up at Russian Gulch. The outgoing tide resurrected one of the bars from its tomb and ran it through the bottom of the *Alex Duncan*.

The Professor went outside and eyed a caravan of wagons being loaded for a rescue mission. *Damn Irish halfwit. Let it be.*

* * *

The sun stretched within a ruby haze as it dipped behind the horizon. Captain L. T. John gave the order to cease operations for the day as he brought the *Whitelaw* another quarter mile from shore. The two-masted steamer was cabled to a buoy and an anchor-watch was set for the night. The crew of eleven were raw-tired having completed another ten-hour day of salvage work, fishing up spools of barbed wire and other cargo from a sunken vessel off the mouth of the Russian River. Along for the adventure was a couple, lawyer Hugh C. Grant and widow Mrs. Esther Noel. They were unmarried and enjoying the isolation away from prying eyes back home.

Without warning, a Northerner swept down the coast and parted the *Whitelaw* from its mooring. An alarm screamed. Men scrambled from their sleep. Captain John rushed topside and ordered the haul up of the anchor as well as the hoisting of the main sail and jib. The wind burst into a gale. Men stumbled into webs of wire. Others curtailed the raising of sheets to untangle their fellow mates. A swell bore down and started the vessel toward land.

* * *

Timber tramps, armed with an attitude, loaded down the wagons. It was vital that the men reach the *Alex Duncan* before others combed and picked it clean. The cargo was one thing. Its engine, sails, masts, anchors and structural bits were something else altogether.

The procession left the village behind and entered the hilly grasslands near the coast. They started to veer north toward Russian Gulch when Duncan slid his vision across the river and eyed the remains of the old mill near Bodega Corner. Charred beams leaned against one another for support as if attempting to outlast the whims of Mother Nature. He looked away, feeling as if he was on the wrong end of a marionette's strings. Insignificant. Under the thumb.

Junior pulled on the reins from his perch atop the lead wagon as a parade of dispirited people blocked the trail ahead.

"What the...?" Alex Duncan said as he stood from his seat, cupping a hand over his eyes for a better looksee.

The group within his study advanced forward with the walk of the dead. Defeated. Tattered. Spent.

Alex alighted from the wagon to judge for himself what the holdup might be. Had to get a move on. With every passing moment, another bit of his schooner might be carried away on the backs of rascals and thieves.

He was about to toss an obscenity toward the oncoming group, to demand they step aside, when the figures of torn men and a lone woman drew themselves closer. Captain John introduced himself in a weak voice, telling of how his schooner had been washed ashore near the mouth of the Russian River in the first hour of that day, how they had walked to this point, saving nothing but what they had on their backs.

Duncan surveyed the survivors. Some half-clad. Others with strips of clothing clinging as might the last strands of a forgotten papier-mâché figurine. They required attention now. Not later.

But what of the *Alex Duncan*? It had been an obsession for years. The first schooner converted to steam along the coast. That was a proud moment, to be sure. And it bared his name. He would be immortalized forever. The vessel, however, was also a reminder of the division between him and his brother, of the fostering of an ego at the expense of family.

* * *

The Duncans took in Mr. Grant and the widow Mrs. Noel, surrendering the guest room at the Victorian. Captain John and his crew received shelter at the El Bonito Hotel. Bed and board were supplied *gratis* as would be the train ride the following day. In the meantime, all gave thanks to a proper soak, clean garments, a hot meal and the hospitality of the residents of Duncans Mills.

Mr. Grant and Mrs. Noel were city folk, unlearned of in the ways of the rugged coast. They were to be married upon their return to San Francisco where they hoped to join family and friends in a formal ceremony at the Palace Hotel. The recent events, however, changed everything. Time was a fragile thing. Not necessarily something to push off for another day. Or even another hour.

Ann loaned Mrs. Noel a bustled dress with frothy confections and layers of ruffles while Alex did his part in outfitting Mr. Grant with a double-breasted reefer coat, silk cravat and top hat. The couple paraded from the Victorian under the escort of Ann and Alex. The small entourage paused upon reaching the hotel where guests, employees and the *Whitelaw* crew joined the proceedings. All stepped to the second floor of the company store where vases of wild irises adorned a makeshift altar. It was a barebones venue but full of dignity, one which not even a collection nearby of white masks could diminish.

Captain John presided over the nuptials, seeing no detriment in hand. After all, he had personally known friends of the widow while living in Los Angeles. In addition, everything appeared straightforward as the couple were of full age and in possession of their faculties. Ann and Alex were pleased to stand-in for the pair, acting as maid of honor and best man respectfully.

With the completion of the "I do's" and a thunderous approval from those in attendance, the newlyweds started to retrace their steps down the aisle when a voice from the sideline requested a moment. Addled looks and murmurings cluttered the space until Alex—after a brief huddle with his wife—made his intent known.

A separate ceremony was promptly reconvened as Mr. and Mrs. Duncan stepped forward to renew their vows. Unrehearsed pledges were exchanged along with a love born of a journey long in the making. Ann choked on her emotions as Alex brushed a finger across the moistness leaking from her eyes.

* * *

In a private celebration of the day's triumphs, Ann summoned Alex to the boudoir. He entered and saw her lift the hem of her lingerie with a playful grin. The door drew shut with a click and he stepped forward with a smile of his own.

He paused and regarded her, saying, "Look at you."

"It's been a while," she said.

He nodded and held her eyes for a long assessing moment.

Her grin turned anxious. "I fear I might have forgotten a thing or two with the lapse of time."

"Like riding a bike, I'm told," and he placed a soft touch upon her waist.

She put aside the cliché and strolled to the bed, released a barrette and shook out her hair. Flosses of her mane came loose and she peered back over her shoulder with an invitation.

His smile grew at the flirtation and he said, "Mrs. Ann Holliday Duncan, I sincerely doubt that you've forgotten a single bit,"

She felt a blush creep up her neck as she edged onto the sheets. He followed, undressing along the way, and formed himself to her as she drew him down.

* * *

The following day Captain John and his crew, along with Mr. and Mrs. Grant, boarded the 3:30 afternoon train for Sausalito. A funnel of black smoke rose from the balloon stack as the engine came to life. Steam hissed from the boiler dome, accompanying two short whistles. Wheels gripped the track and inched forward while the newlyweds waved farewell from the caboose's rear platform. Ann and Alex returned the gesture, wishing the couple well on their journey.

The Duncans peered into the distance long after the train had crossed the Russian River. Reality returned—as it always did—and they pivoted to each other with a kiss, whispered fond adieus and went separate ways to attend to the affairs of the day.

Alex passed between the warehouses and the depot, crossed the tracks and stepped into the saloon where an unexpected assemblage of some size had gathered. "Doesn't anybody care to work anymore?" Duncan said to a row of workers sitting at the bar.

"Decided to take a holiday," William Fraser said.

"Oh, you did, did you?" Duncan asked. "Trying to put me out of purse, is that it?"

"No such thing," Fraser said. "Thought it fitting, seein' as how ya got rehitched and all."

"And did you happen to think of inviting me to my own celebration?" Duncan said in a barbed tone.

"Knew we be forgettin' somethin'," John Orr said as he handed a glass to Duncan. "Quit clattering 'bout and have yourself a drink."

"Any other surprises I should be knowing of?" Duncan said as he lifted the sarsaparilla to his lips.

"As a matter of fact," and a grin grew across the bartender's face as he gestured over the shoulder of Duncan.

Alex followed Orr's look and swiveled on his barstool to a white mask not more than a foot away. "Christ on a bike!" and his drink splashed down his frock. "Like to give an old man a heart attack, this one."

"Wasn't aware I'd be seein' the likes of your Irish gob here," the Professor said as he lowered his mask.

"But saw fit to come and have a drink without me, eh?" Duncan said.

"Sounds 'bout right," and the Professor gestured to the bartender for a whiskey.

The trio chatted a bit regarding the news of the day until Duncan weaved his view between patrons to the rear of the saloon where his nephew was sipping away. Duncan retrieved his drink and walked to the table and seated himself.

"And how are you?" Alex said in a greeting.

"Thanks for the holiday," Junior said as he raised his mug in a salute.

"Not sure who should get the credit for such a thing," Alex said.

"Sorry about your boat," Junior said in a spurt.

"Wasn't a boat. Nor a vessel. More like a pain in the royal arse, is what the *Alex Duncan* was," the uncle said.

"I recall something you handed down to me from your father: *If you look after the pennies, then the pounds will look after themselves.*"

"Aye, remember it well. It was something my da left with me on the day I departed Ireland."

"Seems as if you went adrift of his teaching what with leaving the schooner to the whims of salvagers and such," and Junior took a swig of his ale.

"I was of the same thinking. Until yesterday when I came across the survivors of the *Whitelaw*. I witnessed the desperate look in their eyes, especially those of Mr. Grant and the widow Mrs. Noel. Though they were both from money, the most important item on their minds was each other."

The nephew stilled his mug upon the table. His expression crunched up with an unknowing.

"My da and mum held onto the same warmth," the uncle said to clarify. "Money, or the lack of it, didn't define their feelings for each other."

"Love conquers all?" Junior said, guessing as to his uncle's message.

"More than that. It was the little pieces, the pennies of a life together that multiplied to fill their pockets."

"So, you'd be happy if you died without a coin to your name?"

"Yes," the uncle said before adding, "if you would do me one last favor."

"Of course. Anything."

"Accept my invitation to be the new superintendent of the

mill," and Alex Duncan patted the shoulder of the lad in congratulations. "Your da would be most proud," he continued, knowing there was no more truth packed into a single statement than that.

Junior's skin rippled with the announcement. Emotions welled up.

Within the pause, the uncle raised his glass in a toast. "To your health, lad. *Slainte*."

"No, uncle," Junior corrected. "To *ours*," and they clinked their glasses together.

Chapter Thirty-six

"Goodbye," he said to no one as he shut the door behind him and retreated into the dark crevices of his bedroom.

Epilogue

Thomas Larkin Thompson was elected as a Democrat to the Fiftieth Congress, serving from 1886 through 1889. He failed in his bid for a second term but was appointed as the California commissioner to the World's Fair in Chicago, Illinois and later served as U.S. Minister to Brazil. In 1897 he returned to California and sold his newspapers, the *Sonoma Democrat* and the *Daily Democrat*. There were at least 330 uses of the "n-word" during his tenure as editor. Four months after the sale, the sixty-year-old, suffering from severe depression, committed suicide on February 1, 1898 and was buried at Santa Rosa Rural Cemetery. The coroner's jury ruled he was "mentally deranged" after ranting on several occasions that the Independent Order of Odd Fellows was out to get him.

Alexander Duncan built his mill into the leading producer of lumber along the lower reaches of the Russian River, putting out some thirty-five thousand board feet per day while employing one hundred men. In 1889 his company was the largest owner of timber land in the area with 10,000 acres. Perhaps pleasing him more was his stand against racism and his victory over the Anti-Chinese League on April 17, 1886. Alex Duncan died on February 20, 1903 at the age of eighty-two of valvular heart disease. At the time of his death, only two of his seven children were alive—Jeannie and Sammy.

Ann Holliday Duncan died on September 24, 1898, the same year that Thomas Thompson committed suicide. Her husband often wondered if the coincidence bore any meaning. Perhaps God was of the persuasion that it was necessary to balance good with evil, even during death. Her sister, Frances (Fanny) Holliday, married her spouse's brother, Samuel Montgomery Duncan. Their son, Samuel Montgomery Duncan Junior was made superintendent of the mill.

The **Kashaya** population in 1851 was estimated between 3,500 and 5,000. By 1880, the population had dropped to 1450 people. They occupied an area extending from the Gualala River in the north to Duncan's Landing a few miles south of the Russian River. When the Kashaya people were evicted from Fort Ross, they relocated to the property of Charles Haupt who had married a Kashaya woman. In 1914 the federal government, at the behest of Charles Haupt Jr., started the process of purchasing an isolated forty-acre tract of land four miles inland from Stewarts Point as a permanent residence for the Kashaya. This reservation exists today, high on an exposed ridge possessing poor soil and little water.

Serranus Hastings was chief justice of the California Supreme Court and was elected to the post of attorney general for the state. In 1878 he founded a law school in San Francisco with a donation of $100,000. He died at age 78 on February 18, 1893 and was buried at St. Helena Public Cemetery in St. Helena, California. In 2020 a commission concluded that he participated in the genocide of the Yuki people in Mendocino County. The next year the Board of Directors at UC Hastings College of Law voted to change the name of the institution.

Tyler Curtis drove the Native Americans from Bodega Bay in 1857 to the Round Valley Reservation in Mendocino County. The event became known as the "Death March". Two years later, he hired a militia of some forty men from San Francisco to oust the settlers from his land, but his actions failed in what has become known as the "Bodega War". Upon his wife's (Manuela) passing, he proceeded to sell the land. Curtis also drained the accounts of each of Manuela's three children. The *San Francisco Chronicle* observed that he soon became engaged to six different ladies at the same time while spending the enormous sum of $45,000 (around $11 million in today's money) in an unsuccessful attempt to become mayor of San Francisco in 1871. The *NY Daily Graphic* reported that four years later Tyler Curtis went on a drinking spree and ended his mortal career by dying at Barnum's Hotel in New York, "a victim to rum and loathsome diseases."

Charles Franklin Sloan, a.k.a. the **Professor**, was the lone Black hired in rural Sonoma County during the mid-19th century. At Duncans Mills he operated a barbershop, as well as a news and fruit stand. The *Petaluma Argus* said upon his death in 1899: "Among tourists and campers he was a great favorite, and many will miss the sight of his beaming ebony face. He was a genial, whole-souled fellow." Former historian John Schubert once said that the man received the nickname "Professor" due to the fact that he could tell history by the yard. The casket containing all that was mortal of him was laid to rest at Orr's Cemetery in Duncans Mills.

Guy Ah was registered in the 1870's census as the only person of Chinese descent residing in the Russian River Valley, working at Duncans Mills. It is interesting to note that many officials were incapable of seeing Chinese as individuals. As a result, it became common practice to mislabel many Asian newcomers with the name "Ah". When Guy Ah died is not known.

Duncans Mills was devastated by the 1906 earthquake. Three grand Victorian hotels collapsed, citizens fled and recovery was slow. Swift-growing willows buried the railroad station and other enterprises. The last train to leave the area was in 1935. Christopher Queen's Hotel, DeCarli's General Store, and John Orr's saloon still remain. The railroad station stands proud, having won the California Historical Society Award for the best restoration of 1971. It is surrounded by support buildings in keeping with its history, carefully reproduced by the Wallen and Ferreira families.

Alexander Duncan

Thomas Thompson

Duncan's Landing on Sonoma Coast

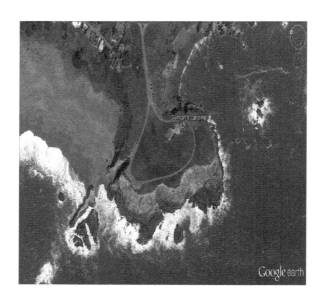

Schooner at doghole on Sonoma Coast

Shipwreck at Russian Gulch

Landscape of Duncans Mill

Alex & Ann Duncans' Victorian

Duncans Mills Company Store

El Bonito Hotel in Duncans Mills

Bull team at Duncans Mills

Timber Tramps on Springboard

R.R. Depot at Duncans Mills

Train crossing Russian River at Duncans Mills

John Michael McCarty is a fourth-generation San Franciscan and retired educator, having taught California History on both the secondary and graduate levels. John is also the recipient of national awards for his historical fiction. He lives with his wife Patricia along the lower reaches of the Russian River in northern California.

For more information regarding the author or to purchase his novels, visit **http://www.johnmccarty.org**

Made in the USA
Columbia, SC
29 August 2023